SAI BABA

Man of Miracles

BY THE SAME AUTHOR

Sai Baba, Avatar
Sai Baba, Invitation to Glory
The Undiscovered Country

SAI BABA

Man of Miracles

Howard Murphet

VRINDAVANUM BOOKS
LONDON

ISBN 0-907555-12-8

First published in Great Britain 1971
by Frederick Muller Ltd.

Paperback Edition by Macmillan (India) Ltd.:
1972, 1974, 1975, 1980 and 1981 (twice).

This edition published by Vrindavanum Books,
43 Ovington Square, London, S.W.3,
and distributed by Element Books Ltd.,
Longmead, Shaftesbury, Dorset SP7 8PL, England.

Printed in Great Britain by Billings, Hylton Road, Worcester

CONTENTS

PREFACE

(to English paperback edition)

Since its first publication in England in 1971, this book has found its way into many foreign languages, both European and Asian. Because of its Western approach, of scientific doubt, I did not expect it to arouse much interest in India where there is a tradition of the miraculous and a preference for devotional literature. But I was wrong. Its publication there in English brought such a tremendous response that it was soon translated into most of the main Indian languages.

In India, America and in all foreign translations the book has appeared in popular-priced editions. But only the original hardcover edition has been offered to readers in the United Kingdom, and this has for some time been out of print. Now I am happy to know that the deficiency is being made good with the publication of the present paperback edition.

This affords me the opportunity to bring several things up to date.

One day at Prashānti Nílayam a young man from England told me that his mother was afraid to make the journey there because of the hardships of travel and *āshram* life as depicted in 'Man of Miracles'. I should write something, he said, to prevent others getting this wrong impression.

What I said about travel and living conditions when I wrote the book, back in the Sixties, was quite correct at the time. But things have changed through the years. Now there is a sealed road all the way from the city of Bangalore to Prashānti Nílayam. The journey takes about three hours by car or taxi. There is also a public bus which takes four or five hours.

The *āshram* has been completely transformed since I first went there. Now the *shānti vedikā* and the open sheds have vanished. Flanking the expanded, lovelier than ever Mandir are blocks of units several stories high. Each unit is owned by a devotee somewhere in the world, but when the owner is not in residence, his unit can be allotted to a visitor by the *āshram* accommodation office.

When all the units are full, which is usually only at the time of big festivals, people are offered dormitory-style accommodation in large halls.

The food situation has changed greatly, too. The canteen now serves non-spiced Western-type meals as well as the traditional Indian dishes. Furthermore, within the *āshram*, there is a bakery where bread, buns, cakes and savouries are baked daily. There is also a number of *āshram* shops where the devotees can obtain many items, including fresh fruit, vegetables, dairy products and breakfast cereals.

A young woman who was studying this book, with a view to translating it into a foreign language, accused me of misleading readers by stating that Sai Baba did not take money from anyone. Well, my research and enquiries on the subject showed that this was the case when I wrote the book.

However, a few years later, when Baba began his costly large-scale education programme, a Central Trust was established into which devotees may contribute funds. The money is used, under Baba's direction, to help in his new spiritually oriented educational work, and also in his extensive health and welfare programmes for the poor.

Yet it is still true to say that he will not personally accept money. I know this from experience, having at times taken donations from various devotees living abroad and offered the money to him. Always he has waved it aside and talked of spiritual matters. So I have had to take the donations and deposit them in the bank where the Trust's account is held.

It is also true that no matter how large the donation, it does not buy the *Avatār's* love. In fact, a good degree of the love relationship and purity of heart must be present before the contribution is acceptable for the divine work.

The main things written in this book, however, are the same as they were when I was the imperfect instrument for bringing them to worldwide public notice. Of course, the wide world as a whole is not yet ready for the *Avatār's* cleansing message. Yet in all countries there seems to be a sizeable nucleus of people who *are* ready — like watchers of the night waiting for a light to shine in a window. When the light shines, they know what it means, and come in thousands, either physically or mentally, to the Abode of Supreme Peace.

May this edition find many more people, hidden away in the nooks and crannies of the English-speaking world, who are ready and waiting for the *avatāric* beacon of joy and hope.

Howard Murphet

Blue Mountains,
New South Wales, Australia.
February, 1984

AUTHOR'S NOTE

This book is intended for three classes of readers: one, the many for whom the mysterious, marvellous and miraculous of life hold interest and appeal; two, the searchers after spiritual light who have not yet found what they seek.

Many in both these classes, especially the former, will not even have heard of Satya Sai Baba of India, let alone seen his miracles and felt his great influence. They will be more than inclined to doubt. Therefore I have tried to present the facts as objectively as possible, keeping the devotional content to a minimum. Other books, from time to time, have dealt in such a way with the subject of miraculous phenomena. But I know of none describing so many and varied events connected with a miracle-saint, still living, and attested to by such an array of witnesses whose real names are given. These witnesses are, in the main, well known in their professions and/or communities and can be contacted by any doubters who would like confirmation of the fantastic, incredible experiences described.

Because the devotional element is minimal, the third class of readers for whom the book is intended, the Sai devotees, will perhaps feel that the presentation is too cold for them. But I beg them to remember that pure devotional literature is of interest only to devotees, and here I am primarily concerned with a much wider field.

But I sincerely hope that even the most ardent and experienced Sai devotee, to whom the extraordinary has become the commonplace, will find in these pages something to interest him - perhaps, some new evidence, aspect or interpretation of the great Sai power. For it is a fathomless ocean and no man can know more than a fraction of it. In this volume, the fruit of long but highly rewarding research, investigation and experience, I would like to share with you the inspiring fraction that I came to know.

Now I want to express some appreciation and gratitude. First and foremost to Sri Satya Sai Baba himself for all that he has so graciously shown and revealed to me personally. Words completely fail me here. So I will pass on swiftly to express my gratitude to those people who so courteously supplied me with the facts about their precious and marvellous experiences, and who also permitted me to use their names in testimony to a truth that is stranger than fiction.

Finally, further sincere thanks are due to my good friend, Mr. Alf Tidemand-Johannessen, who provided some very timely secretarial assistance in connection with the book; and to my wife, who helped so much in typing and checking the manuscript.

PUBLISHER'S NOTE

Many readers of the first Indian edition, arriving in India from different parts of the world, or from within India itself, have tried to contact Miss Leela Mudaliar at Queen Mary College, Madras, in order to locate the Sai Baba temple at Guindy, featured in these pages. As she is now Professor of Botany at another college, we think it may be useful to give the Temple's address here. It is 3I/D Mount Road, Guindy, Madras 32.

Many more readers have been writing to the publishers or the author for the address of Sri Satya Sai Baba in India. To help those who may wish for the same information after reading this latest edition, we give below the addresses most likely to be of assistance to a visitor or would-be visitor:

1) P.O. Prashanthi Nilayam,
District Anantapur, Andhra Pradesh 515134, India:

2) 'Brindavanam',
P.O. Kadugudi,
District Bangalore, Karnataka 560067, India;

3) 'Dharmakshetra',
Andheri West, Greater Bombay, India.

. . . and you find it difficult to believe in miracles? I, on the contrary, find it easy. They are to be expected. The starry world in time and space, the pageant of life, the processes of growth and reproduction, the instincts of animals, the inventiveness of nature . . . they are all utterly unbelievable, miracles piled upon miracles . . .

Professor W. MacNeile Dixon,
Gifford Lectures, 1935–37

INTRODUCTION

Most of us meet the miraculous and magical in the tales of early childhood and, in those plastic years before the "shades of the prison house" have begun to close around us, miracles are part of the accepted order. There is no incredibility, for example, in the magic power of Aladdin's lamp, or in Jack's beanstalk to the land of the giants, or in Christ walking over the storm-tossed water.

Such stories are not, of course, confined to the folklore and religious scriptures of the Western world. The written chronicles of man in all areas unroll a record of miracles that stretches from Lord Krishna, some five thousand years ago, down to the present day. The age of miracles has always been with us. We read of its rosy morning on the far horizons of ancient Egypt, Chaldea, India and Palestine. And in the old Alexandria of the early Christian era there were theurgists who, at public ceremonies, made statues "walk, talk and prophesy".

In Europe, during the Middle Ages, the Church unfortunately claimed a monopoly of the miraculous, and those who worked outside it had to work in secrecy. Such secular theurgical workers, belonging to the Rosicrucian and other brotherhoods of occult practice, did exist, however, and despite ecclesiastical power and jealousy, some great personalities - adepts like Paracelsus and the Comte de Saint Germain - caught the attention of the public, stirring its cupidity, its fears and its suspicions.

But what actually do we regard as a miracle? If in those Middle Ages a single individual had appeared who could do any one of the many things we take for granted today - televise, travel through space above the earth, or to the moon, communicate in a few seconds with someone on another continent, convert matter into nuclear energy, or break matter down to its component atoms and use them like bricks to build an entirely different form of matter — what would have happened to such a dangerous heretic? What would they have done to one who thus flouted the laws of God, undermined the status of the theologians, and took unto himself the powers of angels? Would his life have been worth more than a bundle of faggots for burning? But these 'miracles' around us today have come about gradually through the laborious efforts of science. We know some of the laws behind them. Even if we do not know the laws ourselves we believe that our modern priests, the technologists of science, do. So we accept such phenomena comfortably and admiringly as the products of scientific progress. We do not think of them as miracles.

Yet in a sense they are, just as the whole universe in space and time and the wondrous inventions of the mind are miracles. But provided we can say, "It works according to such and such an equation," or, "Our scientists have discovered the laws, and our technologists operate according to them," we feel that we are on safe ground. It is scientific; there is nothing magical about it.

So the definition of a miracle seems to be that it is a phenomenon concerning which we neither understand the causative laws ourselves, nor believe them to be understood by that large body of scientific workers in whom we put our trust and faith. Christian miracles, such as those at Lourdes, are, according to the theologians, "the suspension of the effect of a law of nature by God as its author". But such an idea does not satisfy the occultist. According to him there is no suspension of law; there may appear to be, but actually the miraculous phenomenon is brought about by a deeper law, not yet discovered and enunciated by exoteric science. When the greater law is known our mental concept of the lesser one will be modified.

Madame H. P. Blavatsky stated the occult viewpoint thus: "A miracle is not a violation of the laws of nature, as is believed by ignorant people. Magic is but a science, a profound knowledge of the occult forces in nature and of the laws governing the visible or the invisible worlds." Such occult laws are known to esoteric science, but those who possess such knowledge have always been few in number and not generally known to the public. So public opinion usually discounts their existence, and the existence of any esoteric body of knowledge.

Miracles, as found in the records, fall into a number of classes. Bhagavan

Das* classifies the miracles of Lord Krishna as follows:

(1) giving illuminating visions;
(2) seeing at a great distance;
(3) multiplying small amounts of food, or other material things, to create large quantities;
(4) projecting his subtle body or bodies to appear simultaneously in several places at once;
(5) healing the sick and deformed by a touch;
(6) on rare occasions bringing the 'dead' to life;
(7) laying dooms on particularly grievous sinners, such as the one who murdered infants and sleepers.

Jesus Christ performed a similar wide range of miracles. But perhaps the emphasis was different. The Nazarene seems to have concentrated more on healing the sick, the maimed and the insane. But he also performed much of what we now call 'phenomena'; he levitated over the water; he made himself invisible; he multiplied food; he turned water to wine; he raised the 'dead'. And, if the records are straight, his greatest phenomenal magic came at the end of the story. After death he dematerialised his body to bring it out of the tomb, rematerialised it into a plastic malleable form, so that at times it was not recognisable by his disciples and, finally, on the Mount of Olives, he raised that etherialised body of earth to another plane of existence.

Krishna and Christ are the two outstanding miracle workers of the world's scriptures. But there have been many others of lesser stature, or sometimes perhaps merely of lesser fame. Some have been able to perform one or two classes of miracles; others have had power over many. The early Christian apostles could heal the sick and perform other wonders. Apollonius of Tyana, in the first century AD, could do likewise, and more. Once, his mere arrival in a town was sufficient to stop an epidemic of plague there. Many saints and mystics have shown miraculous powers such as levitation, bilocation or astral travel. Throughout the centuries there have been ample signs of a hidden brotherhood of occultists who were adepts in various branches of the High Magic.

In the latter half of the last century, Madame H. P. Blavatsky startled an incredulous Western world with a stream of inexplicable phenomena.† Apparently from nowhere she produced a variety of articles when needed: fruit, crockery, cutlery, jewellery, embroidered handkerchiefs, books, letters and other things. She is said to have converted one type of matter into another, to have travelled in her subtle body, and sometimes to have made her physical body invisible. She was able to see things from the past or from a great distance in what she called "the astral light".

To anyone who studies the evidence thoroughly and without prejudice, there is no doubt that Madame Blavatsky was a genuine worker of what the world calls magic. Or perhaps, it might be closer to the truth to say that, in

**Krishna and the Theory of Avatars* by Bhagavan Das

†See *The Occult World* by A. P. Sinnett, Theosophical Publishing House, London.

many cases, the magic was done through her by certain highly advanced *yogis* or adepts whose *chélā* (disciple) she was.

It has been stated that she was a medium but, in its association with spiritualistic practice, this word connotes loss of consciousness, and Madame Blavatsky never lost consciousness when phenomena were being performed through her. She preferred to use the word "mediator", rather than "medium", in describing the part she played. The adepts who worked through her were living far away, but they were not limited by space; they were able to know what was happening at a distance and to take action – either through travel in subtle bodies or by some other means.

Towards so-called miracles, past and present, current public opinion may be said to fall into three categories. There are those (perhaps the majority in the Western world) who say that miracle is all moonshine, that it has no basis in fact. There are, on the other hand, those who through personal experience, or for some other reason, accept the miraculous as quite factual. And, finally, there are some (a growing number) who keep an open mind on the question. They feel that events which are beyond the bounds of rational explanation are not necessarily beyond the bounds of possibility. They feel, indeed, a rationality in the very idea that not all the laws and forces of the universe are yet stated in the textbooks of modern science.

But, while theoretically accepting the possibility of the miraculous, people of this third class are not convinced that miracles do, in fact, take place. Before accepting any event as miraculous, they need strong evidence, preferably the evidence of their own five senses, and even something more than that – an inner intuitive conviction that accompanies the seeing, the touching, the hearing, the testing. I belonged to this third category before I met Satya Sai Baba.

An interest in psychic research, or parapsychology, and a study of its work over the last century had convinced me that many of the miracles were indeed steadily moving across the border into the territory of respectable scientific facts. Telepathy, clairvoyance and precognition are now established phenomena of the laboratories, though as yet there is no satisfactory explanation or scientific hypothesis for them. Furthermore, there is strong evidence for the reality of psychokinesis, the power of man's mind and will to move objects at a distance.

When such phenomena as the power to read minds, see through walls, foretell future events, or mentally to cause or change the motion of physical objects are becoming established beyond reasonable doubt through laboratory experiment and statistical analysis, we begin to have a scientific rationale behind what used to be called "magic".

That is what the majority need today, not a theological explanation as of old, but a rationale acceptable to the new "scientific" outlook, even though many orthodox scientists turn their eyes away from the facts. In all ages there have been diehard dogmatists who preferred the comfort of their own creeds or theories to new facts, new evidence, new thought. In all classes we find this inertia, this *tāmasic* quality that clings to the safety of the *status quo*, eschewing the effort and hazards of the unending search for truth.

But if the "miraculous" really does take place, how does it operate? Can we know or discover something of the means and processes by which a so-called miracle is performed? Could a nuclear physicist explain to a primary school boy how a rocket is sent to the moon? He may give a few hints and an over-simplified explanation but, before the boy can really understand the laws and operations of nuclear physics, he needs to develop his mental capacities and go, step by step, through a long, disciplined course of training.

The development and training required for a schoolboy to become a nuclear physicist is mainly one of intellect, concentration and perseverance. On the other hand, that needed for the ordinary human being to acquire some of the know-how of miracles is mainly one of character, psychic unfoldment and spiritual evolution. With true yogic training, which is in fact spiritual training, miraculous powers *(siddhis)* begin of themselves to make their appearance, as Patanjali points out in his 'Yoga Sutras'.

Many other great teachers have taught the same law in various ways. Sai Baba of Shirdi, for instance, told his followers that in the course of concentration on one's *guru* - or God in any form — one becomes, if sincere, more calm, more placid and, in a number of cases, the latent power of reading the minds of others, or of seeing clairvoyantly, are spontaneously acquired.

But what about the voodoo priests of Africa, the *shamans* of the Siberian tribes, the witch doctors of primitive peoples? Most of these are far from being spiritually evolved. In fact, the magical powers are often used by them for vengeance, personal gain, murder and various undetectable crimes.

This brings us to the question of the different levels of magic, from the high white transcendental type, down through different shades of grey, to black magic or sorcery. Many kinds of miracles are worked through the co-operation of beings from other planes of existence, such as nature sprites, elementals, discarnate humans, and *devas*, or angelic beings. This theory seems to be the most widely held as it has been stated by practically all magicians, high and low, who have had anything to say on their *modus operandi*. Colonel H. S. Olcott, Founder-President of the Theosophical Society, states that the members of the last great school of theurgy, in old Alexandria, "believed in elementary spirits whom they evoked and controlled".

For calling forth and commanding the different classes of beings there is always a secret know-how. This includes not only *tantra, mantra* and *yantra* - the right ritual, right words and right geometrical and mathematical figures - but also certain self-disciplines and, above all, the development of the will power.

The more the will is developed, the fewer the ceremonial aids needed. In *Old Diary Leaves* Colonel Olcott, who spent many years in close association with the theurgist and phenomenon producer Madame H. P. Blavatsky, describes miraculous events that happened frequently in her presence. Some of them, she told him, were performed with the aid of elemental spirits. These seemed to be well under the control of her will, without the use of any ritual, *mantras* or *yantras*.

On the other hand, a *yantra* was employed by an Italian occultist, Signor Bruzzesi, who came to visit Madame Blavatsky and Colonel Olcott one evening in New York. Employing the occult arts he produced a shower of rain out of a clear sky in a matter of minutes. The Colonel observed that the Signor seemed to exercise indomitable will power, but also used a strange geometrical figure on a pasteboard card which he held up to the heavens. He would not let Olcott touch or examine closely this *yantra*. The Italian stated that the shower was produced by spirits of the air under his command.

People of lower levels of spiritual evolution can apparently employ the technique of using entities of the other planes of existence which interpenetrate the earth. However, as like always attracts like, sorcerers with evil motives will attract evil spirit agents to do their bidding. The power of such low-level magic is real enough under certain conditions, but is limited and fraught with danger to the practitioner. He must be ever on his guard lest his weapons boomerang and destroy him. This is one of the hazards of black, or left-hand, magic.

Those who perform the grey, or middle, magic attract allies of a somewhat better type from the subtle planes of being. The motives of such magicians are not criminal. They do not aim at murder, immorality, domination or destruction. Nevertheless, like the average citizen of today's world, their motivation is more selfish than altruistic. Pride, desire for fame, ambition and avarice are among the powers that move them. For example, Mohammed Bey, who earned a chapter in Paul Brunton's book on India, was an average type of the grey magician. His aim was frankly to make money and, for his supernormal feats (mainly reading the contents of sealed documents), he had trained and was employing, he said, the discarnate spirit of his deceased brother. This is no more immoral and unethical, perhaps, than many normal commercial practices, such as the use of industrial spies "in the flesh". But there may be more dangers involved, dangers to the health, well-being and integrity of the one who employs the discarnate forces. Moreover, miraculous powers used for commercial and selfish ends are easily lost, as many professional spiritualist mediums and Eastern pseudo-yogis have found out.

At the other end of the scale from savage sorcery and black magic, through the various shades of grey, we come to the white magic of the right-hand path. This is something entirely different: different in motive, method, power and range. The key to its recognition lies in the motive. This must be pure; that is, entirely dissociated from the personal self of the miracle worker. He must be one who has risen above the normal appeals of nature. Money, ambition, fame, personal power, security – all the usual driving forces of man – must mean absolutely nothing to him. His only motivation is a pure love of his fellow men, with the wish to ease their sorrows and sufferings, and to lift them up to higher levels of understanding and happiness.

If a man has reached such lofty standards of action, perhaps through the evolution of many incarnations spent on earth, then miraculous powers will surely be his. They are part of his pure divine nature. The *Shrimad Bhagavatam* asks: "What power is beyond the reach of the sage who has controlled his mind, senses, nerve currents and disposition, and concentrates on God?" And, in another place, it says: "When a person is merged in God, all powers, all knowledge, all wisdom, all perfection, which are termed divine, shine forth from such a person."

All who have ever written on this difficult subject have said the same thing. Eliphas Levi wrote: "To command Nature man must be above Nature." Joseph Ennemoser in his 'History of Magic', written over a century ago, said that divine miraculous works are possible only to those "who have converted their whole life into a divine one; who are no longer slaves to the senses . . ." And it is well known that in the theurgic schools of old the hierophant who worked the esoteric mysteries lived a life of strictest purity and self-abnegation.

At the highest level we can say that miracles are the work of God coming through a purified person who incarnates (gives earthly human form to) divinity. Christ said, "The father [God] that dwelleth in me, he doeth the works [miracles]. I am in the father, and the father in me . . ."

In the Roman Empire of the first century AD, sorcery had brought the whole of magic into disrepute and it was forbidden by the Emperor. But the great miracle-man, Apollonius of Tyana, pointed out the differences between the lower and higher forms. He said, "Sacrifices have I no need of, for God is always present to me and fulfils my wishes . . . I call sorcerers false sages, for they are attracted only by riches which I have always despised . . ."

The divine miracle workers have no need of the sacrifices and spell-binding enchantments used by magicians of a lower order. One does not read of Jesus or Krishna or Shirdi Baba employing *tāntric* rites or chanting *mantras*. They were beyond the need of such *formulae*. The spiritual will was the creative power. Such a will is both human and divine. It is human in the sense that all men have it potentially, but what most men regard as their will is no more than their own desires, overt or hidden. Only as these selfish desires are eliminated, only as they are polished away like dirt from the surface of a crystal and a man sees himself as one with God, only then does the true spiritual will shine forth. This, being divine, has power and dominion over the worlds of matter.

This is not to say that such an enlightened will does not sometimes employ beings of other planes to do its bidding. Ennemoser, who studied and researched these questions deeply, says that whereas in the lower class of magic the operation depends almost entirely upon element spirits, in the higher, "Man operates principally through his innate power, but not without the assistance of element spirits."

The powers and forces of other worlds which the Godman, or *avatār*, marshals through his pure will must by the very nature of things be of the higher type – not the demons and evil spirits found on the payroll of the sorcerer. And there is no danger of any unseen agents either harming or deserting the great white magician. He will be held in deep reverence by the higher agents, and in fear plus a healthy respect by the lower ones, whether non-human or discarnate human.

To state, as the analysts of magic have always done, that other-world entities, more or less intelligent, are often handmaidens to the miracle worker is not to flout the concept of natural law. That the universe runs according to a pattern of harmony and rhythm there can be no doubt. That man, through careful observation and reasoning, has been able to make certain generalisations which he calls laws of nature is equally true. But such generalisations never fully explain the phenomena. Time brings other generalisations, other hypotheses, other laws, which are closer to the ultimate truth; and in these the old 'law' is swallowed up – shown to be either erroneous or only a partial understanding of reality.

The teachings of occult science, as given in Blavatsky's *The Secret Doctrine* and other works, suggest that living beings beyond the atom, and as unseen as the atom is to human eyes, play a part in the workings of nature. But such beings are not acting according to their own whims and caprices: they are working within, and helping to carry out, that rhythmic harmony which embraces the deepest laws of the universe. Nor does the miracle worker divert such beings from their legitimate business and turn them into law breakers. Through his will they produce surprising effects, but this is still done according to law, though by a deeper law than man has yet uncovered.

If we consider, for instance, that spectacular miracle, the converting of one class of matter into another, we may get some understanding of this principle. All matter, it is believed, emerges from energy and can be reconverted into energy. So the miraculous process is to reduce one type of matter to its fundamental energy form and from that build up another type of matter.

Even without reducing it to the basic nuclear energy, man is today converting one class of matter to another. For example, in the industrial complexes of synthetic chemical manufacture, he is breaking down natural substances like coal and petroleum to their constituent elements and using these as building bricks to construct entirely new types of matter unknown to nature, such as plastics and synthetic fibres. So, what was once a lump of coal or a jar of petroleum becomes a nylon dress, or perhaps a bright plastic housing for an electric razor.

Why then should there not be, in the hidden laboratories of nature, workers capable of similar or even more difficult operations in reduction and conversion? Thus water becomes wine for a wedding feast in old Palestine, or oil for the lamps of a mosque at Shirdi. Such unseen operators, spirits of nature's laboratory, will work according to cosmic laws. They cannot break laws any more than the wizards of modern chemistry can. But their controlling laws are deeper than the ones we yet know. According to these, and without upsetting nature's harmony, why should they not even convert base metals to gold, when this is done under the will of a great alchemist who has lost all personal desire for gold, and who will use it only for the welfare of his fellow men?

Considered on these lines, we see that the miracles of a Christ, a Krishna, a great master of any century, are really no more incredible than the endless miracles forever around us – "the starry worlds in time and space, the pageant of life, the processes of growth and reproduction . . ."

A full comprehension of the *modus operandi* of miracles is no doubt beyond the human consciousness in its present stage of evolution. But an attempt to solve such mysteries must lead us into a fuller understanding of ourselves and the miraculous universe about us.

It was a book* written by an Englishman and published in England which first introduced me to the strange, fascinating figure known as Sai Baba of Shirdi. Later I learned more about this miracle-working God-man from other writings, including the four-volumed biography by B. V. Narasimha Swami, but from the first introduction to him I felt a stir deep inside me – as if something pulled on a cord attached to the core of my innermost self. I could not understand what it meant.

Mystery surrounds the birth and parentage of Sai Baba. All that is known are a few remarks dropped by Baba himself and these, often symbolical, do not always appear consistent. However, it does seem that his birth took place about the middle of last century in the Nizam of Hyderabad's state, probably in the village of Patri. Apparently his parents were (Hindu) Brahmins but, at a tender age, Baba seems somehow to have come under the care of a Muslim fakir, a saintly man and probably a Sufi, who became his first *guru*.

After four or five years, either through the death of the fakir, or for some other reason, Sai Baba came into the charge of a noted government official at Selu named Gopal Rao. This remarkable man was not only rich and liberal but also pious, cultured and deeply religious. He was a warrior-saint with powers both temporal and spiritual.

When he first saw the young Sai Baba he recognised him, it is said, as an incarnation of the great saint, Kabir. Gopal Rao was therefore happy to have the boy live at his residence and take part as a constant companion in the activities of court, field and temple. Thus the child received from Gopal

**The Incredible Sai Baba* by Arthur Osborne, Rider & Co., London.

Rao, his second *guru*, a training and education of the highest, though not of the bookish, kind.

But after some years the warrior-saint decided that the time had come for him to leave the earth. Accordingly, at the time fixed by himself for departure, he sat in the midst of a religious group performing rituals of worship and by his own yogic power left his body. Before doing so he pointed westward and bade the young Sai Baba to travel in that direction to his new abode.

Sai Baba went westward and eventually came to the village of Shirdi, in the Bombay Presidency (as it was then). He was not at first made very welcome there. Arriving at a Hindu temple on the outskirts, he was attracted by its solitary calm and wanted to live in it. But the priest in charge took him for a Muslim and would not let him put a foot inside the temple.

So Baba took up temporary residence at the foot of a *neem (margosa)* tree. He left Shirdi and returned several times; then, eventually, in the year 1872, he settled down permanently in the village. A dilapidated Muslim mosque of Shirdi became his home. Here he kept a fire burning constantly, and oil lamps lit the interior of the mosque throughout the night. This was according to the view, common to both Hindus and Muslims, that places of worship should be lit up at night.

A few people recognised Sai Baba's divine qualities and came to pay him homage (among the first was the priest who had driven him away from the Hindu temple), but most of the villagers regarded him as a mad fakir, and of no account. In the tradition of holy men of India, he depended on charity for food and other material needs. These were few, but he did need oil for his earthen lamps. One evening the shopkeeper who supplied Baba with oil, *gratis*, told him untruthfully that he had no supplies. Perhaps this was a joke to amuse the village loiterers. Anyway, a group of them, together with the oilmonger, followed the mad young fakir back to his mosque to see what he would do without his religious light – and maybe to have a good laugh at his expense.

Water jars are kept in mosques for people to wash their feet before entering the sacred precincts. In the dusk, the villagers saw Baba take water from the jars and pour it into his lamps. Then he lit the lamps and they burned. They continued to burn, and the watchers realised that the fakir had turned the water into oil. In consternation they fell at his feet, and prayed that he would not put a curse on them for the way they had treated him.

But Baba was not what they thought. He was not a sorcerer resenting their contempt, and ready to seize an advantage. His nature was pure love. He forgave them and began to teach them.

This was the first miracle Sai Baba performed before the public, and it was the match that lit the fire which became a beacon drawing thousands of men to him from afar. Many became his devotees. He used his miraculous powers to cure their ailments, to help them in their day-to-day problems, to protect them from danger wherever they happened to be, and to draw them towards a spiritual way of life.

A great many found their sense of values changing. Some surrendered themselves entirely to the divine will which they saw in Baba, gave up their worldly lives, and came to live at Shirdi as close disciples. Sai Baba taught them according to their needs and capacities. Learned pundits, who thought him illiterate, found that he could discourse on spiritual philosophy and interpret the sacred writings of India more profoundly and clearly than anyone else they had ever known. But, always, he led his disciples along the *bhakti mārga*, the radiant pathway of divine love, self-surrender and devotion.

Loving care of his devotees was the ruling *motif* of all Baba's actions, and many of them have stated that in his presence they always felt a spiritual exaltation. They forgot their pains, their cares and their anxieties. They felt completely safe and the hours passed unnoticed in blissful happiness.

One devotee, a Parsi woman, wrote: "Other saints forget their bodies and surroundings, and then return to them, but Sai Baba was constantly both in and outside the material world. Others seem to take pains and make efforts to read the contents of people's minds, or to tell them their past history, but with Sai Baba no effort was needed. He was always in the all-knowing state."

Many quaint, amusing and illuminating stories are told about him in the volumes on his life and teachings. But for our purposes there are just a few points we might note. One object of the fire he kept burning always at the mosque was to provide a ready supply of ash. This he called *ūdhi*, and he used it for many kinds of miraculous purposes, particularly for curing ailments. The miracles he performed cover the full range of *siddhis*, or supernormal powers, as expressed in such spiritual and *yogic* classics as the *Shrimad Bhāgavata* and Patanjali's *Yoga Sūtras*. Many times he proved to his devotees that he knew what they were thinking and saying and doing when hundreds of miles away from him. Frequently, in crises, he appeared wherever he was needed, either in his own form or apparently in some other body – a beggar, a hermit, a workman, a dog, a cat or something else. There was plentiful evidence that he could project himself through space and take any material form he chose. Those who were in the best position to know, his nearest disciples, had no doubts whatever on this point.

Baba gave visions to people, as for instance, to the visiting high Brahmin who was dubious about going into the Muslim mosque. From outside the mosque the Brahmin saw Sai Baba as the God-form he worshipped, Shri Rāma. So convincing was this vision of Rāma that he rushed in and fell at Baba's feet. Other types of miracle include the giving of protection at a distance – protection against accident, plague, ill fortune and imminent death; the granting of issue to those who were childless or desired to have a son; appearing to people in dreams with advice and help in their problems.

Like Jesus, Baba was able to cast out evil spirits from those obsessed and cure the most terrible diseases, such as blindness, palsy and leprosy. For instance, he allowed Bagoji, a man with advanced leprosy, to come and wash his feet and legs. People were afraid that Baba would himself be infected but, on the contrary, Bagoji was completely cured of his leprosy, only scars and marks remaining, while Baba remained in good health.

By the end of the last century, in spite of India's primitive communications at the time, Sai Baba's fame was snowballing rapidly. The high peak was reached by about 1910, when an endless stream of visitors began to flow in from Bombay and other places. Pomp and ceremony were thrust upon the rugged, unsophisticated old saint. Loaded down with jewellery, seated in a silver chariot with fine horses and elephants, he was taken in grand and colourful procession through the streets.

Baba, it is said, disliked all this show, but he submitted to it to please the people. Yet, despite the royal treatment and the riches offered him, he continued to beg his food as of old; perhaps this was to show that humility is more than ever necessary when wealth and pomp and power are striving to seduce the soul of man.

When, in 1918, Sai Baba died at Shirdi, he had just enough money to pay for his burial, and no more. It is the tradition in India that a God-realised person should be buried and not cremated. So all devotees agreed that Baba must be buried, but they quarrelled about the method. As had happened in the case of Kabir, centuries before, both Hindu and Muslim sections of his followers claimed the right to inter the body according to their own particular rites. Being in the majority, the Hindus won the day. But, through the wisdom and diplomacy of Mr. H. S. (Kaka) Dixit, acceptable concessions were made to the Muslim following. Sai Baba's *samādhi* (tomb), the mosque where he lived for over forty years and where the sacred fire is still kept burning, and other spots associated with him in Shirdi, are today the Mecca of thousands of pilgrims – Hindus, Muslims, Parsis, Buddhists and Christians.

If therefore ye are intent upon wisdom,
a lamp will not be wanting . . .

Anonymous

1

THE SEARCH

After spending some time in Europe, my wife and I decided to stop for a while in India on our way home to Australia. We had two purposes in view. One was to go more deeply into Theosophy by attending the six months' School of Wisdom course at the international headquarters of the Theosophical Society in Adyar, Madras. Let it be said, incidentally, and in case of misunderstanding, that this school does not pretend to offer a brief course on how to be wise; its object is simply a study of the ageless wisdom, the perennial philosophy found mainly in the ancient writings of the East.

Our second purpose was to travel through the country to discover whether there was any deeper spiritual dimension in the life of modern India. Was there, we wondered, anything left of the mysterious India described in the pages of Paul Brunton, Yogananda, Kipling, Madame Blavatsky, Colonel H.S. Olcott and other writers? Were there still hidden fountains of esoteric knowledge or had the ancient springs dried up? Would it be possible to find somewhere, in *āshram* or jungle hermitage, a great *yogi* of supernormal powers who knew the secrets of life and death? We thought that about a year should suffice for this programme.

The Theosophy School was enjoyable and enlightening. As a *sortie* into the wisdom teachings ranging from the ancient Vedas to *The Secret Doctrine*, published in 1888, it prepared our minds for our coming exploration "on the ground". We understood better what we were looking for and felt better equipped to appreciate it should we find it.

Our search took us to several of the well-known *āshrams* throughout the length of India, and to a few little-known ones. We sat and talked to hermits and ascetics in their caves in the Himalayas. We met a goodly variety of *sādhus, sādhakas* and teachers of different types of yoga.

From the hermitages of the Himalayas and *āshrams* along the sacred Ganges we came back to New Delhi. There, at a leading social club, we met a top business executive who said, over his beer, "So, you're looking for the spiritual life of India. There is none. That's all past. We are looking for what you have in the West - material progress."

In another place, a professor of history also tried to dampen our enthusiasm. "Believe me," he said, "there is no spirituality left in this country. In the India of old there was, of course, but it died a thousand years ago."

However, we knew that the men who spoke this way, the men of the modern India with its thirst for Western technology, were wrong about their own country. We had seen enough and sensed enough to feel quite sure that the yogic treasures of old were still to be found in her deep recesses.

We had sensed it; we had caught some drifts of its perfume on the breezes; we had met brotherly love in the *āshrams*; we had found men who were happy to teach, for the sake of teaching, the eternal truths of Hindu religio-philosophy.There was no dearth of inspiring words and noble theories. But we had not yet met a man of real power; one who had himself lived the yogic life long enough and truly enough to have broken through the limitations that bind man in his present unhappy state. But, with all the promising material there was surely hope that one such might exist. Yet we also knew that spiritual treasures are not handed out on a platter. There are always *tapas*, labours, austerities to be performed.

Train and bus journeys on the plains of India in burning June were, we thought, austerities enough for anyone. From the oven that was Delhi we went to the fiery furnace of Dayalbagh on the outskirts of Agra. We wanted to see what had happened to the Radha Soami religious colony there which Paul Brunton had admired so much thirty years before.

We found that its educational institutions had progressed and its factories and farms seemed to be thriving, but that it had a weary air. There was none of the dynamism that Brunton had found there. It was like an old tired man who had had rosy, optimistic dreams in his youth which had never come true. Perhaps this was because the energetic, inspiring leader of the Brunton days, His Holiness Sahabji Maharaj, was dead. Just before dying he had passed on the leadership to a retired engineer among his followers, one Hazur Mehtaji Maharaj. Now he was God Incarnate on earth to the Dayalbaghites.

He proved to be a very elusive God. We tried to meet him but were not encouraged. On one occasion we went out early in the morning with a large party that does a few hours' work in the fields before starting duty in office, school or factory. The *guru* was with the group and we had great hopes of finally making the contact (in fact, that was our reason for going), but he all the time managed to put a few acres between himself and us.

At last, however, on the day before we left, the secretary of the colony managed to pin him down in his office long enough for us to have an interview. On the way to the interview we were shown the house in which the leader lived. It was just one in a row, indistinguishable from its modest neighbours.

In the office we found a shy little man who seemed quite ashamed of the fact that there was an air-conditioning unit in his simple room. This was not common in the colony, and he made it clear to us that his followers had forced the exceptional luxury upon him because of the indifferent state of his health. He was friendly in a self-effacing way, but he said nothing of importance that I can recall. And we felt nothing, except that, if God is utter humility, then this man might be God Incarnate; but he was certainly a reluctant Incarnation, and kept any other signs of his divinity well hidden – from us, at least.

The Secretary, Babu Ram Jadoun, made up in open-hearted hospitality and helpfulness any lack on the part of the modest leader. He spent the evenings sitting with us on easy chairs in front of the small guest house talking about the Radha Soami faith and its *shabda* yoga, in which one concentrates in meditation on listening for the inner *anāhat* sounds. He also liked to recall the old days and tell us anecdotes about the two English writers, Yeats-Brown and Paul Brunton, who had once stayed together at this same guest house in the early 1930s.

I knew that there were now about twenty of these Radha Soami colonies in India, each with its own *guru*. We had visited a number of them, including the big one at Beas, near Amritsar, where some 600,000 people believe that their benign leader, Charan Singh Maharaj, is the true Incarnation. We had found that each group we visited had exactly the same idea about its leader.

On the evening before we left Dayalbagh, I decided to ask the Secretary, an intelligent man, what he thought about this division of belief that had developed in the cult during the century of its existence since 1861.

"Do all the leaders have the divine current?" I asked. "Do you think they are *all* Incarnations of the boundless Brahman?" My wife and I were the only ones sitting with him under the trees before the guest house.

He shifted his seat in the warm air that wrapped us around like a blanket and, after a minute's silence, replied, "No, there can be only one Incarnation at the same time."

"And that is *your* leader?"

"Yes."

"So all the rest are wrong?"

"I'm afraid so."

"Well, you no doubt have your good reason for feeling so sure," I remarked, "but how can we – how can any outsider – know who is right? How can we decide in which of the many leaders, if any, divinity is enshrined?"

The wrinkled kindly little man seemed to ruminate for a time before he said, "Thirty years ago I was a lecturer in the Engineering College here. One evening I was sitting with a few people where we are sitting now, listening to our leader, Sahabji Maharaj. Paul Brunton, who was with us, asked him the same question that you have just asked me. I remember very well the answer His Holiness gave . . ."

"What was it?" Iris asked.

"It was: 'Pray every day to God that He will lead you to the man in whom He is at present incarnated'. I suggest the same to you now. Such a prayer will undoubtedly be answered." He paused, then added with a gentle smile, "And when it is, when you find Him, please write and let me know."

I wondered if he meant, "Write and say you are on your way back here." Then I remembered that Brunton did not go back and become initiated into the Radha Soami faith at Dayalbagh, but found his great *guru* in Ramana Maharshi of Tiruvannamalai.

It was all very strange. I was not sure that I believed in modern Incarnations. Maybe in ancient times, as the scriptures taught, there had been such – men like Rāma, Krishna, Christ and others. I knew that many in India regarded some comparatively modern spiritual teachers, such as Paramhansa Ramakrishna, as Incarnations or *Avatārs*, but I had never hoped or expected to meet one in the 1960s. The idea had not occurred to me. I was prepared to settle for a great yogi who had climbed to the rare heights of God-realisation. But, what was the difference, if any? It was all beyond my understanding or hopes.

Still, my wife and I decided that, if among the teeming millions of India there was an Incarnation today, we would love to find Him. So the prayer could do no harm. It might, at least, help to lead us to the great master we sought.

I don't think we repeated His Holiness Sahabji Maharaj's prayer in actual words very regularly, or for very long, but the strong yearning was deep in our hearts, the yearning to find the highest manifestation of God in man – and that in itself is a prayer.

Truth is always strange; stranger than fiction.

Lord Byron

2

SATYA SAI BABA

I first heard the name Satya Sai Baba from a wandering yogi. He had not himself met this holy man, he said, nor been to his *āshram* at a village called Puttaparthi. This, he had heard, was a difficult place to reach, being in the wilds of the interior: one had to do the last part of the journey by bullock cart or on foot over rough tracks. Still, the *swāmi* was no doubt worth the effort, the yogi thought, if I had time and was interested in phenomena. He was known to have *siddhis*, to be a great miracle worker.

"What kind of miracles?" I asked.

"Well, it's said that he can, for instance, produce objects from nowhere. Of course, there are other men to be found who have some of the *siddhis*: they can do a few supernormal feats, but from reports Sai Baba's powers are much greater. And he performs miracles frequently. Anyone can see them."

Such talk certainly aroused my interest and curiosity. I had heard (who has not?) that India was the crucible of wonder workers. I had read of the great adepts, occultists, saints of the past who knew nature's inner laws. But I half doubted their actual reality. And even if they did once exist, could they still be around?

This, I thought, might be my great chance to find out if the fantastic tales that have come out of India belong to the realm of fact or fiction. I decided that I must see Satya Sai Baba as soon as convenient. Later, when I heard that his followers regarded him as a reincarnation of Sai Baba of Shirdi, my desire to meet him became even stronger.

But the bullock cart safari into the interior of southern India would have to wait a little while, however. It sounded more than arduous, and we had recently discovered, on our northern journey, that ordinary travel in India saps one's vitality. On our return, we were glad to recuperate for a time in the tranquil tree-filled Theosophical estate.

One day, several months after our return, a young pale-faced woman wearing the ochre robe of a monk came on a visit to the Theosophical headquarters. She was introduced to us by a mutual friend as Nirmalananda, and we took her to our sitting room for morning coffee. She told us that she was an American from Hollywood, an odd place of origin for an ascetic, we thought. "Nirmalananda," she said, was the Hindu name given her by Swami Sivananda when he initiated her into the monastic life. After he had died she left his *āshram* at Rishikesh and became a follower of Satya Sai Baba. At Puttaparthi she had witnessed many wonderful miracles. Now Sai Baba was on a visit to Madras and she was one of a small party of disciples he had brought with him.

This seemed to be our golden opportunity. Iris was not feeling well enough to come, but Nirmalananda conducted me to the place where Sai Baba was staying. It was a pleasant house, standing behind lawns and flower gardens. Later, I learned that it was the home of Mr. G. Venkateshwara Rao, the mica magnate who was also a devotee of Sai Baba. The lawns and pathways in front of the house were covered with people sitting quietly cross-legged on the ground - white-clad men to one side and women in saris like bright-coloured flowers to the other. There were hundreds of them, obviously waiting for a sight of the great man.

Nirmalananda led me through the crowd to the front verandah and there introduced me to a pleasant, red-haired American named Bob Raymer.

"I think Sai Baba has finished interviews for the morning, but I'll go and find out," he said.

He took me into a small sitting room and left me there. Nirmalananda had already gone off somewhere. In the room were only two Indian men, both standing and apparently waiting for someone. I also stood waiting.

After a few minutes the door from the interior of the house opened and there entered a man the like of whom I have never seen before - nor since. He was slight and short. He wore a red silk robe that fell in a straight line from shoulders to feet. His hair stood up from his head in a big circular mop, jet black, crinkly to the roots like wool, and seemingly vibrant with life. His skin was light brown but seemed darker because of the thick beard which, though closely shaven, still showed black through the skin. His eyes were dark, soft and luminous, and his face beamed with some inner joy.

I had never seen a photograph of Sai Baba. Could this be he? I had expected someone tall and stately with a long black beard, and dressed in white robes. I had a preconceived image of what a great yogi or master should be like, perhaps derived from early Theosophical descriptions of the Masters.

He came swiftly and gracefully across the carpet towards me, showing white, even teeth in a friendly smile.

"Are you the man from Australia?" he asked.

"Yes," I replied.

Then he went to the Indians and began talking to them in Telegu. Presently I saw him wave his hand in the air, palm downwards in small circles, just as in childhood we used to wave our hands when pretending to perform some abracadabra magic.

When he turned the palm up it was full of fluffy ash, and he divided this among the two men. One of them could not contain his feelings; he began to sob. Sai Baba patted him on the shoulders and back, and spoke to him soothingly like a mother. I did not understand at the time that these were what are called *bhakti* tears – tears of overwhelming joy, gratitude and love. Later, I heard that Baba had cured this man's son of some terrible disease, but as I did not check the story, I cannot vouch for it.

After a while the small figure turned to me again. Standing close in front of me, he began circling his hand again. This time, I noticed, he pulled his loose-fitting sleeve almost up to the elbow. Much later, I learned the reason for this. In my mind was the suspicion that he might be doing conjuring tricks like a stage magician, perhaps bringing the ash out of his sleeve. Baba has no difficulty in reading minds and knew my suspicions. So he pulled his sleeve high to allay them.

When the mound of powdery ash appeared suddenly in his palm, he tipped it into mine. For a moment I stood there wondering what to do with it. Then a voice to my left said, "Eat it, it's good for your health." This was Bob Raymer who had just returned to the room.

I had never expected to eat ash and enjoy it, but this brand was fragrant and quite pleasant to the taste. Baba stood there watching me. Halfway through the strange snack I said to him, "May I take some of this to my wife? She is not very well."

"Bring her here tomorrow at five o'clock," he replied, and then he was gone.

The next afternoon found Iris and myself at the same house. In the entrance we met Gabriella Steyer of Switzerland, one of the small Western contingent in Baba's travelling party. She, very friendly and sympathetic, led us to an upstairs room where about a score of women, most of them Indian and all in sāris, sat cross-legged on the carpet.

We sat down near them and Gabriella began to tell us about some of the miracles she had seen at Puttaparthi. Taking out my notebook I asked her for the full address of the *āshram* and directions on how to get there. At that moment Bob Raymer's wife, Markell, came up and said that Baba was on his way, and that I should go and sit on the other side of the room, the men's proper territory. The males now filled their area of the floor but I found myself a place by the wall. I noticed that Bob Raymer and I were the only two white faces in the group of men.

Suddenly, Sai Baba appeared in the doorway. His robe was old gold in colour, but like the red one it fell from shoulder to floor in a simple line with no pockets, appendages or folds. All his robes are of this same style. They fasten right up to the neck with two gold studs – the only jewellery he ever wears – and the loose sleeves come to the wrist or elbow, depending perhaps on the temperature. Under the robe he wears a *dhôti* (a cloth tied around the waist and reaching the ankles like a skirt) and this has no pockets in it either. I now know these things for sure because, later on when we were staying at a guest house with Sai Baba, my wife used sometimes to iron his robes and *dhôtis* in our room. So although sceptics, without examining the matter properly, have said (and will doubtless say again) that he conceals the things he produces miraculously somewhere in his robe, I know beyond doubt that this is quite wrong and quite impossible.

From the doorway Baba pointed his finger at me and said, "Did you bring your wife?" I was pleased that he had remembered.

He took us both into another room and talked to Iris about her health. He seemed to know just what was wrong with her and the basic causes of the trouble. He gave her much advice and then, with his handwave, produced from the air some medicinal ash for her to eat.

I was standing close by, keenly watching the production, because I still doubted that it was genuine magic. Now he turned to me, smiled, pulled his sleeve up to his elbow, and waved his hand under my nose. As he turned the palm up I expected to see the usual ash, but I was wrong. Lying in the middle of his hand was a little photograph of his head with the full address of his *āshram*. The photograph had a freshly glazed look as if straight from a photographic laboratory. He handed it to me saying, "You've been asking for my address. Here it is. Keep it in your wallet."

"May I – may we – come there sometime?" I managed to ask.

'Yes, of course. Whenever you wish. It's your home."

Since that day I have seen many wonderful and rare things produced by the wave of his small brown hand, but I still carry in my wallet that little photograph which came out of "nowhere" in answer to a question in my mind. There were no ordinary means of his knowing that I had asked Gabriella for the address.

After our interview, Sai Baba gave a discourse to the people assembled in the room and, later, as we went home, we saw him walking among the people in the gardens. Many of them tried to touch his robe or his feet. He spoke to some and 'produced' something for others, usually ash, I think.

This constant production of ash, or *vibhūti*, as it is called, seemed to have a special significance. It made me think of Sai Baba of Shirdi and the fire he always kept burning to produce the *ūdhi* which he gave to his followers for curing their ailments, and for other purposes. Now it was as if Satya Sai, who perhaps really was his reincarnation, could produce this ash from a fire that burned in a dimension beyond the range of our mortal eyes.

Ash is a spiritual symbol and has been used as such by many religions, including the Christian. Like all symbols it has different levels of meaning. An obvious one is that it reminds us of the transitory nature of all earthly things and the mortality of man's body. It is meant to lead our thoughts to the eternal beyond the transitory, to our own immortal selves beyond the little mound of ash or dust to which our bodies will some day be reduced. For the Hindus ash is especially sacred to the God Shiva, or that aspect of the Godhead concerned with the destruction of all material forms. Destruction is considered a divine attribute because only through destruction can there be a regeneration, a rebirth of new forms through which life can flow more freely, more fully, more vitally.

During the next few days we talked a good deal about our strange experience. Apart from his miraculous abilities, Sai Baba had a powerful effect. He seemed to lift us up to some high level where there were no more worries. Life became larger than life, and the usual difficulties and conflicts of the mundane world were far off, unreal. There seemed to be an aura of happiness around us. Iris mentioned that she could not stop herself smiling for hours after Baba had talked to her.

As for miracles themselves – well, as time went on I began to ask myself if I had really seen them. It all seemed so unlikely, so far outside the commonplace everyday order of things. It is very difficult for the mind trained in logic and the physical sciences and believing implicitly in the rational order of the universe to accept the reality of such apparently irrational phenomena. Even after seeing such miracles it is difficult to believe in them.

So a doubt hung in my mind like a morning mist. Was I, after all, fooled? Was it, after all, just a clever sleight of hand? Going over the facts and conditions carefully I failed to see how this could be so. Ash would be a difficult if not impossible thing to hold in the palm of a hand waving in circles, wide open and turned downwards. How could he bring it out of a pocket or a sleeve, even if he had pockets, which he did not, and even if the cuffless sleeve was down to the wrist, rather than pulled up nearly to the elbow, as it often was?

Perhaps there was some way in which he could have done the things I saw by brilliant conjuring. Perhaps his apparent mind-reading and his inside knowledge of one's personal problems were no more than clever guessing.

Inwardly I felt from the elevating splendour of his presence that he was not an impostor. I could not be absolutely sure, however: I could not be quite certain that I had met a man of truly supernormal powers, that I had witnessed genuine miracles. No, I could not feel sure until I had investigated further. I would have to observe such phenomena many times in many different circumstances and conditions. I would have to get to know the miracle man himself, learn his character, his background, his life, and the kind of people who followed him. And I certainly would have to visit that *āshram* in Puttaparthi.

This earth alone is not our teacher and nurse,
The powers of all the worlds have entrance here.

'Sāvitrí', Sri Aurobindo

3

ABODE OF PEACE AND MANY WONDERS

I travelled by bus from Madras to Bangalore. Some friends in that city provided me with a car and I set off north along a country road to find the retreat of the wizard of Puttaparthi. I was travelling alone with an Indian driver as Iris was not able to get away from her duties at the Theosophical Society headquarters.

The way led out of Mysore State* into Andhra Pradesh, mainly through barren, open country pimpled here and there with outcrops of round, stoney hills. I did not see even a mention of Puttaparthi on the signposts until we reached the last stretches of the hundred-mile journey.

Then we were on a road of broken rocks and loose sand, like a track for country carts. At one place it became a narrow alley, squeezing itself between the tumbled buildings of a lonely village. In other places the road sauntered across the sandy, near-dry beds of rivers. Such crossings are fordable except in seasons of very heavy rain. But I was told that if the cunning rogues living nearby are in need of money they dig a deep ditch in the shallow water of the ford. Then they wait for cars to get stuck, and bargain for a high price to push them out.

Gone, however, are the days when visitors finished the Puttaparthi

*Mysore State is now called Karnataka, though the city of the same name retains its old nomenclature [Ed.]

journey by bullock cart, or on foot across slushy fields of paddy. Despite the rugged road in the year of my first journey there – 1966 – cars and even big buses could negotiate the final obstacles and reach the *āshram* gates.

Sai Baba's retreat is beside the village of Puttaparthi, which nestles in a narrow farming valley between pewter-coloured hills of bare rock. The valley, gentle green in the season of young crops, is remote and silent, untouched by the twentieth century. As I drove in through the gate, the sun was setting, spreading a golden glow over the buildings. Most of them stood around the perimeter of the large compound, facing inwards towards a large, white central building.

It was the time of the evening *bhajan*, that is, singing of sacred songs and chants. I was informed that Sai Baba was with the crowd in the big hall which occupies most of the ground floor of the central building, and as apparently only he could say where I must sleep, I sat on my bedroll outside the hall and waited.

The rhythmic sounds of the singing deepened the peace of the evening hour. Dusk gathered, the lights came on gently, the haunting music continued. It seemed to seep through me, soothing my tired body, and calming my impatience, washing away my worries and anxieties.

Presently someone came and took me to the room Baba had allocated to me. It was in the small guest house and was well furnished, with its own private washroom and a flush lavatory. This was much better than I had been led to expect or had dared to hope for.

One of the first people I met at the *āshram* was Mr. N. Kasturi, a retired history professor and college principal at Mysore University. He was now the secretary of the āshram, editor of its monthly magazine, *Sanāthana Sārathi*, and the writer of a book on Sai Baba's life. He had also translated into English many of Baba's public discourses which had been delivered in Telegu. These, published in several volumes, contain the miracle man's spiritual teachings and give an idea of his mission and message.

On my first morning, Mr. Kasturi arrived at the guest house with copies of all the books which had been printed in English.

"They are a present to you from Baba," he explained. Mr. Kasturi is not only a scholar, but a deeply religious man whose face glows with devotion and benevolence.

Now he told me something about the *āshram*. Its name is Prashānti Nílayam, meaning 'abode of great peace'. About seven hundred people live here permanently, while hundreds are coming and going all the time. The residents occupy the inward-facing terraced houses around the perimeter. The visitors occupy whatever space is available at the time – perhaps a room in one of the large buildings, perhaps a spot of floor in one of the open sheds, perhaps a corner on the post office verandah or, at times of great festival crowds, the bare, brown earth beneath a tree. People like myself, who have been softened by the creature comforts of Western civilisation, Baba usually puts in the furnished guest house.

In the early morning I had heard strange but soothing sounds of Sanskrit chanting. Now I learned that it came from the school where boys and youths are studying the 'Vedas'. They are not only learning to read the Sanskrit of these works but also to recite it by heart. They are being taught by pundits to chant the texts with the correct intonation and emphasis, as was done in India's ancient days. The reason for this is that the uplifting spiritual benefits of the Vedas come from the *māntric* effect of the sound as much as from the meaning of the words. That is what the ancient writers tell us and, having been subjected to some of the chanting myself, I do not find it hard to believe them. There are very few schools like this one in India today; perhaps because it normally takes about seven years to learn one 'Veda', as Mr. Kasturi informed me, and there are four of them. Over twenty years to master the lot, and no commerical rewards to speak of at the end of it all! But Sai Baba seems determined, against the surging tide of materialism in modern India, to revive her ancient spiritual culture.

The *āshram* also has its own canteen where I had been invited to have my meals, but I was told that as I was Baba's guest I must not pay. The accommodation was also free and I had been given a set of free books! It seemed I was not allowed to pay for anything. Perhaps I could make a donation at the end of my stay, as one does at most *āshrams* in India. This point I queried with Mr. Kasturi.

"No," he said emphatically, "Baba will not accept donations. He never takes money from anyone."

"He seems to have some wealthy followers," I replied. "Perhaps they give financial help to the *āshram*."

"No," Mr. Kasturi smiled. "But don't take my word for it; ask them yourself. Many will be arriving in the next few days for Shivarātri."

"What's that?" I queried.

He explained that it was the great annual festival to the God Shiva, that many thousands came to Prashānti Nílayam for it and that, during the festival, Baba always performed two great miracles in public.

I decided then and there to wait for the festival of Shivarātri (Shiva's night) and see the miracles. In the meantime I would read Sai Baba's story as written by N. Kasturi, talk to his followers, and get close to the great man himself whenever I possibly could. Kasturi gave me hope that I might be called for an interview fairly soon, although Baba was very busy.

During the next few days, in fact, I was fortunate in being invited to several group interviews. For these, about a dozen people gather in one of the interview rooms at either end of the *bhajan* hall, or "prayer hall", as it is sometimes called. Sai Baba sits either on the one chair, or else on the floor - depending, it seems, on his whim - and the people sit cross-legged on the floor, fanning out in a rough circle about him. On each occasion I managed to get as close as possible to him and sat to his right within a couple of feet of the hand that performs the magic.

These group interviews usually begin with some talk on spiritual subjects.

Baba invites someone to ask a question; then in the answer he expounds on such matters as the meaning and purpose of life, man's true nature, and the way he should strive to live in order to reach the goal. The teachings are always clear, vivid, and intensely practical.

Towards the end of each meeting, if some people have personal problems, he may take them into another room one by one or in family groups. But never a meeting went by without Baba producing at least one item besides the *vibhūti* he always produces, with his theurgic handwave. Pendants, chains, rings, necklaces and other objects I have watched him pluck from the air in this way and then give to some delighted individual.

He apparently knew my suspicions of him were not yet dispelled, because he still pulled his loose cuffless sleeve up before taking an object from nowhere. But on one occasion he did not need to raise the sleeve above suspicion. It was a very hot day and he was wearing a robe with short sleeves that came only to the elbow. Now, as if he would exorcise, once and for all, the sceptical spirit within me, he let his right hand lie open, palm upward, on the arm of the chair within a few inches of my eyes. If I had been a palmist, I might have read the lines and mounds on the small palm and slim graceful fingers. I could certainly be quite sure that no items, however small, were concealed there.

Then he lifted his hand from where it lay, and began to circle it in the air about eighteen inches from my face. One moment the hand was empty, the next it was holding something big that protruded brightly on either side of his fist. He shook this out to reveal a long necklace of coloured stones. It was what the Indians call a *japamālā* which, like the Christian rosary, is used for prayers. Its regulation size is one hundred and eight stones or beads. There was nowhere in three-dimensional space that a conjurer could have hidden such a bulky object to produce it in such circumstances. Baba gave it to a grey-haired lady on his immediate left. When he placed it around her neck, she was so overcome that her eyes filled with tears and she went down on her knees to touch his feet.

Every day now saw the crowd swelling. The buildings were all full and people were beginning to spread their beds under the trees. In this gathering tide of dark-faced white-robed Indians, I was the only Western male, Bob Raymer having returned to his home in California. Among the ladies there were only two pale faces left: ochre-robed Nirmalananda and Gabriella Steyer.

Yet I did not feel like a foreigner: I felt that I was among brothers, and was completely happy. One could hardly be otherwise with brotherly love shining in every face and inspiring every word and action. Any stranger was your acquaintance in minutes and your close friend within an hour, anxious to help you in every way and eager to tell you about the wonderful things that Sai Baba had done for him or some member of his family.

I soon found that the followers were from all parts of India and from all classes of society – princes, businessmen, doctors, lawyers, judges, civil servants, scientists, soldiers, clerks and tradesmen. Filling the guest house there were, in the ladies' suite, the Rani of Sandur, her daughter, and Nanda, a princess of Kutch. Among the men were the Kumaraja (prince) of Venkatagiri, the Kumar of Sandur, Mr. G. Venkateshwara Rao, the mica magnate, and myself.

These people were all quite rich so, remembering Mr. Kasturi's challenge, I questioned them as well as other wealthy followers about money donations to Sai Baba. From all of them, and later from many others, I had the same answer. They would, they said, love to help support Baba's *āshram* with funds, but he would never accept any money from them. Nor did he take any donations from anyone they knew.

I thought what a fertile field was here for those religious leaders and their organisations, always on the look-out for funds – not only the wealthy nucleus, anxious to give, but the huge numbers that congregate at Baba's discourses, sometimes up to two hundred thousand. What a collection could be raised from such crowds by a good rousing evangelist! Sai Baba, however, refuses to take a *paisé*. How then does he get the money he needs? To this question they smile, as if to say, 'How does Baba do anything? He is a mystery we can't solve.' Anyway, it soon became quite clear that whatever the motive for his miracles it was not money.

Everyone I spoke to had at least one and usually many more miracles to tell me from his own experience. My notebooks began to swell with fantastic stories, many of which I could never hope to verify. But there were others which could be cross-checked and verified in a number of ways. Apart from the materialisation phenomena of the type that I had already seen there were tales involving almost every kind of miracle found in the historic and spiritual records of the fantastic. Among them were the healing miracles – the curing of many kinds of diseases, some deep-seated and chronic, some considered incurable by medical opinion.

At the *āshram* there is a small hospital with two doctors on the staff, and occasional helpers from outside. The two full-time workers are the Medical Superintendent, Dr. B. Sitaramiah, and his assistant, Dr. N. Jayalakshmi, a woman doctor. The Superintendent told me that when Sai Baba asked him some years ago to take charge of the hospital he had already retired from practice, and felt disinclined to take the responsibility. Baba said that the doctor would be only a figurehead, and that he himself would do the healing. Then Dr. Sitaramiah, who was a devotee, had no more fears about the job, and that was the way it had been.

"Apart from the routine treatments, I have had Baba's directions always," he told me. "And there have been many cures of cases that were quite incurable by any known medical treatment. From the scientific point of view the cures are quite inexplicable."

For my benefit he went into several case histories in full detail, showing me X-ray photographs, records of medical diagnoses, and any other documents that were relevant. Below are a few sample cases to indicate some of the diseases Baba has treated at the *āshram*. They also show that he has, as he puts it, "different prescriptions for different patients".

A woman devotee from Mangalore was suffering from tuberculosis. There was bleeding, and X-rays showed a cavity of the right lung. Medical opinion was that the disease was probably curable but that effective treatment would take about two years. Instead of undergoing the prescribed treatment, she came to Prashānti Nílayam.

Sai Baba gave her *vibhūti* from his hand, and she was put in the hospital. About a week later, when I visited the hospital myself, she was still there convalescing. All symptoms of the tuberculosis had gone, the doctors assured me. She had been cured in a week instead of two years.

A young man living in Bombay, but recently returned from Switzerland, was suffering from internal trouble which doctors in both Europe and Bombay had diagnosed as cancer. He was not a devotee of Sai Baba, but a friend had urged him to go to Prashānti Nílayam. In desperation he went and stayed, not in the hospital, but in a building near the canteen. There he waited and prayed to Baba for help.

One night he had a dream in which someone visited him, carrying a shining knife. When he awoke that was all he could remember, he told Dr. Sitaramiah and others; the vague visitor and the clear, bright knife. Perhaps it was not really a dream. To the canteen manager who took him breakfast in the morning he showed a large, mysterious blood stain on his sheet. Had Baba performed an operation while he slept? Such strange things had been known before. Anyway, all signs and symptoms of the cancer had vanished.

It was about a year after this experience that I wrote to the young man to enquire if the cancer cure had been complete. His reply came from Switzerland where he had returned to his job. He was in sound health and not a day passed, he said, in which he did not think of Sai Baba and offer a heartfelt prayer of gratitude for his miraculous cure.

A fifty-eight-year-old man, suffering from hyperpyrexia, was brought into the hospital. He had at another hospital been under treatment for fever and dysentery for about two months without relief. At the *āshram* hospital various treatments were tried by the doctors – quinine, penicillin, chloromycetin – but all to no avail. The patient's temperature kept above 103 degrees; he was delirious, and his general condition worsened. He lost consciousness and there seemed to be no hope of his recovery.

Then Sai Baba came to the hospital to see him. Taking *vibhūti* from the air in his usual way, he smeared it on the forehead and put some in the mouth of the unconscious man. Within a short time the temperature began to drop, the patient regained consciousness, and his condition improved rapidly. Soon he was back to normal with no signs of the dysentery. When strong enough he was discharged from hospital.

A cripple, unable to walk, stand or even sit, was brought to the *āshram*. This man, a wealthy coffee planter from Mysore State, was about fifty years of age, and for the last twenty of those years, he had suffered from severe rheumatoid arthritis. He had been through a variety of medical treatments without any success. Now, in addition to his other troubles, he had a damaged kidney which was not functioning. His temperature stayed around 103 to 104 degrees.

At Prashānti Nílayam hospital he refused any orthodox medical treatment, saying that he had complete faith in the power of Sai Baba to cure him. On this occasion Baba waved his hand to produce a small bottle of liquid medicine and prescribed two drops to be taken daily in water. Fifteen days after the treatment began, the planter could walk with the help of a stick. Now Baba gave him a *mantra* to repeat as he walked daily a certain number of times around the prayer hall. Within a month he was walking without the help of a stick. Furthermore, there was no more trouble from the kidney: it was functioning normally again.

Before returning to his plantation, he tried to express his deep gratitude to Sai Baba. The latter replied, "Don't thank me. It was your own faith that cured you."

I asked Dr. Sitaramiah if the cure had been permanent or if, perhaps, the troubles had returned.

"It seemed to be permanent. I heard a long time afterwards that the planter was still quite fit and well," he said.

In the months ahead, I was to meet many people who had themselves experienced dramatic and miraculous cures of serious, sometimes deadly diseases; and others who could bear witness to such fantastic healings among members of their families or friends. A good proportion of these were well-known leading citizens of their communities; they have permitted me to use their names, and their cases will be described in later chapters.

Then, at Prashānti Nílayam, Dr. Sitaramiah informed me that Sai Baba's own temperature was up over the hundred mark. The doctor had been checking it each morning as he always did at this time of the year, with Baba's permission. The high temperature was a sign of the approaching miracle that takes place annually at the Shivarātri festival, the doctor explained.

I awaited this event with eagerness, having heard devotees' descriptions of the miracles performed on previous occasions. And yet I felt a little sceptical as there was, to my knowledge, nothing like it in the chronicles of miraculous phenomena.

O world invisible, we view thee,
O world intangible, we touch thee.

Francis Thompson

4

O WORLD INVISIBLE

In 1966, the Mahāshivarātri Festival, generally known simply as Shivarātri, took place on 18th February. As I walked back from breakfast at the canteen that morning I had to step carefully between groups of visitors camping on the ground. All the buildings were full, all the space under the trees was occupied, and now people were making their temporary residences anywhere on the open ground: comfort is of no concern to the Indians on such occasions.

I joined the crowd standing in front of the Mandir, the big central building. Thousands were waiting for Sai Baba to appear on the balcony and give his morning blessings. Presently, the small red figure with the dome of black hair came to the balcony. He lifted his arm in blessing, rather listlessly for him, I thought, and returned quickly to his room. I had the impression that he was not well. Then Dr. Sitaramiah, who had just come down from seeing him, informed me that Baba's temperature was 104 degrees.

"I suppose it has something to do with the *Shivalingam* forming inside him. It's a great mystery," the doctor declared.

Baba, however, carried on throughout the day as if there was nothing the matter with him. I saw him walking around distributing packets of sacred ash to the crowds sitting on the ground waiting for it, and waiting also for the chance of touching the edge of his robe. Then, during the morning, the first of the day's two public miracles was performed. It took place in a large open-sided shed where thousands could sit on the floor packed close together in a manner achieved only by tinned sardines and Indian crowds. Fortunately, I was sitting near the stage among a bunch of photographers where a little more elbow room had been allowed. Here is my diary entry on what took place that morning:

> On the stage is a large silver statue of Sai Baba of Shirdi in his characteristic sitting posture. Mr. Kasturi takes up a small wooden urn, about a foot in height, and filled with *vibhūti*. This he holds above the head of the silver statue, and lets the ash pour over the figure until the urn is empty. He shakes it well to make sure that the last grains have fallen out, then continues to hold it above the statue with its open top downwards.
>
> Now Sai Baba thrusts his arm as far as the elbow into the vessel and makes a churning motion with his arm, as women did when making butter in the old days. Immediately the ash begins to flow again from the vessel and continues to do so in a copious stream until he takes his arm out. Then the flow of ash stops. Next, he puts in his other arm and twirls that around. The ash streams out over the statue again. This process goes on, Baba using alternate arms, ash pouring from the empty vessel while his hand is in it, and stopping immediately he takes it out. Finally, Shirdi Sai is buried in a great mound of ash – much more then the vessel could possibly have held. Now the urn is placed on the floor: the miraculous ceremonial ash bath is over.
>
> There is a joyous, elevated atmosphere all around: Mr. Kasturi's face is more radiant than ever, Baba's movements and manner are the acme of unselfconscious grace. It's all wonderful, yet having watched him pull handfuls of ash out of the empty air, I am not so greatly surprised to see him stir it in large quantities from an empty pot.

But the big climax of the day was to come, and many people talked to me about it. They told me that every year one or more *Shivalingams* have materialised in Baba's body at this sacred period. He ejects these *lingams* through his mouth for all to observe. They are always hard, being made of crystal, clear or coloured stone and sometimes of metals like gold or silver.

"Are you sure he does not pop them in his mouth just before he goes on stage, and then eject them again at the right moment?" I asked.

My hearers looked at me with amusement and pity. One of them said, "He talks and sings for a long time before the *lingam* comes out, and it's always much too big to hold in the mouth while speaking. Last year it was so large that he had to use his fingers to pull it out through his lips, and it stretched them so that the sides of his mouth bled." Another added, "There were nine one year. Each was about an inch and a half in height. Imagine holding all those in your mouth while you talked for nearly an hour!"

Well, I thought, even if he does bring these things up from somewhere inside him, what is the point of it? Certainly, it's a most miraculous phenomenon, but has it any significance? What is a *Shivalingam*, anyway?

To this question I had a number of answers from the people at the *āshram*, but it seemed to me that the most satisfactory explanation of the *Shivalingam* I had heard to date was the one given by Dr. I. K. Taimni at the Theosophical Society's School of the Wisdom at Adyar. I could only recall this vaguely, but later when I returned to Adyar, I looked up my notes. Briefly, the following is what he taught.

The *Shivalingam* belongs to the class of "natural" Hindu symbols, which are usually mathematical in form. Such symbols are called "natural" because they not only represent a reality, but to some extent are the actual vehicles of the power within that reality. The *lingam* is an ellipsoid. It symbolises Shiva-Shakti: that is, the primary polarity principle of positive and negative forces. On this principle of opposites the whole universe is founded.

Why is an ellipsoid used to symbolise the polarity principle? Dr. Taimni explains it in this way. The ultimate reality, the Absolute or Brahman or God, or whatever we are to term it, has no polarity, no pairs of opposites: all principles are balanced and harmonised within it. Therefore, the ultimate reality is represented by the most perfect mathematical figure, the sphere.

If the centre, or the one focal point of the sphere, divides itself into two we get the ellipsoid. So this figure gives a symbolic representation of the primary pair of opposites out of the original harmonious one. And from this first duality comes all manifestation, all creation, all the multiplicity of things in the universe. The *lingam* is therefore the basic form lying at the root of all creation, as "AUM" is the basic sound.

To put the matter in Hindu terms, from the one Brahman emerges Shiva-Shakti, the father and mother of all that is. We must note in this connection that Shiva is not only an aspect of the Triune Godhead - the destruction-regeneration aspect - he is also the highest God, the father of all the gods, the cosmic Logos.

Like all the gods of Hindu thought, Shiva has his consort, Shakti, or female aspect, and whereas the male, or positive, aspect represents consciousness, the female, or negative, aspect symbolises power. Both are necessary for creation or manifestation in the planes of matter.

It is significant too that the ellipsoidal or *lingam* form, which symbolises the Shiva-Shakti principle, plays a fundamental part in the structure and working of the universe. It lies, for instance, at the base of all matter within the atom where the electrons apparently move in elliptical courses around the central nucleus. Again, at the solar level, we find the planets describing not circular but elliptical orbits around the sun.

Some people have considered the *lingam* to be a mere sex symbol. But sex is only one of the many manifestations of the Shiva-Shakti principle inherent in the *lingam*. The principle is demonstrated in all the pairs of opposites, and nothing can exist in this phenomenal universe without its opposite or contrast. In fact, the concept of opposites is basic to our very thinking at this level of consciousness; we cannot know light without darkness, and so on.

So, to say that man's worship of this symbol is derived entirely from primitive phallic worship is to take a false view. The *lingam* has a much more profound and significant connotation. The word itself in Sanskrit simply means a symbol or emblem, which in itself suggests that it is a basic, primary symbol. In fact, representing in concrete form the fundamental principle and power of creation, it is considered the highest object of worship on the physical plane and, as it has a true mathematical relationship to the reality it symbolises, it can bring the worshippers *en rapport* with that reality. Just how it does this, Dr. Taimni points out, is a mystery which can only be resolved and understood by one's inner realisation.

Nevertheless, it is claimed that this sacred ellipsoid of stone or metal does have the occult property of creating a channel between man and the divine power on the inner plane it represents. Through such a channel many blessings, benefits and auspicious conditions will flow to the worshippers. But the mystic link must be established by someone with the necessary understanding of the principles, and knowledge of the forms of the ritual required.

Would thirty thousand people travel many arduous miles to see Sai Baba produce an ordinary stone from his interior, miraculous though it may be? I doubt it. But the stone expected that evening, the *lingam*, is not ordinary. It lies at the very heart of India's ancient spiritual culture.

Shadows were lengthening, but the afternoon was still quite hot when I made my way from the guest house to the small rotunda called the Shanti Vedika where the event was to take place. The building stands some distance in front of the Mandir and is rather like the open bandstands in parks of Western cities. It is circular with an elevated floor, a low fence and narrow pillars supporting the roof.

Not only were the big unwalled sheds along one side choked with spectators, but the wide grounds stretching from the central rotunda to the perimeter of the *āshram* were a solid mass of sitting figures. I was led by a guide through this silent forest of heads, along a coir-matted lane between the women to my right and the men on my left. I wondered if there was a square yard anywhere on which I might sit.

Near the Shanti Vedika a space had been reserved for officials, the closest disciples, photographers and a few people with tape recorders. Being a pale-faced foreigner, I was courteously placed there, but even this privileged enclosure became so packed that I began to wonder if I would ever be able to vary my cramping cross-legged posture. If I was to be there for over three hours, as predicted, my legs would probably set permanently in the position and I would have to be carried out.

At six o'clock Sai Baba, accompanied by a small group of disciples, came onto the Shanti Vedika and soon after that the speeches began. Several men spoke but I remember most clearly one speaker, a leading Sanskrit scholar of southern India, Surya Prakasa Sastri. Not that I understood what he said, for he spoke entirely in the ancient tongue of the Vedas,* but there was something appealing in his lined, scholarly, benign face and his cloak of heavenly blue.

It was about eight-thirty p.m., powerful electric lights illuminating the group on the platform, when Sai Baba rose to his feet. First he sang a sacred song in his sweet celestial voice that touches the heart. Then he began his discourse, speaking, as always on such public occasions, in the Telegu tongue. The thirty thousand or so people were as one, expectant and utterly silent, except when Baba told a funny story or made a joke. Then a ripple of laughter would pass over the starlit field of faces. On the platform Mr. Kasturi was busy making notes of the address which would be published later, in both Telegu and English.

Sai Baba's eloquence had been flowing in a steady stream for some half an hour when, suddenly, his voice broke. He tried again but only a husky squeak came. Bhajan leaders among the devotees, knowing what was happening, immediately gave voice to a well-known holy song and then the great crowd joined in.

Baba sat down and drank from a flask of water. Several times he tried to sing, but it was impossible. Now he began to show signs of real pain. He twisted and turned, placed his hand on his chest, buried his head in his hands, plucked at his hair. Then he sipped some more water and tried to smile reassuringly at the crowd.

The singing continued fervently, as if to support and help Baba through this period of pain. Some men around me were weeping unashamedly and I myself felt a flow of tenderness towards the man suffering there before us. I could not grasp the full significance of the event that caused the agony, nor perhaps could most of the great crowd watching. To understand a thing with the mind is one matter and to feel its meaning in the bones and blood is another. Inwardly I felt that I was sitting at the very heart of something profoundly significant to mankind.

But another cautious, rational part of me was not even convinced that a genuine miracle would indeed take place, let alone a spiritually important one. So, instead of blurring my eyes with the tears of sympathy, I kept them fixed on Baba's mouth; my whole attention was glued to that point so that I would not miss the exit of the *lingam* – if, in fact, it would come from there.

After about twenty minutes or so of watching Baba's mouth, while he writhed and smiled and made attempts to sing, I was rewarded. I saw a flash of green light shoot from his mouth and, with it, an object which he caught in his hands, cupped below. Immediately he held the object high between his thumb and forefinger so that all could see it. A breath of profound joy

*Sanskrit.

passed through the crowd. It was a beautiful green *lingam*, and certainly much bigger than anything an ordinary man could bring up through his throat.

Sai Baba placed it on the top of a large torch so that the light shone through its glowing emerald-like translucence. Then, leaving it there, he retired from the scene.

Sunderlal Gandhi, a young volunteer guide for the festival, who had become my friend, took me out of the crowd. My legs felt like knotted spaghetti but they carried me to the guest house. Every time I awoke during the night I could hear the crowd still chanting and singing around the illuminated *Shivalingam*, and when I came down at daybreak the people were just dispersing. Among them I met Gabriella Steyer who told me that most of the great gathering had remained for the nightlong worship of this symbol of the highest divinity, which had formed miraculously in the body of their leader.

Shiva is the god of yogis, the one who helps man to conquer his lower nature and rise above it into his true divine nature. To make this transition the mind must first be mastered. Mind is said to be somehow related to the moon, and it is believed that there is an astronomically favourable time when the moon is right for success in man's efforts to transcend his mind. It is at this most favourable time, in February, that the great Shivarātri festival is held. But at Prashānti Nílayam this lunar festival is doubly auspicious: not only are the celestial conditions correct, but the miraculously produced physical symbol of Shiva is there before all eyes, a glowing focus for the supreme effort of meditation.

It is interesting and appropriate to note here that in the Uttara Gita, Lord Krishna says that the word *lingam* comes from lina, which means to unite. This is because the *lingam* makes possible the union of the lower self with the higher self and with God -- with *jivātma* and *Paramātma*.

Later, the Raja of Venkatagiri, a pious Sai Baba devotee with a good knowledge of orthodox Hinduism, told me that it was essential for regular and correct *pūjās*, or ritualistic worship, to be performed for such a sacred symbol. As few people could carry these out, most of the Sai Baba *lingams* were dematerialised: that is, they went back to the realm of the unmanifest from whence they had come. Several other devotees supported his opinion.

Several of my new-found friends saw the *lingam* at close quarters on the morning after its production. There was a good deal of talk about this and comparisons were made with other specimens produced in previous years. I asked what had happened to them all and was told that some were given to very devout devotees, but others - well, no one knew.

Nevertheless, I know for a fact that some are given to devotees. Over a year later a very sincere follower of Sai Baba showed me a beautiful *Shivalingam* which had come from Baba's body, and which he had presented to her. She carried it about with her, carefully wrapped in a cloth, and would let nobody touch it.

"Don't you have to perform regular *pūjās* to it?" I asked.

"Yes," she replied, "Baba told me just what to do and I do it. But I don't know why he gave it to me: I'm not worthy of it." But I could feel that she was. Baba, who sees the deep heart of all his devotees, knows who is worthy.

I was able to inspect the 1966 *Shivalingam* at close quarters a couple of days after it was produced. I had, at Prashānti Nílayam, gone with a small group of people into the Mandir for one of the much-coveted private interviews with Sai Baba. We were ushered into a downstairs room. After a few minutes Baba came in and placed the *lingam* on the window ledge for everyone present to inspect. It was of emerald green colour, as it had appeared in the artificial light on the night of its emergence. Mr. Kasturi, who had been present on the platform of the Shanti Vedika when it was produced, thus described it later in print: "An emerald *lingam*, three inches high and fixed on a pedestal five inches broad that had formed itself in him [Baba], emerged from his mouth to the unspeakable joy and relief of the huge gathering..." When I saw it standing on the window ledge, I did not realise that its big pedestal had also emerged from Baba's mouth, but I estimated the size as about what Kasturi stated later.

After we had all had a good look at the *lingam*, but without touching it, Baba sat down on a chair and we sat on the floor around the walls. I was on the floor to his right, as close as possible.

For a while he chatted in what seemed a light and easy manner. He asked people individually what they wanted from him and laughed at some of the responses. He was rather like a mother with her children, happy to give them the things they wanted, anxious to bring them joy, but hoping that they would learn to want the more important things of life, the treasures of the spirit.

Suddenly, turning to me, he said in a teasing manner, "If I give you something, you will probably lose it?"

"No, Baba, no, I won't," I protested.

Pulling up his sleeve he stirred the air with his hand about on a level with my eyes; I could see under as well as over it, yet I saw nothing there until he turned the hand up and a large shining ring had appeared in his palm. It seemed to be of silver and gold; but he told me later that the silvery looking metal was *panchalôhā*, the sacred alloy of which many temple idols are made.

Fascinated, I held out my hand for the gift but he laughed and passed it in the opposite direction. It went around the circle, each person inspecting it, most of them holding it reverently to their foreheads before passing it on. When it had returned to Baba he placed it on my third finger. It fitted exactly.

I felt quite overwhelmed, and even more so when I saw that the figure embossed in gold on the *panchalôhā* was Sai Baba of Shirdi. I had never told Satya Sai or any of his followers about my deep affection for the old saint. Was it, then, something that he could read in my mind?

Soon after that he began taking us separately into another room so that we could ask him private questions. When my turn came he talked to me about my personal life and health. He seemed to be not only a father and mother but the very essence of parenthood itself, the archetype of all fathers and mothers. It was as if a warm beam of love came from him and entered into the depth of my being, melting my very bones. This, I felt, must be the pure high love which in Sanskrit is called *divya préma*, the love that has no hidden selfish motive, the love that is simply a spontaneous expression of the highest, the divinity, in man.

My wonderful inner experience matched what several devotees had already told me about their own personal contacts with the universal yet individualised Baba *préma*. So, one way and another, by the end of my first visit to the 'Abode of Great Peace', I began to understand that, whatever this miracle man might be, he was not just a clever conjurer. Nor was he a "street magician" with a limited repertoire of psychic tricks for extracting a few *rupees* from the passing crowd.

Sai Baba did not belong to either of these well-known categories. What was he, then? That remained a deep mystery, perhaps unfathomable – but anyway a challenge.

But trailing clouds of glory do we come
From God, who is our home.

William Wordsworth

5

BIRTH AND CHILDHOOD

During visits to Prashānti Nílayam I was able to inspect the village of Satya Sai Baba's birth and talk to members of his family living there. The village, Puttaparthi, lies about a quarter of a mile from the *āshram* itself. It is a small sun-bleached place of white-washed houses and narrow, sandy streets.

The actual house where Baba first saw the light of day is now reduced to a few bits of broken brick wall, but his two elder sisters and a younger brother still live in the village in houses of their own. His elder brother resides in another town, his mother lives in the *āshram* and his father is dead. However, although I met and talked to members of the family and some old friends, it was from the historian Kasturi that I had the main facts about Sai Baba's background, birth and childhood.

The most outstanding figure in his family background was his paternal grandfather, Kondama Raju. This gentleman seems to have been a small landlord, owning farmlands even some distance away from Puttaparthi. He was not rich but he was sufficiently well off to dedicate a temple to the goddess Satyabhāmā, the consort of Lord Krishna. He is remembered chiefly for the devout religious life he led. Also as an outstanding musician and actor, he took a leading part in the village religious dramas and operas, produced at Puttaparthi and other centres nearby. In those days this was the main form of village entertainment. Many of the dramatic performances were drawn from the great Indian spiritual epics such as the 'Rāmāyana'. One version of this very long work is given as a series of songs, and Kondama Raju knew the whole of it by heart.

In his old age, his many grandchildren used to gather around him in the cottage where he lived alone, as he brought to life the wonderful 'Rāmāyana' tales of gods and god-men. A constant member of his young fascinated audience was the little boy Satyanārāyana, known today as Satya Sai Baba. This education of the grandchildren in the mythology and spiritual lore of the great epics and 'Purānas' went on for many years; the grand old man lived to be one hundred and ten years old, dying in 1950 at Puttaparthi with a song of the mighty Rāma on his lips.

Twenty-four years earlier, in the year 1926, at the home of Kondama's eldest son, Pedda Raju, a coming event was being signalled by some strange signs. Pedda's offspring at this time consisted of one son and two daughters and now, following a long period of hopes, prayers and *pūjās* to the household gods, his wife Easwaramma was again pregnant. Her prayers had been for another son and, as the time drew near, her hopes were high. But she was puzzled too, for many unheard of things were happening in the house.

For instance, the big *tambūrā* leaning against the living room wall would sometimes twang in the middle of the night when no one was near to play it, and the *maddāla* (drum) on the floor would throb in the darkness as if an expert hand were beating it. But no hand could be seen. What could be the meaning of such things?

A priest, learned in the lore of the unseen, told them that these events indicated the presence of a beneficent power and foretold an auspicious birth.

The year 1926 was known as *akshaya*, meaning the "never declining, ever full" year, and 23rd November* is always, according to the old calendar, a day to be devoted to the worship of the god of great blessings, Shiva. Moreover, in this year a certain juxtaposition of the stars made the day even more auspicious for Shiva worship. So the villagers were already out chanting the names of Shiva when the rising sun outlined the purple rocky hills beyond the yellow sands of the Chitrāvati river. It was just at that moment, as the sun showed its face above the horizon, that under the eaves of Pedda Raju's cottage the child Satyanārāyana was born. He was given this name because the mother's *pūjās* and prayers had been to that particular form and name of God. Actually, Nārāyana is another appellation for Vishnū, the second in the Hindu Trinity, while *satya* is Sanskrit for truth, or reality; so Satyanārāyana can be taken to mean the "true all-pervading God". There is nothing odd or profane in the Hindu custom of naming a child in this way; most Hindus, men and women, bear one or more of the thousands of names of God.

*The Indian lunar equivalents of this date and this year are what it should mean [Ed.].

Soon after his birth the baby was placed on some bedclothes on the floor. Presently the women in the room saw the clothes moving up and down in a peculiar way as if there were something alive underneath. There was: a cobra. The snake did not harm the child, however.

Whatever the people present may have thought at the time, this appearance of a cobra in the lying-in room is now regarded by many of Baba's devotees as very significant, the cobra being one of the symbols of Shiva. Also Sai Baba of Shirdi had, it was said, on several occasions appeared to his followers in the form of a cobra.

From the beginning the baby was the pet of the village, loved for his beauty, ready smile and sweet nature. When Satya began to run about the dusty street and venture across the mud of the paddy fields and the barren hills beyond, there were certain characteristics that made him stand out from his young companions. Unlike most boys, he had a tender heart for all creatures, human or otherwise. He could not bear to cause or to see suffering. This made him a natural vegetarian from an early age among the meat-eaters around him.

Said Mr. Kasturi: "He kept away from places where pigs or sheep, cattle or fowl were killed or tortured, or where fish were trapped or caught; he avoided kitchens and vessels used for cooking flesh or fowl. When a bird was selected and talked about by someone in connection with dinner, Satyanārāyana, the little boy, would run towards it and clasp it to his bosom, and fondle it as if the extra love he poured on it would induce the elders to relent and spare the fowl. He was called by the neighbours *Brahmajnāni* on account of this type of aversion and his measure of love towards creation."

Furthermore, although fleet of foot, fond of outdoor sports and a leading scout, Satya would have nothing to do with sports involving ill treatment to animals, such as cock-fighting, bear-baiting, or the cruel bullock-cart races that were sometimes held in the soft sands of the dry riverbed.

Many beggars came to the cottage door and if little Satya were there none would be turned away without something to eat. More than this, when he met cripples and blind people in the street, he would bring them home and insist that his mother or elder sisters gave them food. Sometimes the family became irritated by these constant and expensive demands. Once, his mother said, "Look here! If we give the beggars food you will have to starve yourself." This threat did not daunt the child at all. He agreed at once that he would stay away from lunch that day, and he did. Nothing could persuade him to come to his plate.

The same thing happened frequently, and it was through such events that the family had a first glimpse of the strange things which were to take place concerning the child. On one occasion, when he had really outshone himself with beggar-feeding from the family larder, he decided to stay away from meals for several days. Although he persisted in this he showed no indications of hunger, and he carried on his activities without any signs of weakness. When his worried mother begged him to eat he told her that he had already filled his stomach with delicious balls of milk-rice. Where did he get them? she asked. Why, an old man, Tata, had given them to him. No one had ever seen or heard of such a person, and the mother would not believe little Satya's story. But he held up his right hand for her to smell, for, like most Indians, the Raju family ate with their hands rather than with cutlery. From the boy's palm the mother inhaled a fine fragrance of *ghee*, milk and curds - of a quality she had seldom experienced before. So the child whose sympathy for hungry strangers robbed his own plate was nourished by some mysterious unseen visitor. What could this mean?

Satya began his formal education at the village school where he showed himself bright and quick in learning. His special talents were, like those of his grandfather, for drama, music, poetry and acting. He was even writing songs for the village opera at the age of eight.

At about that age he went on to the Higher Elementary School at Bukkapatnam about two and a half miles away. One of the teachers who knew him there remembered him as an "unostentatious, honest, well-behaved boy". Another wrote in a book, published in 1944, that Satya often used to come a little early to school, collect the children around him, and conduct worship (*pūjā*) using a holy image or picture and some flowers he had gathered for the purpose. Even if the boys were not attracted to the religious ceremony itself, he had no difficulty in gathering them around him because of the things which he used sometimes to "produce" for their pleasure or help. From an empty bag he would take sweets and fruits, or if a comrade had lost a pencil or rubber, he would "produce" one of those from the bag. If someone was sick, he would bring out "herbs from the Himalayas", and give these as a cure.

When the children asked him how he performed such wonderful, magical feats he would say that a certain grāma shakti obeyed his will and gave him whatever he wanted. The children had little difficulty in believing in unseen beings, or in accepting that Satya had a faithful invisible helper. After all, he was their leader in most activities, in dramatics, athletics and scouting, for instance, and some boys began to call him their *guru*.

So when Satya went on to high school at Uravakonda, he found that his fame had spread there before him. Mr. Kasturi writes in his book* on Sai Baba:

> Boys told each other that he was a fine writer in Telegu, a good musician, a genius in dance, wiser than his teachers, able to peer into the past and peep into the future. Authentic stories of his achievements and divine powers were on everybody's lips. . . .
>
> Every teacher was anxious to be assigned some work in the section to

*The Life of Bhagavan Sri Sathya Sai Baba by N. Kasturi.

> which he was admitted; some out of curiosity, some out of veneration, and some out of a mischievous impulse to prove it all absurd. Satya soon became the pet of the entire school. . . . He was the leader of the school prayer group. He ascended the dais every day when the entire school assembed for prayer before commencing work, and it was his voice that sanctified the air and inspired both teachers and taught to dedicate themselves to their allotted tasks.

Satya's elder brother, Seshama, was a teacher at this high school, and he did his best to promote the family's ambition, that young Satya might be educated for a good position as a government officer; but things were moving rapidly towards an event that was to change all such worldly ambitions. It was one of those profound and shattering experiences which, in one form or another, seem often if not always to precede the missions of great teachers and inspirers of mankind.

At seven o'clock on the evening of 8th March 1940, Satya, while walking barefoot on the open ground, leapt into the air with a loud shriek, holding one toe of his right foot. In the area there were lots of big black scorpions and his companions immediately thought that he must have been bitten by one, but in the dusk they could not find the black culprit. Everyone was very concerned because of the local belief that no one could survive either a snake or scorpion bite in Uravakonda. This superstition seems related to the fact that Uravakonda is dominated by a hill crowned by a hundred-foot boulder in the shape of a hooded serpent. In fact, the place name itself means "serpent hill".

However, Satya slept that night without any signs of pain or sickness and seemed quite normal next day. Everyone was greatly relieved. Then, at seven in the evening, twenty-four hours after the supposed scorpion bite, the thirteen-year-old boy fell down unconscious; his body became stiff and his breathing faint. His brother, Seshama, brought a doctor who gave an injection and left a mixture to be taken when the boy regained consciousness. But Satya remained unconscious throughout the night.

Next day consciousness returned but the boy was by no means normal in behaviour. He seemed at times to be a different person. He seldom answered when spoken to; he had little interest in food; he would suddenly burst into song or poetry, sometimes quoting long Sanskrit passages far beyond anything learned in his formal education and training. Off and on he would become stiff, appearing to leave his body and go somewhere else. At times he would have the strength of ten, at others he was "as weak as a lotus stalk". There was much alternate laughter and weeping, but occasionally he would become very serious and give a discourse on the highest Vedanta philosophy. Sometimes he spoke of God; sometimes he described far-off places of pilgrimage to which – certainly during his life as Satyanārāyana Raju – he had never been.

The parents came from Puttaparthi, several doctors were consulted and prescribed various treatments, but there was no change in the patient. Many people thought that an evil spirit had taken possession of the boy, perhaps as a result of someone's black magic. So a number of exorcists tried their arts to invoke the evil spirit and transfer it to a lamb or fowl. But all to no avail.

Finally, the parents took Satya to a place near Kadiri where there was an exorcist of great repute. This expert in devilcraft was a Shakti worshipper before whom, it was said, "no evil spirit dare wag its poison tail". His appearance alone was enough to scare minor fiends away: he was of gigantic stature, with blood-red eyes, wild aspect and untamed manners. He seemed to work on the general principle that if he made the body of his patient suffer sufficiently the occupying demon would grow tired of the discomfort and leave it.

First of all, the fierce exorcist went through the ritual of sacrificing a fowl and a lamb and making the boy sit in the centre of a circle of blood while he chanted his incantations. Then he shaved Satya's head and, with a sharp instrument, scored three crosses on the scalp, scratching so deeply that the blood flowed. On these open wounds he poured the juice of limes, garlic and other acid fruits.

The parents, who were watching this treatment, were appalled at its severity; they were also amazed that Satya made not the slightest murmur and gave no sign whatever of suffering. Apparently, if there was a spirit tenant he too was immune, for he gave no notice of intention to quit.

The relentless exorcist arranged that every day in the early morning, one hundred and eight pots of cold water be poured over the markings on the scalp. This was done for several days, while other rough treatments went on, such as beating the boy on the joints with a heavy stick.

Finally the Shakti worshipper decided to use his strongest weapon, reserved for the most recalcitrant demons. This is the *kalikam*, which is described as a mixture of all the painful acidic abracadabra in the repertory of torture. He applied the *kalikam* to Satya's eyes. The boy's body shook under the impact of pain, his face and head turned red and swelled beyond recognition, the eyes shrunk to thin tear-exuding slits.

The parents and elder sister, who was also present, wept in anguish at the sight. Satya did not speak, but made signs for them to await him outside. When he came out he asked them to go and fetch a remedy he knew. It was brought and applied to the boy's eyes: the swelling subsided and the eyes opened to their normal size.

When he discovered what had happened, the witch doctor was enraged at this "interference with his treatment", as he called it. He had been within an inch of driving the demon from the boy, he fumed. But the parents had witnessed quite enough. They paid his fees and mollified him with the statement that they would build up the boy's stamina and then bring him back for a further course of the great man's learned exorcism. Then they took Satya away, still evidently possessed by the 'demon' who would quote long Sanskrit verses, discourse learnedly on Vedanta philosophy and cryptically on ethics, could sing lovely sacred songs, and call for the performance of *aarati* (a sacred ritual and song) because "the gods are passing across the sky".

The parents continued to take Satya to medical doctors and various kinds of healers, but no treatment seemed to make any difference. Two months passed by in this vain endeavour to get the boy back to a normal state. He had not returned to high school, and was still at home in Puttaparthi.

On the morning of 23rd May Satya called around him the members of the household, except his father who was busy at his produce store. With a wave of his hand the boy took from the air sugar candy and flowers and distributed them among those present. Soon, the neighbours began to crowd in. Satya, in a jovial mood, 'produced' more candy and flowers, and also a ball of rice cooked in milk for each person. The news that his son was performing apparent *siddhis* before a crowd of people reached Pedda.

Suddenly the father overflowed with anger and resentment. Was it not enough that the boy had caused them all this worry and strain over the last two months? Now he must be making a public show of himself with stupid tricks, hiding things and producing them by sleight of hand, no doubt, although where the boy had learned such *legerdemain* he had no idea. As Satya had for a long time been able to do inexplicable things, perhaps it was not just jugglery after all but something worse - black magic, sorcery!

Thus, with bitter thoughts, Pedda found himself a stout cane and went to the house. As he pushed through the crowd someone ordered him to go and wash himself before approaching the giver of boons. This incensed and angered him still more. Standing before his thirteen-year-old son and waving the stick threateningly, he shouted:

"This is too much! It must stop! What are you? Tell me - a ghost, or a god, or a madcap?"

Satya regarded his wrathful, distraught father and the upraised stick. Then he said calmly and firmly, "I am Sai Baba."

Pedda stood staring silently at his son while the cane slid from his hands. Satya continued, addressing all present, "I have come to ward off your troubles; keep your houses clean and pure."

A member of the family approached him and asked, "What do you mean by Sai Baba?"

He replied enigmatically, "Your Venkavadhūta prayed that I be born in your family; so I came."

In the Raju family there was a tradition of a great age named Venkavadhūta, an ancestor who had been looked upon as a *guru* by the people of hundreds of villages around the area. But only a few of the old folk gathered that morning around the Raju cottage had ever heard of anyone called Sai Baba. Those who had heard the name had no idea who he was. "*Baba*" was, they all knew, a Muslim word, and Pedda thought that perhaps his son was possessed by the spirit of a Muslim fakir.

The villagers who heard about it felt some trepidation and a great deal of wonder. That there was something special about little Satya they had long known. Otherwise how could he do such strange miraculous things? Since his illness, he often spoke like an old sage or seer. But who was this Muslim, Sai Baba? And what could he possibly have to do with the little boy they had all known, admired and loved for nearly fourteen years?

Truth is not that which is demonstrable, it is that which is ineluctable.

St. Exupéry

6

THE TWO SAIS

There were a few people in the district who had heard of a great wonder-working fakir named Sai Baba. Some thought he was still alive while others declared that he had been dead for years. Some said that he was a Muslim, others that he was a Hindu saint with a great following. In any case, he seemed very remote from the Raju family and the village of Puttaparthi.

Then, some friends told the family that there was in Penukonda, a town twenty-five miles away, a visiting government officer who was supposed to be an ardent devotee of the fakir, Sai Baba. It was decided to take Satya to him: perhaps that would clear up the mystery, or at any rate throw some light on the boy's strange announcement and behaviour.

Satya was quite willing to go, and the government officer condescended to see him. But when they met, the officer could not accept the idea that his great *guru*, who died at Shirdi in 1918, had been reborn as this wild talking boy.

"It's a mental derangement," he told the adults, "the child should be taken to a psychiatric institution for treatment."

Here young Satya interposed, "Yes, it's a mental derangement, but whose? You're just a *pūjāri*; you can't recognise the very Sai whom you are worshipping." Saying this, he took handfuls of ash from nowhere and, scattering it in all directions, left the room.

Reincarnation is part of the Hindu religion, and Satya's acquaintances had no difficulty with that idea in itself. But how were they to accept the boy's statement that he was actually Sai Baba of Shirdi reborn? The government officer had not helped them to swallow this big improbability.

Of course, considering Satya's miraculous powers, it could be true. It *might* be true. But they needed some proof, some strong convincing sign.

Thursday is regarded as *guru's* day in India and, on each Thursday, some people gathered around their new *guru*, young Satyanārāyana Raju. Once, soon after the visit to Penukonda, someone at a Thursday meeting voiced the desire that was in many minds.

"If you are really Sai Baba, show us a sign."

Satya saw the need of this. "Bring me those jasmine flowers," he said, pointing to a large bouquet in the room.

The flowers were placed in his hands and, with a quick gesture, he threw them on the floor. All present looked in awe: the flowers had fallen to form the name "Sai Baba" in Telegu script, the language spoken in the village. This flower writing was not something that required imagination to help; the words were strikingly clear, as if arranged with meticulous skill, all the curves and convolutions of the Telegu letters perfectly reproduced.

As the days and weeks passed there were other outward signs that the claim coming from the boy's lips was more than a childish fancy, more than something that could be explained away as a "mental derangement".

Nevertheless, in spite of all this. Satya submitted to the family's insistence that he go back to high school in Uravakonda. He returned in June, six months after the mysterious "black scorpion" had bitten his toe – or whatever happened to trigger off the psychic crisis leading to the emergence of new personality facets, and to the shattering announcement.

Thursdays soon became big events at Uravakonda. For the people gathered around him Satya Sai would, with a wave of his small hand, produce items which linked him with the deceased Shirdi saint: photographs of the old body, *gerua* cloth which he said was from the *kafni* that Shirdi Baba used to wear, dates and flowers which he declared came directly from the shrine at the Shirdi tomb, where they had been taken as offerings by worshippers.

Perhaps the most interesting phenomenon was his regular production of ash. Shirdi Sai had always kept a fire burning to have a ready supply of holy ash, which he called *ūdhi*. Now young Satya Sai took it as if from an invisible fire in a hidden dimension of space. This was a miracle that he had not performed until after the announcement of his identity with Sai Baba. The announcement also marked the beginning of the mysterious flow of photographs, drawings, paintings, and figures of Shirdi Baba which still goes on, as I personally experienced on a number of occasions.

A strange story of the production of a colour print of Shirdi Sai is told about these early days. It seems that before Satya returned to Uravakonda from Puttaparthi his eldest sister, Venkamma, had asked him for a picture of this Shirdi Baba about whom he was talking and composing *bhajan* songs. He promised to produce one for her on a certain Thursday.

However, on the day before that particular Thursday, Satya returned to his high school. "Well," Venkamma thought, "he has forgotten; it can't be helped; some day he will give it to me, no doubt."

On the promised Thursday night she was awakened by a strange sound, as if someone was calling outside the door. She sat up but all seemed quiet so she lay down again. Then there was a sound behind a bag of *javār* in the room. Perhaps it's a rat or snake, she thought, so she lit a lamp and searched. She found something white sticking out from behind the bag; it was a roll of thick paper. She unrolled it in the lamplight to find a picture of an old man seated with his right leg resting across his left knee. Soft but penetrating eyes looked out at her from below a knotted head-cloth. "It must be the promised picture," she thought, "delivered to me by some invisible messenger." Venkamma still has this coloured picture of Shirdi Sai and showed it to me when I visited her once at Puttaparthi.

But high school was not really the place for a boy who, like Jesus in the temple, could teach the teachers; in fact several of them, including the headmaster, used to bow before him and, seeing through the illusion of his youthful body, would listen to his inspiring words.

The final break from schooldays came on 20th October 1940. That morning, at his brother's house, where he was residing, Satya threw away his books, and announced that he was leaving. "My devotees are calling me. I have my work," he said. His sister-in-law says that when she heard these words she saw a halo around the boy's head which almost blinded her, so that she covered her eyes and cried out in alarm.

Nevertheless, she and his brother tried to persuade Satya to remain and continue his schooling. But he marched off to the home of an excise inspector who was very much attached to "little Baba". There the boy spent three days, mostly under a tree in the garden while people gathered around him. Some brought incense and camphor for ritualistic worship, some came to learn, some to pry into this great curiosity, and some to have a good laugh.

Satya led the group about him for hours in *bhajan* songs. Here in the garden another phenomenon occurred linking him further to Sai Baba of Shirdi. A photographer arrived to take a photograph of the little newsworthy prophet. A large crude stone seemed to spoil the composition of the picture, so the photographer asked Satya Sai to change his position. No co-operation seemed forthcoming, so the photographer clicked his camera and hoped for the best.

He got more than the best. When the film was developed and printed, it was found that the obstructing rock had become an image of Sai Baba of Shirdi. Both forms of Sai were in the picture though only one had been seen by the people assembled there.

During the three days Satya spent in the garden his parents arrived again at Uravakonda. Deciding, at long last, that school was out of the question they asked Satya to come home. He refused. They pleaded. Finally, after they had assured him that they would not in future obstruct or interfere with his mission, he agreed to return to Puttaparthi. There he began to gather more devotees around him; first in his father's home, and later in the spacious house of a disciple.

Throughout the years since the fourteen-year-old boy in the obscure village of Puttaparthi made the astounding claim that he was the reincarnation of India's most mysterious and powerful modern saint, there has been much interesting outward evidence to support that claim.

One story related in detail by Mr. Kasturi in his book on Baba's life tells how, about a year after the announcement, when Satya Sai was fifteen, he was visited by the Rani of Chincholi. Her late husband, the Raja, had been a very ardent devotee of Shirdi Baba and used to spend a few months every year at Shirdi. It is stated by the Rani and some old servants of the Palace that Shirdi Baba on several occasions came and stayed at Chincholi. He would, they say, ride with the Raja far out of town in a *tonga* drawn by bullocks. Incidentally, this *tonga* was later taken from Chincholi to Puttaparthi and left there.

During her visit to Puttaparthi to see this reincarnation of the old saint, the Rani persuaded him to accompany her to Chincholi. Perhaps she wanted to test him. There had been a number of changes at the Palace since the days when Shirdi Baba visited there. Although theoretically accepting the boy as a rebirth of the Shirdi saint, the Rani was startled when he immediately commented on the changes. He asked what had happened to a *margosa* tree that had once been there; he mentioned the previous existence of a well which had been filled up and was no longer in evidence; then pointing to a line of buildings he said, "They were not built when I was here in my previous body." This was all true.

Later he told her that there should be in the Palace a small stone image of a certain kind which, as Shirdi Baba, he had given to the Raja long ago. The Rani did not know of its existence but a thorough search was made and the image found. These were some of the many extracerebral memories that helped to establish the truth of the reincarnation.

There is significant interest in the experience of His Holiness Gayathri Swami, a disciple of the Shankaracharya of Sringeri Peetham. It happened while he was on a visit to Prashānti Nílayam *āshram*, after Satya Sai had moved there from his home village. The *swāmi* had once spent a whole year with Baba at Shirdi back in 1906, and often visited him in the later years. He was, perhaps, only partly convinced that Satya Sai was his old *guru* reborn. Anyway, on the night before he left Prashānti Nílayam, he had a vision. In this Shirdi Baba came to him and said that he had returned from his *mahāsamādhi* (the word used for the death of a great yogi) after eight years, and that he had brought all his "properties" with him fifteen years later. "What could this vision mean?" the *swāmi* wondered.

He understood its meaning next morning. When discussing his vision with devotees he was told that Satya Sai was born eight years after the passing of Shirdi Baba, also that he assumed the name of Sai Baba in his fourteenth year and was manifesting the full powers associated with Shirdi Baba by his fifteenth year. These powers, the *swāmi* felt, must be what his *guru* meant by 'properties', and the vision had been given to confirm in his mind that his Lord was again walking the earth.

Sai Baba of Puttaparthi has given many people visions of his old Shirdi form when they have requested it - and sometimes without request. One way in which he does this is to hold out both open palms to show on them bright shining images of the Shirdi and Puttaparthi bodies, one on each palm. Another way is to lead the person to be blessed with the vision into some quiet secluded room of whatever house he happens to be in. There in a corner of the room is seen the glowing, three-dimensional figure of Shirdi Baba.

One woman described such a vision in these words: ". . . there sat Shirdi Sai Baba on the floor in his characteristic pose, but with eyes closed and ash marks on his forehead and arms. The incense sticks before him were burning, and the smoke was rising straight into the air. His body was glowing with a strange effulgence, and there was a beautiful fragrance around."

It might be argued - and perhaps rightly - that the power to produce hallucinations of the Shirdi form is no proof that Satya ever lived in that form. None the less there are many other types of evidence pointing to the fact that the two Sais are in spirit one and the same.

The men who as adults were close disciples of Baba at Shirdi have most of them passed on with the passing years. But there are still a few old gentlemen around who as boys visited Shirdi when the old saint was still there. These he recognises even though their own mothers would not easily see the boy of long ago within the ageing body.

One of these is Mr. M. S. Dixit who, having retired, now lives at Sai Baba's summer retreat at Whitefield near Bangalore. While I was there with Baba one summer, I had many wonderful talks with Mr. Dixit on his experiences of the two Sais.

He was born in 1897, the son of Sadashiv Dixit, an advocate who was at one time *diwān* (prime minister) of the royal state of Kutch. Sadashiv's eldest brother, Hari S. Dixit, was a solicitor in Bombay and a member of the Legislative Council. It was this Hari Dixit who became a close devotee of Shirdi Baba. In the company of his uncle Hari, M. S. Dixit told me, he made his earliest visits to Shirdi, first in the year 1909, and again in 1912. Before this second visit he had been suffering what he called "half-headaches". At sunrise half his head would start to ache agonisingly; then a little before sunset it would stop. This would go on each day for about two months at a stretch; it was very distressing. His uncle took him to Sai Baba, hoping for a cure of the strange headaches. Mr. Dixit recalls vividly how he was sitting near Sai Baba one day when Baba suddenly said to him, "Why are you sitting there? Go home!"

Young Dixit replied that he had a bad headache and the heat of the fire near which he was sitting brought him some relief. But Baba insisted that he must go. It was the custom when leaving to take some ash from the fireplace and put it in Baba's hand, so that he might give it with his parting blessing. The fourteen-year-old boy did this. Baba held the *ūdhi* for a moment and then applied it to the lad's forehead with some force.

Young Dixit felt that he had been slapped on the head as well as ordered to go away, so he told his uncle that he would not visit Baba any more.

Hari Dixit replied, "Are you a fool? The slap means that your headache will not recur."

This turned out to be true. The strange and terrible half-headaches never came back after that day, and young Dixit understood that Baba had been in his enigmatic way ordering, not the boy, but the headache to go away.

Six years later, in July 1918, M. S. Dixit found himself ill again, this time with bad haemorrhoids and an anal fistula. The medical men of Bombay where he was living said he must undergo an operation, but he felt very nervous about having surgery and did not want it. Yet he was suffering a lot and there was much bleeding. He felt very miserable about his condition.

At one of the regular Thursday evening gatherings of Shirdi Baba's Bombay devotees, M. S. Dixit was somehow overcome by the devotional atmosphere combined with his own misery. Although a young man of twenty, he broke down and cried like a child. That night he had a dream in which Shirdi Baba came to him and chided him for "weeping like a girl". Then the old saint told him what to use as a cure for his ailment. After waking, Dixit could remember everything except the name of the medicament which Baba had prescribed. He was very distressed about this and decided to go to Shirdi as soon as possible and get the name from Baba's lips.

But before he could go he heard that Baba had died. "Now," he thought gloomily, "I shall never know and must go on suffering."

Then, at the next Thursday evening meeting, following the news of Baba's passing, he found himself again overwhelmed with sorrow for himself, and wept once more. The same night brought him another vivid dream. In this Baba stood before him again, still in the old Shirdi form. He said, "What! Crying like a girl again!" Then he told the young man to take seven seeds of pepper, crush them to powder, and each day take a pinch of the powder mixed with *ūdhi*. All devotees, incidentally, kept some of Baba's *ūdhi* in their homes.

M. S. Dixit remembered these dream-instructions clearly next morning and carried them out. On the third day of treatment the pain stopped; on the seventh the bleeding stopped. A complete cure took place and the complaint never returned.

The years passed and the pages of Dixit's life turned over: he was in business; he was married; he was a major and Brigade Education Officer in the army during the Second World War and for some years afterwards. The year 1959 found him back in commercial life in the west coast city of Mangalore. During leisure time he was reading a famous Hindu religious work entitled *Guru Charitra*. If this is read through completely within seven days, it is said, great spiritual benefits will ensue.

On the evening of the sixth day of the reading he had a dream. In this he was walking along a broad avenue of trees, and felt that someone was following him. He looked back. There was a man, a very distinctive man, close behind him. Dixit asked, "Who are you and why are you following me?" But there was no reply, the figure just continued to follow silently. After a few minutes Dixit looked back again and saw the man still following him. Neither said anything. Soon the footsteps drew closer, and Dixit felt that something was being poured over his head from behind. He realised that it was ash. . . .

That was all of the dream he could remember on waking, but very clear in his mind remained the striking, unique figure and face of the man who followed him.

Some months afterwards, through an odd set of circumstances, he heard that there was a reincarnation of Shirdi Baba but did not believe it. Then later on he heard the same story again from another quarter, and was shown a photograph of Satya Sai Baba. It was the man who had followed him in the dream. Now his interest was really aroused. He remembered his uncle's story that Shirdi Baba had once told him: "I will appear again as a boy of eight years." Was this the boy, now grown to manhood? He decided to go as soon as possible to Puttaparthi and find out all he could.

It was early in 1961 when he managed to get there, as one of a party of about thirty people. The *āshram* was choked with the Shivarātri thousands, and Dixit stood among them waiting for a view of Satya Sai Baba on the high balcony. When the little red-robed, dome-haired figure with the sweet, lovable face appeared, Dixit knew for certain that it was the figure of his strange dream.

Yet, he thought, how can this be the old saint of Shirdi? With his coloured silks, hair like a woman and the big crowds around him, this man is more like a film star. Shirdi Baba was rugged, homespun, simple; how can this possibly be the same man? Suddenly he wanted to go home.

However, he stayed to watch Satya Sai pour huge quantities of sacred ash from a small bowl over the statue of Shirdi Sai, and the same evening take nine *lingams* from his mouth. Then during a public discourse next day Baba said, "Some who have come here think I am too much like a film star, they object to my bright-coloured robes and the style of my hair. . .". With consternation, Dixit heard all of his own unspoken critical thoughts being repeated from the platform. Then Baba went on to explain the reasons – good reasons Dixit felt – for the striking attire, the unique hair style and the other features of this incarnation.

Well, Dixit decided, he is certainly something very special. There is no doubt about his supernormal powers, but. . . he is so different from old Shirdi Baba. Can it, really, be the same soul?

On a second visit to Prashānti Nílayam three months later he was called into a room with a group of half-a-dozen people for an interview. Baba came in, spoke to a few people, and then went up to M. S. Dixit, who was holding a small photograph of his uncle, H. S. Dixit, in his hand. Baba took the photograph from him, looked at it, and said, "That's H. S. Dixit, your uncle, your father's elder brother, and my old devotee at Shirdi. Now have you any more doubts?"

His doubts were fewer because all that Baba had just said was true. Dixit had told no one his name at the *āshram*. He was there *incognito* - just an unknown member of a crowd of visitors, but Baba had recognised the face of his uncle in the photograph at first sight.

After that, Dixit often made trips to the *āshram* and, through the years, enjoyed the wealth of Sai Baba's miraculous powers, great compassion and spiritual teachings. Once, speaking of Shirdi Baba's remark to his uncle Hari about coming back to earth "as a boy of eight years", Baba told Dixit that what he had really said was that he would return as a boy in eight years, that is, eight years after his death - which he, in fact, did. Satya Sai added that H. S. Dixit must have misunderstood him.

But it was the many, many little things, more than these big ones, that finally convinced him that the two Sais were one, Dixit told me. He went on to describe these important little things; the similarities in the *siddhis*, the parallels in the teachings and manner of instruction, the subtle echoes from the past in gesture, phrase and attitude. "Sometimes I even see on his face the same old smile that I saw long ago on the face of Shirdi Baba," he said.

Of course, the differences which he felt so sharply at first are indeed there, he admits. But there is, after all, a different body, a different setting, a different period in time - a different environment for the Sai mission. And therefore the mission, while in spirit the same, cannot be precisely the same in form and style, and it is to be expected that the outer personality through which the message comes to the world will also be different. Sai Baba himself comments that he is not as hard or angry now as he was in the earlier manifestation. He is more tolerant and gentle. He explains the difference by means of a simile: "The mother is usually hard when the children enter the kitchen and disturb the cooking, but while serving the food she is all smiles and patience. I am now serving the dishes cooked then. Wherever you may be, if you are hungry and if your plate is ready, I shall serve you the dishes and feed you to your heart's content."

At another time, concerning the controversy about whether he is the same Baba or not, he said, "When there are two pieces of candy, one square, another circular, one yellow and the other purple in colour, unless one has eaten and realised the taste of both pieces one cannot believe that both are the same. Tasting, experiencing - that's the crucial thing for knowing the identity."

Sai Baba of Shirdi, the *guru* from whom Satya Sai Baba believes himself to be reincarnated.

Another person who met Shirdi Baba is an old lady now living at Prashānti Nílayam. N. Kasturi writes in the second part of his *Life of Satya Sai Baba* that this lady was, when a child, taken to Shirdi by her father, a collector in the Nizam's dominions. Later, after all her four children had died, she went again to Shirdi in 1917 and asked Baba for permission to stay on with him for spiritual initiation and training.

But Baba said, "Not now. I will come again in Andhra; you will meet me then and be with me."

She returned to the Nizam's dominions and spent her life doing welfare and charitable works. During her travels, collecting money and support for her home of refuge for orphan girls, which she had called "Sai Sadan", she heard that there was a boy in Uravakonda who had announced himself as Sai Baba. Remembering what Baba had told her in 1917, about reincarnating in Andhra, she hastened to Uravakonda, arriving there on a Thursday. She joined the crowd that went to visit the young Sai Baba on that day, and sat near him.

She says that Baba spoke to her in a low voice in Hindi, as at Shirdi, "So you have come, my child."

Then he told her that she owed him sixteen rupees, reminding her that of forty rupees she collected for religious celebrations at Shirdi, sixteen were still on loan to a friend of hers. Then smiling he whispered, "I am telling you this only to convince you that I am Shirdi Sai Baba."

The lady is now with Satya Sai Baba at Prashānti Nílayam, Andhra Pradesh, happy that what he told her half a century ago at Shirdi has come true.

Yet it is not the outer but the inner evidence that will lead to conviction in this deep question. People who have stayed with Satya Sai Baba a long time, and also known Shirdi Baba - either directly or through the written records - have no doubt that both are incarnations of the same divine being.

A number of books have now been published on Sai Baba of Shirdi, including Narasimha Swami's excellent four-volume work on his life and teachings. I find that when deeply absorbed in these, I often think I am reading about Sai Baba of Puttaparthi; I must continually remind myself that these are the teachings, sayings, doings of Shirdi Baba, not the present-day Satya Sai, there is such a profound similarity.

Before describing my further personal experiences with Satya Sai Baba I must return for a while to those early days at Puṭtaparthi. Satya Sai himself has said that the first thirty-two years of this incarnation would be marked mainly by *leelās* and *mahimās* (miracles), and the subsequent years by discourses and verbal teachings. He pointed out that this was just a question of emphasis, that both aspects would be in evidence at all times.

Considering the many miracles I have witnessed during this, his teaching phase, I wondered what life must have been like with Satya Sai during the years of his miracle phase. So I sought out and talked to men and women who had known him then. Amongst them were practical men of business and affairs, well-travelled people of the world, high-ranking civil servants and highly educated people of the professions.

All were happy to tell their strange and wonderful stories.

The spirit shall look out through matter's gaze,
and matter shall reveal the spirit's face.

Sri Aurobindo

7

ECHOES FROM THE EARLY YEARS

When Satya Sai Baba finally returned from high school to the village of Puttaparthi just before his fourteenth birthday, he went first to live at his father's house but, before very long, moved around the corner to the home of a Brahmin family named Karnum. This was the place to which he had often run as a child to have vegetarian meals when there was a meat meal at his own home. Now he took up his residence there and the housewife, whose name was Subbamma, not only tended him with love and care but also welcomed the growing number of his followers to her home, which was much more spacious and suitable to the purpose than the cottage of Satya Sai's parents.

So it was at the Karnum house, still standing today in the main street of Puttaparthi, that Sai Baba's mission had its firm beginnings in 1941. The gatherings were at first held in a room, but the crowd soon overflowed into the road outside. So a shed was built; as the months passed this was enlarged and then a tent was added. Still the numbers continued to burst all accommodation. Furthermore, Baba insisted on feeding visitors who came from a distance. Often the amount of food cooked threatened to be totally inadequate, and it was here that he first showed the Christ-like power of increasing the food supply to meet the need of the moment.

A lady who used to help the devoted Subbamma in those early days describes the ritual Baba used for this. When quietly informed that the food was not sufficient, he would ask for two coconuts – always important items for religious ceremonials in India. He would strike one against the other so that they both broke exactly in half, and then "he sprinkled the coconut water on the little heaps of rice and the vessels containing the other items, and gave the signal to proceed with the task of serving all who had come, or who might yet come before dusk". There was always plenty for everyone.

It was in those days of cramped sitting space that he began taking his followers to sit on the sands of the Chitrāvati. This today is a river of sand, three or four hundred yards broad, near the village, and dry except in the rainy season. In the early 1940s it was much the same, except that most of the time there was a narrow stream of water running through the sands. Here the young Sai would sit with his crowd of followers. Here on the sands he would lead them in *bhajan* singing, advise them on their personal problems, teach them the way to live, and build up their faith by various miraculous phenomena.

On the crest of a rocky knoll on the left bank of the river, about half-a-mile from the village, grows a solitary tamarind tree. In those early years it acquired the name of *kalpatāru*, or wish-fulfilling tree. This was because Sai Baba used to take his devotees – or at least those who could climb – up to this tree and ask them what fruit they would like to pick from it. When they named the fruit it would be seen immediately hanging from a branch of the tree. Apples, pears, mangoes, oranges, figs and other varieties of fruit, out of season, and some not ever grown in the district, were plucked from the wild tamarind tree.

There were other strange, deeply moving events around that tree. Sometimes Baba would challenge the youths of his own age to a race up the hill from the sands to where the tree showed its foliage against the sky, some hundred and fifty feet above. It was a steep, rocky climb, almost vertical in places; yet before the others had taken more than a few steps, young Satya Sai would be up there, calling from the summit.

The young men would then stop and with the other devotees below watch the youth on the hill top, knowing that something amazing would certainly take place. One of the competitors in the hill-climbing contest, then a college student, tells what he saw there: "The time was a little past seven," he says, "with evening closing in. Suddenly, a great ball of fire like a sun pierced the dusk around the youth on the crest. The light was so bright it was impossible to keep your eyes open and watch it. About three or four of the devotees fainted and fell."

Different visions are said to have been seen on different occasions. Sometimes it was a great fiery wheel or a full moon with Baba's head in the centre, sometimes a blinding jet of light from his forehead – from the third eye centre – sometimes a pillar of fire. I have spoken to a number of people who personally witnessed those miracles of light.

Small wonder that echoes of these village happenings were heard in Madras and other faraway places, and that the curious, the distressed and the true seekers began to arrive from a wide circumference. No doubt there would have been an even greater influx had the journey been less difficult. But only the valiant-hearted travellers would tackle the exhausting trip with its final stage by bullock cart or on foot.

Even so, in 1944, because of increasing crowds, what is now called the Old Mandir was built on the edge of the village. This is a kind of double barn with a galvanised iron roof and enough space for fair-sized *bhajan* crowds. At the back are rooms for sleeping and eating, and some of the visiting devotees used to stay here, or camp nearby. Nowadays it has only historic interest. Visitors to Prashānti Nílayam walk down the two furlongs of dusty road to be shown over the Old Mandir. Its walls are lined with quaint old photographs of the young Sai and groups of his devotees which illustrate, as much as anything, the poor level of provincial photography here in the 1940s.

In the world outside it was an eventful decade, seeing World War Two and the start of India's independence. But to a growing number of people the most exciting and most important events were taking place at Puttaparthi, and the Old Mandir could not always seat the numbers arriving. So gatherings on the sands of the Chitrāvati river remained popular.

Some of the visitors who came simply out of curiosity remained to pay deep homage, and returned there again and again. Some from distant centres persuaded the young Sai to visit their cities and stay in their houses, where their friends could meet him too. Many of the earliest devotees are still, more than twenty years later, going to the *āshram* to see him as often as possible and begging him to bless their homes with his presence whenever he is in their vicinity.

The long-standing devotees whom I met proved to be an inspiring aspect of my research into this great miracle man. They are not, as some readers might suspect, uneducated, fanatical, vague or visionary. On the contrary, they are well-educated, rational, practical citizens of the kind whose integrity and reliability would be accepted in any court of law.

I needed to assure myself of such things – as I assure the reader now – because at the time I gathered some of the stories in this book I had not yet personally experienced much of the type of phenomena they describe. Now I have seen so much that my attitude has completely changed. The miraculous has become familiar.

Most of the old devotees have given me permission to use their names, placing the cause of truth and their belief in the transcendental powers of Sai Baba above all other considerations. In this chapter are some sample stories told by men and women who have known Satya Sai since the 1940s.

Mr. P. Parthasarathy is a well-known businessman of Madras, being part-owner of a company connected with shipping. He told me that he first met Sai Baba in 1942 when the latter came to Madras to stay at the home of a neighbour of his. Soon after that he and other members of his family went to Puttaparthi.

He stayed there a whole month and witnessed Baba's levitation up the hill to the wish-fulfilling tree, seeing both a bright halo of flame around the young Sai's head and a shaft of light from his forehead between the eyes. He says: "All the time in those days Baba was full of laughter and fun. He would sing songs, and many times a day he would perform some miracle – often as a prank, such as making a clock run backwards, or holding people to their seats by some invisible force. At picnics he would tap empty dishes and, when the lids were removed, the dishes would be full of food, sometimes hot as if straight from the kitchen. I have also seen him multiply small amounts of food to feed big crowds.

"These outings were very happy events always. Often Baba would turn some wild tree at hand into our *kalpatāru* tree; any fruit we liked to name could be picked from its branches."

Mr. Parthasarathy had been suffering from asthma for many years and, soon after his arrival at Puttaparthi, Baba materialised an apple with a wave of the hand and told him to eat it as a cure. He has never had another attack of asthma in the quarter-century since that day.

But he says that the most important miracle of those early experiences was connected with his mother. She was completely blind with cataracts when the family first met Sai Baba. His treatment of her was simple – as simple as the paste of clay and spittle that Christ used on a blind person. Baba put jasmine petals on the woman's eyes and held them in place with a bandage. Each day he changed them for fresh ones and at the same time insisted that she should go daily to *bhajan*. This went on for ten days, and when he took the bandage off for the last time she was able to see again quite clearly. "She lived for ten years after that," Mr. Parthasarathy told me, and had no more trouble with her sight.

Mr. G. Venkatamuni was a leading figure in the fertiliser business in Madras when I used to talk to him about his early experiences with Sai Baba. Unfortunately he has since died, but his son, Iswara, also a devout devotee, carries on the same family business. Baba, when in Madras, always stays at least part of his time at the Venkatamuni home.

An honest, matter-of-fact person, Mr. Venkatamuni, far from exaggerating, was inclined towards understatement in all his descriptions. This I found out when I checked some of his stories with other witnesses present at the time. I give here just one or two of the many incredible experiences he had with Baba, as he told them to me.

In the year 1944 he began hearing strange stories about a wonder boy in a village of Andhra Pradesh, the state from which his own ancestors had come. He decided to go and see for himself what truth there was in the stories.

On the day of Venkatamuni's arrival at Puttaparthi, Satya Sai, then seventeen years old, took him with a small party to the sands of the river. As they sat there talking, Baba put his hand in the sand and took out a handful of sweets, distributing them among the party. "They were hot," said Mr. Venkatamuni, "as if just out of an oven. I had to let them cool before I could eat them." From this he knew that what he had seen was no mere sleight-of-hand trick.

He stayed on at the village, hoping to see further wonders. His hopes were more than fulfilled, he said, and he described the same copious stream of marvels witnessed by the early devotees.

"I was young then," Mr. Venkatamuni said, "and it was all great fun. I used to go swimming with Sai Baba and the other young men, and it was then that I saw the *shankha* and *chakra* on the soles of his feet."

"What is that?" I enquired.

"It's a circular mark - you might call it a birth mark. Hindus believe it's one of the signs of an *avatār*."

Mr. Venkatamuni and his wife became close devotees of Sai Baba, going to his *āshram* regularly, and having him stay for days or weeks at their home in Madras.

It was in 1953, nine years after the first meeting, that they experienced some Sai magic that was in its way unique. They had set off on a global journey that was to begin in Europe and include the Far East. Travelling by air, their first stop was Paris where they planned to spend several weeks.

While out walking in the streets on the first day, they decided to change some traveller's cheques and go shopping. Mrs. Venkatamuni was carrying the folder of cheques in her handbag; or, at least, she thought so until she opened the bag and found they were not there.

Both decided that she must have put them in her suitcase, after all, so they went straight back to the hotel. But the traveller's cheques were neither in her nor her husband's suitcase. After a more thorough search, a repeated combing through all their belongings, it became painfully obvious that the precious folder was lost. Where it was lost they had no idea. Mrs. Venkatamuni had last noticed it, as far as she could recall, in her handbag some time before they left Bombay. It was an awkward and very unhappy situation. Here they were in a foreign city at the beginning of a world tour with hardly enough cash to pay their first hotel bill. They sat depressed and forlorn in their bedroom, wondering what they could do.

What they did would seem utterly crazy to anyone except a close Sai Baba devotee. To him it would seem the only sensible thing to do. With the few *francs* they had brought to France in cash they sent a cable to Baba asking for his help. After that they felt better, knowing that assistance would come in some form. But they hardly expected what, in fact, happened.

A day or two later they went window shopping again. Mrs. Venkatamuni decided to make a list of the things she would buy when she had some money. She opened her handbag to take out her pencil and notebook, and her heart gave a great bound. There, right on top of everything, lay a folder of traveller's cheques, which proved to be their own. It was the folder dropped or left behind in India. Mr. Venkatamuni told me that his wife's handbag was a medium-sized one, and that they had both searched through it many times, emptying everything out on the bed to do so. There was, in the circumstances, no possibility whatever that they could have overlooked the folder if it had been in the bag earlier. Mr. Venkatamuni had no doubt that Baba had teleported the folder from wherever it had been lost. A most useful miracle!

They sent another cable from Paris, one of thanks. When they returned from the enjoyable world tour, they were able to tell Baba personally how deeply grateful they had been for his timely and superhuman help. He just smiled, saying nothing - and they asked him for no details.

A well-known and highly honoured citizen of Madras who confirms what others have said about Baba's early miracle phase is Mr. V. Hanumantha Rao. This man, now retired, was Transport Commissioner of Madras Presidency (which then included part of the present state of Andhra Pradesh) when he first met Sai Baba in 1946.

The relationship between Baba and this grand old philanthropist and his wife is a moving story, involving aspects other than the early miracles and pranks of the fun-loving Sai. I will tell it in another chapter where it belongs. But here I want to mention an interesting little story that may throw light on the *modus operandi* behind at least some of Baba's phenomena production.

Both Mr. and Mrs. Hanumantha Rao have often told me about the wonderful celestial quality of those early Sai Baba years when he used to drive with them in their car, how he would sing beautiful songs and ask them to name whatever food they wanted, or whatever out-of-season fruit they fancied. Then, with some gesture, he would produce instantaneously the things they had requested. They also told how, when he stayed in their home, he was as natural, spontaneous and carefree as a child, and yet seemed to have the power to command with his will all the forces of the three worlds.

Once, they said, on the birthday of Lord Krishna, Baba was walking aimlessly, it seemed, about the sitting room of their Madras home. Suddenly he turned to Mrs. Hanumantha Rao and remarked, "There are some *devas* [angels] here waiting to give me a bowl of sweets."

As she looked, seeing nothing, he held out both hands and took from the air, as if from some invisible person, a large, carved glass bowl. The bowl seemed suddenly to materialise. Baba handed it to Mrs. Hanumantha Rao. It was filled, as they described it, with "divine-tasting sweets of many varieties from different parts of India".

After this incident Satya Sai asked for an apron. When it was brought he put it on and began singing lullaby songs. He acted the part of a nursemaid carrying the baby Krishna, and soothing it to sleep. Then from the folds of the apron he took a carved sandalwood idol of Krishna which had certainly not been there, or anywhere else in the house, before.

Mr. and Mrs. Hanumantha Rao showed me, when I visited them, the glass bowl and the Krishna statuette, two treasured items brought long ago into the home of the transport commissioner by some mysterious method known only to the young Satya Sai. It seems from his remark that he has beings of another plane of existence under his command for such transportations.

Mrs. Nagamani Pournaiya, who lives in Bangalore, is the widow of a government district transport officer and the mother of the popular novelist Kamala Taylor, who is married to an Englishman and lives in England. Nagamani first met Sai Baba in 1945 and spent many long periods at his *āshram*. I found her always happy to talk about Baba and she helped fill out my mental picture of the early period, confirming the main features and adding some new ones to the bright tapestry of those years.

Nagamani has herself written a book on Sai Baba, but there are one or two of her experiences that bear repeating here. Many have described to me Sai Baba's miraculous production of figures – usually statuettes of Hindu or other gods – from the sands, and I have seen it myself. But Nagamani told me that, on one occasion, when a party went with Baba to the sands of the Chitrāvati river, she saw idols rising up out of the sands themselves. Baba simply scraped away a little sand to reveal the top of the head, then the figure itself began to rise, as if driven up by some power beneath.

First, she said, came a figure of Shiva, then his consort Parvati, and then a *lingam*. As each rose a few inches above the sand Baba pulled it out and threw it quickly to one side. This was because the objects were made of metal and were quite hot, too hot to hold for more than a second. After they had cooled, he took them back to the Old Mandir for *pūjā* (ritualistic worship).

But one of the most striking of her many fantastic experiences has to do with a surgical operation by Baba. I have had from devotees several descriptions of such operations. But Nagamani reports the earliest one of which I have heard.

A man and his wife came to stay at Puttaparthi. Nagamani observed that the man had a bulbous, tremendously swollen stomach. He spent all his time lying down, either in his room near the Old Mandir or outside in the open. She heard that he was not able to eat anything, nor even to take coffee. This latter seemed the "last straw" to Nagamani, who loved her coffee. She went to Baba and asked him to cure the man.

But the days passed and nothing happened, so she said again, "Please do something for that poor man, Baba!" He smiled and answered, "Do you think this place is a hospital?"

Then one evening all the devotees were going with Baba to the sands of the riverbed. It was not a very large party, and each of the women decided to take some item of food for a picnic. Nagamani took the coffee. She also left a pot of water on an outside wood fire, not far from the Mandir. With this warm water, she said, she was hoping to bathe Baba's feet on their return from the sands.

At the riverbed they all had a wonderful time singing songs. Baba told them beautiful stories about the gods, occasionally producing some appropriate object from the sand. All this kept their spirits at a high level, so that when three wild panthers came near them to drink at the stream they felt no fear whatever. The panthers seemed to regard them as friends and went about their business unperturbed.

When they returned to the Mandir, Nagamani went to stir up the fire under the pot and Baba disappeared into the room of the sick man. After a while he came running towards the fire, asking her for some warm water to wash his hand. She looked and saw that his right hand was all red.

"Have you been painting, or something?" she asked in fun.

"It's blood," he replied.

Then peering closer in the fading light she saw that he carried in the blood-smeared hand something that looked like "a dirty coloured ball of old banana leaf". This he tossed away, and then washed the blood from his hand in the water she gave him. "Well," he said teasingly, "you've been insisting that I turn this place into a hospital, so I've just done the necessary operation on the man."

Was he joking? She had seen blood and something horrible that he had thrown away. Had he removed a growth from the man? Sai Baba, apparently reading the queries in her mind, handed her a roll of cotton-wool and said, "Take this and help the man's wife put a fresh bandage on him."

She went to the door but remained outside. She wanted very much to see what had happened but somehow felt afraid to go in. Presently Sai Baba came and took her into the room. The man was still lying down, his wife sitting beside him. Baba went and pulled up the man's shirt to show her the operation.There was no bandage, but across the stomach was a thin mark, like a cut that had already healed, and the stomach was no longer large and swollen. Both the man and woman were looking silently at Sai Baba as if he were God. No word was spoken. Baba led Nagamani out again, and finally permitted her to bathe his feet.

Next morning, dying to know just what had taken place, she returned to enquire about the health of the patient. He was sitting up eating a hearty breakfast. He told her that Sai Baba had come into the room on the previous evening; and, waving his hand, produced from the air a knife and some other instrument. Next he produced some ash and rubbed it on the sufferer's forehead. This seemed to act as an anaesthetic because the man lost consciousness and knew no more until the operation was over, and Baba was telling him that all was well. The cut had felt just a little sore, but now it was quite normal.

Nagamani wanted to know how it had healed so quickly. The wife told her that Baba had simply held the opening together with his fingers and it had healed up immediately. Then he had smeared some *vibhūti* on the wound, held his hand there for a while, assured the patient that he would be all right, and left.

Nagamani realised that Baba's instructions to her the evening before about a bandage were simply to give her an excuse for going to see the patient. She was surprised that he had been pleased to satisfy her curiosity, but perhaps it was because she had shown concern for the sick man. She felt no amazement, only awe, at the discovery of this new wonder. Nothing Baba ever did surprised her any more; everything simply added to her profound love of him.

There are other types and varieties of phenomena in the chronicles of the early years but, as I actually saw examples of these with my own eyes during the 1960s, it is better that I describe my personal experiences.

Come to me with empty hands.
I shall fill them with gifts and grace.

Satya Sai Baba

8

WITH BABA IN THE HILLS

One winter in Madras Sai Baba invited my wife and myself to spend the following June with him at his summer retreat at Whitefield, near Bangalore. We were filled with joy at the prospect, but we had learned by then that it is far wiser to have no firm expectations about Baba's future movements. There is such a colossal demand for his presence and time, and it seems that he goes wherever he is most needed; or, in other words, he does whatever is most relevant to the advancement of his mission. At least that is the interpretation we put on Baba's movements, but the fact is that they follow some law beyond our comprehension. So we told each other that we might, if lucky, be with him for a day or two at Whitefield. As for spending a whole month in his presence - well, it was all right to hope, but presumptuous to expect.

Still in that state of mind, we arrived in Bangalore at the beginning of June and stayed the night with a fellow member of the Theosophical Society. He drove us in his car the next morning to Whitefield, which is on rising ground about twelve miles outside the city. On the way he explained that Whitefield had come into being as a British community, but that now there were very few Europeans left. It was, we found, a widely spread out place, with most of the houses large and in broad, pleasant gardens. Eventually, set in a high brick wall, we found a gate with the name "Brindāvanam" above it and a khaki-clad Gurkha on guard. We knew from the name that this was Baba's residence.

Just inside the gate was a cottage from which came a benign, snowy-haired man who proved to be Mr. M. S. Dixit. He installed us in a room of his cottage, which I supposed had been the lodge in former days, and gave us the good news that Sai Baba was in residence. We could see no signs of another house, and I wondered where Baba actually lived.

However, a little later in the morning Mr. Dixit led us across the tree-studded grounds, through wandering tribes of monkeys, and up a flight of steps to a higher terrace. Here was a park-like garden of shrubs and covered walks and a good-sized house where we found Sai Baba surrounded by a party of resident guests, with many day visitors from Bangalore.

"Swami", as his devotees mostly address him, welcomed us like a mother who is happy that her children have come home. He offered us the choice of moving into the big house with him, in which case we would have to separate, Iris sleeping dormitory-style with the women on one side of the house and I in the men's dormitory on the other; or we could lodge where we were with Mr. Dixit, but have our meals and spend as much time as we wished in the big house. We chose the latter.

That morning we watched a sacred thread ceremony in the central hall of Baba's residence. The boy receiving the sacred thread was the son of Mr. Jawa, owner of the Joy ice cream factories. The parents, grandmother and other family members, all of whom are Baba devotees, were present for the ceremony and the hall was crammed with spectators. Under Sai Baba's supervision, pundit priests from Prashanti Nilayam carried out the ritual. At the right moment Baba stepped into the centre of the scene, waved his hand in the now well-known manner and, from that occult niche in space which he sometimes calls "the Sai Stores", produced the necessary thread to place around the boy's neck.

After the ceremony came a feast on the broad verandah. We sat cross-legged on the floor in two long rows, eating Indian dishes from plantain leaf plates while a servant kept the monkeys at bay with a pole. Swami walked around making sure that all his guests were happy. On this festive occasion men and women ate together, but normally at Brindavanam they use the dining room at separate times, Baba eating with the men and sometimes visiting the ladies to talk to them during their meals.

Sai Baba has found that it certainly would not pay him to advertise. Even without the benefits of publicity, crowds tend to impede his movements. So my wife and I felt honoured when he confided to us quietly that he was taking a small party to spend a couple of weeks with him at Horsley Hills, some ninety miles north of Bangalore, and we were overjoyed to learn that we were to be included in the party. All accommodation arrangements had been made by one of his devotees, Mr. T. A. Ramanatha Reddy, the

Superintending Engineer of Roads and Buildings in the large area which included Horsley Hills. We should be ready to move, Swami said, in a couple of days' time. We understood that this was confidential information.

As we had expected to be away from headquarters at Adyar for the whole summer in various types of climate, we had a good deal of luggage with us. So we began to plan what to take and what to leave stored at Brindavanam. It was good, we thought, that Swami had given us plenty of warning. If anyone else at Brindavanam knew about the pending move, they said nothing – and we said nothing to anyone.

We prided ourselves on having learned to keep a secret, but we still had an important lesson to learn. Like Yama, the god of death, Baba may sometimes give you a warning, but you can never know the exact time when his beckoning finger will be seen. Next morning we were awakened from our slumbers about six o'clock by a stern voice saying, "What, aren't you ready? Swami is leaving in five minutes' time."

It was a terrible situation: our things were scattered everywhere. We had neither showered nor dressed nor had a cup of tea, let alone packed. And Baba was waiting to take us away for two weeks. How long would he wait? Would he go without us? We staggered around blindly trying to think and throw things into suitcases.

The stern voice of the devotee at the window agreed to give us a quarter of an hour. But even that still presented an impossibility. When we came out in about half-an-hour with our cases and valises, we were told that Swami had left. Our hearts sank, but it was not as bad as it seemed, he had gone on ahead in one car, but left another for us. In it we found a few other lucky devotees bound for the hill station, including Mr. Ramanatha Reddy who was to guide us there.

In a forest a few miles along the route we were happy to see Baba's white car waiting beside the road, his red-robed figure and a small group of men standing beside it in the morning sunshine. He teased us a little about taking so long, looked startled at the amount of our luggage, then led the whole party in among the fragrant trees for a picnic breakfast.

After that there was a reshuffle of passengers and I had the privilege of my first journey with the great man himself. Raja Reddy, perhaps Baba's closest disciple at the time, was driving the car, two teenage boys sat in the back with Baba, while Ramanatha Reddy and I were in front with the driver. We rolled on through empty barren country and an occasional village or town with people teeming like ants over sugar. Slate-coloured rocky hills began to outline against the sky. The last town we passed through was Madanapalle, the birthplace of J. Krishnamurti. Just before we climbed the steep Horsley Hills we passed a road sign to Rishi Valley where the well-known school run by Krishnamurti's followers is located.

Right on the crest of the hills, some 4,800 feet above sea level, we came to the white Circuit House, our destination. It is not very large but has the comforts of a first-class hotel, being intended primarily as a guest house for government ministers and important official visitors. Our host, Mr. Ramanatha Reddy, had been able to secure it for what was to his mind the V.I.P. of all V.I.P.s: Satya Sai Baba, plus whatever party the latter cared to bring along.

Besides the host and myself there were four males in the group. Dr. Sitaramiah, Mr. V. Raja Reddy and two teenagers, and there were half-a-dozen women, including three Indian princesses. Being the only married couple in the party, Iris and I were given a suite to ourselves. This was only two doors from Baba's suite, and opened onto a broad balcony from which there was a wonderful view of the country far below.

The plains were a smokey dun and green carpet, with isolated hills like children's blocks scattered carelessly over it, and the scores of water "tanks" shone like broken pieces of mirror fallen on the giant carpet. We were living up in the sky – in more ways than one. Here, we thought, we could at last have Baba to ourselves, just a small group of us. At last the ubiquitous crowds were left behind. We could live on intimate terms with this superhuman being from morning till night. We could see what his life was like and enjoy his wonders to the full.

No matter how early we arose in the crisp mornings we found that Baba was already up, usually sitting writing by his open door; he attends to his large correspondence himself besides writing regular articles for his *āshram* magazine, 'Sanāthana Sārathi' (The Timeless Charioteer).

Sometime during the morning, after breakfast with us, he would gather all of us into a room for a spiritual discourse. This would often take the form of narratives from the 'Rāmāyana', the 'Mahābhārata' or the 'Shrimad Bhāgavatam'. Interpreting the stories, Baba would reveal in sharp relief the profound wisdom of *bhakti* yoga.

After a walk in the gardens, followed by a lunch and a siesta, would come afternoon tea in the lounge. The first difficulty here was to persuade the Indian women to sit on chairs, for they thought it incorrect to be on the same level as their Swami. Indeed some, to the very end, insisted on sitting at his feet on the carpet, leaving empty chairs. But when Baba had managed to get the majority onto seats, albeit stiffly and ill at ease, he would usually launch into some comic theme, making us all laugh. Nevertheless, this always had practical hints and implications on the ethics of right living.

In the late afternoon or evening the party frequently went for a drive, followed perhaps by a walk, weather permitting. Otherwise there might be another enlightening discourse by Baba. On one occasion we all visited an Indian village, far off the busy highways and beautifully, unbelievably silent. Here at the home of some Baba devotees we were entertained to dinner, while the whole village crowded around in the courtyard to see and be blessed by the *avatār*.

Within the first few days another element began to disturb the even tenor of our Horsely Hills idyll. Even in this remote spot the crowds began to gather. Somehow the word had spread that Sai Baba was in the area and people came from far and near, by car, by bus or on foot. Before breakfast the first few would appear, and then throughout the whole day a crowd would be standing in the grounds looking up at the balcony, waiting for the blessings of a look and a sign from Sai Baba.

And he never disappointed them. Often he would go out onto the balcony, look on them with loving compassion and raise his hand in a characteristic gesture of upliftment and benediction. Sometimes he would go down and walk among the visitors, talking with them and producing *vibhūti* or something else to help those who were sick or in trouble. If a crowd of poor people had come a long way on foot, he would give them all money so that they could go home by bus. Every evening he would bring all who were there into the large foyer and front corrider of Circuit House, and lead them and us in beautiful *bhajan* songs for half-an-hour or more.

Interspersing all these daily activities were the miracles of physical phenomena, several each day. Here are some of the more outstanding ones.

One afternoon, soon after our arrival, we all went for a drive and, leaving the cars, strolled about on a rocky knoll of the hills. Baba several times picked up a piece of broken rock, played with it a while, and then threw it away. Finally, just as we were returning, he kept a piece about the size of a man's closed fist and carried it back to Circuit House.

Arriving there, he took us into one of the suites and sat on the carpet while we sat in a semi-circle around him. He began to talk conversationally on everyday topics, occasionally throwing the piece of rock a couple of feet in the air and letting it fall on the floor. Presently he tossed it over to me, asking, "Can you eat that?"

I examined the rock closely. It was hard granite, streaky and rather lightish in colour. I admitted its inedibility and bowled it back to him - he was not more than two yards away from me.

He took the stone and, still chatting casually, threw it in the air again, while a dozen pairs of eyes watched expectantly. I felt that something strange was going to happen and never let the stone out of my sight. Now as it lay on the carpet I could see a slight change in its appearance. Although of exactly the same size and shape, and still streaky, it was a little lighter in colour than before.

Swami rolled it back to me across the carpet. "Can you eat it now?" he asked. To my amazement and joy it was no longer rock but sugar candy. Baba broke it into pieces, giving us each a portion to eat. It was sweet and delicious as candy should be. Is this an illusion, I wondered, are we all hypnotised? So I put a piece in my pocket. I still have it and it is still sugar candy.

I thought of the popular song about 'the Big Rock Candy Mountains' and jokingly said to him, "I wish you would turn the whole mountain into candy or chocolate." Baba seemed to take this seriously or, maybe, as a kind of challenge. Anyway he replied solemnly that it would not be right to interfere too much with nature's housekeeping.

Then it occurred to me that my joke was rather superficial. If will power, or whatever power it is, can transmute a small piece of igneous rock into an entirely different substance, why not a large piece? And why not into any substance? Gold, for instance. So how very important it is that a man who understands and can employ the occult laws of nature must be above nature: must be beyond normal human desires for such things as power and material gain. Otherwise what might happen?

Writing on this theme in the last quarter of the nineteenth century, when a good deal of "physical phenomena" came before the public eye, A. P. Sinnett said: "It is enough to say that these powers are such as cannot but be dangerous to society generally, and provocative of all manner of crimes which would utterly defy detection, if possessed by persons capable of regarding them as anything else but a profoundly sacred trust."* He goes on to say that such powers in the hands of people willing to use them for merely selfish and unscrupulous ends are productive of disaster – as it is said to have been for the Atlanteans.

Today in our world, men of exoteric science have learned the secret and hold the power of disintegrating matter into atomic energy, and this stands as a constant threat to the very existence of humanity on this earth. They have also learned to transmute base metal to gold though the process is too expensive to be economically and socially disruptive. A safeguarding law of occultism is that spiritual and moral advancement should keep pace with the growth of the intellect and the acquisition of the knowledge of nature's deeper secrets. When this law is broken a dangerous situation must inevitably arise.

One sparkling morning I was walking with Swami and the two teenage youths in the gardens of Circuit House. Baba was wearing an ochre-coloured robe which fell like a smooth cylinder from shoulders to ground. As Iris had ironed some of his robes a couple of days earlier, I knew for certain that they contained neither pockets nor places where anything could be concealed. His sleeves were straight and loose, without cuffs. He carried nothing in his hands.

One of the young men was returning to Bombay next day and wanted to take photographs of Swami, so the latter posed for several pictures. Occasionally, as we strolled and talked, he paused to pick a berry or a bud from one of the shrubs. This he would examine with the concentration and thoughtfulness of a botanist: then, after a while, he would throw it away as if it were not quite suitable to some purpose he had in mind. Finally, he picked a small bud from a bush, examined it, seemed satisfied, and handed it to me saying, "Keep that."

Soon afterwards we went back up the steps to the front entrance. Baba did not go to his own suite but walked straight into ours. He sat on an

*'Esoteric Buddhism' by A. P. Sinnett (now out of print).

armchair while the young men, my wife and I gathered around him on the carpet.

Swami asked for the bud that he had given me. I handed it to him, and he held it in his fingers for a while, discussing it.

"What flower is it?" he asked.

We confessed our ignorance. He suggested that it might be a button rose and we agreed.

Then, looking at me, he asked, "What do you want it to become?"

I was at a loss to know what to say, so I replied, "Anything you like, Swami."

He held it in the palm of his right hand, closed his fist, and blew into it. Then he asked me to stretch out my hand. I gasped, and my wife gave a squeal of delight, as from the theurgic hand that held the flower bud there fell into my open palm a glittering diamond of brilliant cut. In size it matched the bud, which had completely vanished.

Baba graciously presented me with this beautiful and amazing product of transmutation magic. I still have it.

We were on the floor around Baba, expecting a morning discourse, perhaps one of those wonderful stories from Indian mythology which lead the mind to the deeper truths of life. However, before talking, he showed us a green leaf and wrote on it with his fingernail. Then he handed the leaf to me, but I could make nothing of the writing, which he said was a *mantram* in Sanskrit.

Next, he asked for a book, and one of the ladies who occupied the suite passed him her Telegu grammar. Placing the leaf between the pages, he shut the book and tapped its cover several times. Now he opened it and took out the leaf. The writing was still on it, but instead of being green and fresh, as it had been a moment before, it was brown and so dry that it easily crumbled into dust.

Baba tossed the book on the carpet nearby and, after talking for a while, left the room. Well, I thought, on the face of it this miracle would not stand up to the sceptic; the brown leaf could have been somehow "planted" in the book earlier. So I picked up the volume and searched its pages for the missing green leaf, but could find nothing.

Why am I doubting, I asked myself, when I have seen him do so many things equally inexplicable and incredible? Sai Baba had somehow blasted this leaf, as another One who stood above nature had blasted a fig tree two thousand years ago. It was as if, for the leaf, many months of summer had been telescoped into that one magical moment when Baba tapped the book.

On the subtle planes of being, interpenetrating our physical plane of existence, there may well be classes of entities for whom our physical space would be actually non-existent: our "here" and "there" would be all one to them. The ancient wisdom teaches that there are such beings. It also teaches that a physical object can be disintegrated into a subtler substance, or "energy system", which can be moved by some agency at near light speed, and reintegrated to form the original object. This is the general principle behind the phenomenon known as an apport, that is, as far as it is understood.

At Horsley Hills Sai Baba produced a particularly striking example of such telekinesis. One evening a party of us were sitting on the carpet in his suite: Ramanatha Reddy, the doctor, the young men, Iris and myself were there. Swami asked the year of my birth and, when I told him, he said that he would get for me from America a coin minted there in that same year.

He began to circle his down-turned hand in the air in front of us, making perhaps half-a-dozen small circles, saying the while, "It's coming now . . . coming . . . here it is!"

Then he closed his hand and held it before me, smiling as if enjoying my eager expectancy. When the coin dropped from his hand to mine, I noted first that it was heavy and golden. On closer examination I found, to my delight, that it was a genuine milled American ten-dollar coin, with the year of my birth stamped beneath a profile head of the Statue of Liberty.

"Born the same year as you," Swami smiled.

What would the sceptics say about this? I wondered. Would they suggest that Baba carried around with him a stock of coins so that he would have one to match my year of birth? Such old American coins, now long out of circulation, would not be easy for him to obtain in India through normal channels.

I have no doubt whatever that this was one of Baba's many genuine apports. While he circled his hand before us, some agency under his will had dematerialised this gold coin at some place somewhere, carried it at space-annihilating velocity, and rematerialised it in Sai Baba's hand.

From where did it come? Who knows? Baba would never say; perhaps from some old hoard, hidden, lost, forgotten long ago, and now belonging to no one alive.

Although I had come to know through first-hand experience that Sai Baba was certainly not an impostor and that his miracles were genuine, I could not help thinking that the use of sand as a medium for production was something which gave fuel to the sceptic. Admittedly, several of his followers had told me that, in fact, everything he had produced from sand he had also produced at other times without it, that is, from the air.

Even so, an objective psychical researcher, hearing the stories of the sand wonders, is bound to raise the queries: are the objects previously "planted" in the sand? Or does Baba, by some lightning sleight of hand, slip them in just before he digs them out? In fact, for anyone who had neither seen the miracles for themselves nor felt the spiritually elevating presence of Sai Baba, I suspected that "sand productions" must leave a bigger question mark in the mind than "other productions".

But this was because such events had not hitherto been fully and thoroughly reported to me by a careful observer. At a later period I had my own close observations of the sand miracles confirmed by several of India's leading scientists - but that is jumping ahead of the story.

The first point I want to make clear about my Horsley Hills experience of Baba's "sand productions" is that on the journey from Circuit House to the place of the miracles I sat in the front of the car with Sai Baba and Raja Reddy, who was driving. Baba carried nothing in his hands, and he was wearing his usual robe; none of the objects later produced could have been concealed on his person.

A few miles from Circuit House the car, and several other vehicles following it, stopped by the roadside. We all got out and went to a patch of sand some fifty yards away which had been seen from the road on an earlier journey.

Baba asked the young men in the party to make him a sand platform, so they scraped and pushed the sand with their hands to build a flat stage about a foot high and four feet square. Baba sat cross-legged in the middle of this and the party clustered in a semi-circle around him. I was in the front row of the spectators, right at the edge of the sand platform. The thought passed through my mind that if any object had previously been buried here, near where Baba was sitting, he would have to dig down more than a foot through the newly piled sand to reach it.

He began as usual with a spiritual discourse which, apparently, always has the effect of harmonising and purifying the psychic atmosphere around. Maybe this is a necessary preparation for the miracles. Then with his forefinger he made a drawing on the surface of the sand just in front of him, and asked me what it was. From where I sat it looked rather like a human figure, and I told him so.

Laughing, and with the expression of a happy child playing on a beach, he scooped up the sand to form a little mound above the drawing, about six inches high. Still with an air of happy expectation he put his fingers lightly into the top of the mound, perhaps an inch down, and drew out, head first, a silvery shining figure, like the drawing he had made. It was a statue of the god Vishnu, about four inches in height. He held it up for everyone to see, then put it to one side, smoothed out the mound before him to make a flat surface again, and began once more to discuss spiritual topics.

Soon he made another drawing in the sand on the same spot as before. Again he scooped sand over it, making a mound, a wider flat-topped one this time. Again with a happy chuckle he felt with his fingertips into the top of the mound and scraped a little sand away; less than an inch down was a photograph. He pulled it out, shook the yellow grains away, and held it up for us to see. It was a glossy black-and-white print, about ten inches by eight.

He passed it around for some of us to look at closely, and later I examined it at leisure back at our quarters. It was a photograph of the Hindu gods and *avatārs*, standing in two rows to form a forward pointing arrowhead, with Lord Krishna in the foreground at the tip. Heads of Satya Sai Baba and Shirdi Sai Baba could be seen as small inserts on the body of Krishna. This print, I felt, was not produced in any earthly studio. Baba later gave it to Mr. and Mrs. T. A. Ramanatha Reddy, our hosts. It stood with the unearthed statue of Vishnu for some days on a side table in the dining room at Circuit House.

Other objects produced from the sand in the same manner went to various people in the audience. There were, for example, a *japamālā* (rosary) for Nr. Niak, the Collector of Kolar District, and a pendant which was given to a revenue officer.

But there was one supreme production from that sand patch of which we all had a share. Baba did his outline sketch, which I could see from where I sat was a little container of some kind. Then, in the usual way, he scraped the top sand with his open hands to make a tiny hill above the drawing. Pausing a moment with a delighted smile, he felt into the crown of the hill and took out a silver-coloured container. This was of circular shape with a neck and a screw top. At a guess its spherical bowl would be perhaps two and a half inches in diameter.

Sai Baba unscrewed the lid and a wonderful perfume pervaded the air. Putting the container to one side, he went through the same process again of drawing and mound building. This time the product was a golden spoon like a small teaspoon. With this he stirred the contents of the bowl and, standing up, began to give some to each of his spectators.

Like the others I opened my mouth while he poured a spoonful onto my tongue. The word that came into my mind was "ambrosial": it seemed nothing less than the food of the gods; it suggested a mixture of the essences of the most heavenly fruits, the divine archetypes of the loveliest fruits of earth. The taste is quite indescribable; it has to be experienced.

The devotees call this glorious nectar *amrita*, which has much the same meaning as ambrosia, the food of the Immortals. Several devotees, including some Westerners like Nirmalananda and Gabriella, had told me about seeing it produced on rare occasions from the sand, and all tried in vain to describe its exquisite taste and aroma. Others, including Dr. Sitaramiah, had witnessed Baba produce *amrita* by squeezing his own hand, and in other ways. But no one at this time had seen a manifestation of *amrita* for about three years, and I was very grateful that Baba had given my wife and myself this personal experience of a thrilling, deeply moving miracle. It was witnessed on this occasion at Horsley Hills by about forty-five men and more than a dozen women. Baba went around giving some to all, except to the women who were staying at Circuit House. There was enough *amrita* for everyone to have a spoonful each and the bowl was still not empty.

Baba handed it to me to carry back to our quarters. I felt very honoured and held it carefully in my hand as we drove up the sharp bends to the crest of the hill. Sand still clung to the designs carved on the silvery metal, which I was told was the sacred alloy *panchalôhā*. On the balcony of Circuit House I handed the container back to Baba and he straight away walked around giving some to each of the ladies who had not yet tasted the "food of the gods".

I sometimes wondered afterwards what had happened to the little bowl but, about a year later, a Bombay devotee told me he had visited Baba at Horsley Hills a day or two after the event and been presented with the *panchalôhā* container. It still held some *amrita* which he and his family enjoyed, and the miracle bowl now occupies a place of honour in his home.

So here are the answers to the two points raised by my inner psychical researcher. First, the objects could not have been previously hidden in the sand patch ready for Baba to take out because they came from the top of a mound, made before our eyes, on the top of a foot-thick sand stage, also built while we watched. Secondly, even if Baba could have carried the objects to the sand patch that night without my seeing them, an utter impossibility, he could not by the most expert *legerdemain* have slipped such articles as a glittering idol, a large photograph, a bulky *japamālā* and a shining bowl of nectar into the sand under our noses without our being aware of the fact.

Quite apart from the miraculous production of such objects there is the strange mystery of the *amrita* itself, its ambrosial, out of this world quality, its power (shown on various occasions) to increase in quantity to meet the needs of whatever numbers happen to be present. What, I wondered, was its actual significance? I determined to ask Sai Baba about this at the first opportunity.

Unknown to me, my king, thou didst press the signet of eternity upon many a fleeting moment . . . .

Rabindranath Tagore

9

RETURN TO BRINDAVANAM

At a group meeting on the day after he had produced *amrita*, I asked Swami about its inner meaning. He related the Hindu myth about its creation, which is briefly as follows.

Once, in days of old, a great *rishi* cursed Indra, the king of the lesser gods (some *rishis*, apparently, had such tremendous power). As a result, the gods and the three worlds began to lose their vigour. Vishnu the Preserver (one of the trinity forming the Hindu Supreme Godhead and therefore higher than Indra), offered the gods a solution. He told them that to save themselves they must churn the ocean of milk until from it they produced the invigorating elixir called *amrita*. This nectar would overcome the *rishi*'s debilitating curse and renew the strength of the gods, and hence that of the three worlds over which they hold dominion.

For the churning operation, Vishnu told them, they could employ Mount Mandara as a stick and the great serpent Vasuki as a rope for turning the stick. Also, he said, the gods must make an alliance with the demons and persuade them to pull one end of the rope (the serpent) while the gods pulled the other. In this way Mount Mandara could be turned, just like the stick in an old fashioned Indian churn.

Many difficulties arose in the great churning operation. For one thing, the poor snake was badly battered and venom poured from his mouth in a great river which threatened to destroy all creatures. To save the situation

Shiva, another member of the High Trinity, appeared and drank the poison. The only harm he suffered was a slightly burned throat, causing a blue patch there; and this is why Shiva is also known as *Nīlakanttha*, meaning "blue throated one".

Eventually, however, the stirring up brought good results, and many wonderful things came out from the ocean of milk as by-products of the churning. Finally, the main product appeared: Dhanavantari, the physician of the gods (and, incidentally, the inventor of the *ayurvedic* system of medicine, still practised in India) stepped forth from the ocean. In his hand he carried the gleaming cup of *amrita*, the elixir of eternal youth and vigour.

Immediately the quick-thinking demons grabbed the cup from him and fled. But to help the gods Vishnu appeared among the demons as a seductive woman. Then, forgetting the precious liquor of immortality, they began to fight amongst themselves for possession of the woman. During the conflict Vishnu snatched the cup of *amrita* and bore it to the disconsolate gods. They eagerly drank, each having a share before the cup was empty. Thus they regained their immortal strength, and released new power and vigour into the worlds of gods and men.

Baba then spoke of the symbolic meaning in the story. The cream of truth, wisdom and immortality, symbolised by *amrita*, must be churned from the great cosmic ocean, the phenomenal universe in which we live and move. Because this universe is based on and must always operate on the principle of opposites, the evil forces (the demons) are as necessary as the good forces (the gods) for the churning – that is, for the continuous struggle in the lives of men; but, unfortunately, most men are like the demons: they forget the priceless product, immortality, in their chase after transient sense pleasures, symbolised by the illusion of a seductive woman.

"Once *anrita*, that is falsehood or unrighteousness, enters into the character," Sai Baba said, "men lose contact with *amrita*. He dies many deaths who is false, afraid of truth, blind to his own glorious heritage of immortality." So, he explained, when people fall prey to pride, to attachment, to unreality, their thoughts and feelings have to be churned to bring out the cream of spiritual truth. The groups on either end of the churning rope are always the "forward leading influences and the backward pulling influences", the gods and the demons, or, looked at in another way, the divine and animal forces within ourselves.

After about twelve days on the Olympian heights of Horsley we returned to Whitefield. On this journey Iris and I had the honour and joy of sitting with Swami in the leading car. For miles along the road Baba led the carload in songs of praise to God, most of which were composed by himself. These were some of the songs used daily in the *bhajan* sessions at the *āshram*, or anywhere else that Sai Baba happens to be.

As we were entering a village along the route, two busloads of people passed us and recognised Baba. In the village street just ahead they stopped, piled out and formed a human road block. My own instinct would have been to sound the horn loudly and force a way through what looked like a rough crowd. But Swami seems never to feel any alarm or annoyance with the milling mobs that often surround him. The only reactions I have ever seen from him are love and understanding, though sometimes people lose all restraint in their desire to get near him and touch him. On this occasion he told the driver to stop, then, opening his side window, he leaned out and gave his blessings. As the crowd, now smiling happily, parted for us we drove slowly through, while Baba waved and spoke to the people on either side. It was like riding with a royal personage, only much more than that. On the faces of these country folk there was a radiance that nearly moved one to tears.

At Brindavanam Swami decided that the two of us should stay with him in the big house, but not dormitory style, as the crowd was now smaller than before. He gave us a room and a bathroom to ourselves. Here we saw some new facets of his character.

Before we moved in, he called some of the young men who are ever happy to serve him, and set them to work cleaning the room thoroughly and re-arranging the furniture. I have never seen Indians move so fast or work so efficiently as they did under Swami's supervision. He would let neither my wife nor me move a finger to help, yet he himself gave a hand in the work. From somewhere he brought attractive carpets, curtains and drapes. Finally, he installed us, apologising that the room was not more comfortable. But we loved it. And we could not help admiring Swami in his new role of works supervisor and interior decorator. Whatever is done by him, at whatever level, is done supremely well.

One thing we liked about living in this room was that Baba would often pop in casually, unannounced; he would sit for a while and talk, answering any questions in our minds, or enquiring about how our stomachs coped with the hot Indian dishes served in the dining room. The food was, admittedly, well laced with chillies, so that we found it advisable to skip some of the meals and just eat fruit in our room.

On one occasion we asked for a few slices of bread, an item unknown to the dining room. Baba sent a car to Bangalore for bread and other foodstuffs suitable to the Western palate. It came back with a fine parcel of things - bread, butter, pots of jam, cake, cheese, and tins of special drinks such as Ovaltine and Bournvita. But some of the devotees must have heard that we had asked for bread, because messengers kept arriving at the door laden with loaves. We soon had enough to start a baker's shop, but this is typical of the brotherliness and generosity among the Baba devotees.

Baba decided to give my wife and myself the Hindu ceremony known as *shashtipūrti*. This is a kind of remarriage performed when the husband has reached his sixtieth birthday. For the ceremony Swami presented Iris with a beautiful new silk sari and myself with a white silk *dhôti* and *angavastram*, saying that it was correct for us to wear new attire on the occasion.

A young couple belonging to a family of Baba devotees was married first, and we were able to sit and watch this with the large crowd that had gathered in the central hall. After about an hour came our turn. We sat cross-legged on the low stage while two priests from Prashanti Nilayam performed the colourful ritual. Before us was a large coconut, some bananas, bowls of rice, sandalwood paste, saffron, *kūmkūm* (a red powder), incense and other things. These were essential items of the ritual. The priests chanted Sanskrit *mantrams* and, at specified times, they (or we, under their instruction) sprinkled something from one of the bowls onto the coconut, or smeared it with a paste.

Baba was sitting to one side watching and sometimes directing the proceedings. At the right moment he stepped forward, waved his magic hand in the accustomed way, and materialised two gold rings, each set with a large precious stone. One was for me to put on my wife's finger, and the other for her to put on mine. After that Baba handed us long garlands of flowers with which to adorn each other, and one was given for both of us to place together over Swami's head. The ceremony finished with a chant by the two pundits in unison, invoking, we were told, the blessings of a long life under the protection and guidance of Sri Satya Sai Baba.

The whole ritual was radiant with the warm love that flows from Swami. One could not help feeling that for some forty minutes unseen beneficent powers had been focused on us and on our marriage union. Thus it was renewed and supremely blessed.

Next day came the ceremony which, Baba said, must follow *shashtipūrti*: feeding and clothing the poor. Word had gone out to the villages in the neighbourhood, and about a thousand paupers - men, women and children - were shepherded into the grounds of Brindavanam. They sat in rows to receive a substantial rice meal, cooked and served by a number of Baba devotees.

Then sixty of the most destitute men and the same number of women were brought to sit on either side of the drive within the inner garden. Each woman was to receive a sari and each man a *dhôti*. As it was our ceremony, Iris and I were to have the job of handing out these goods but it was Sai Baba who had provided them.

Swami, the giver, kept out of sight while Raja Reddy, who has witnessed many such occasions, supervised the handing out. He organised several young devotees to carry the big piles of clothes, while on one side my wife gave out the saris, and on the other I distributed the *dhôtis*. Some of the poor souls tried to touch my feet in gratitude and, feeling embarrassed by this, I told each that the gift was from Sai Baba. Whether they understood English or not, they knew the blessed name.

For multitudes of the destitute Sai Baba has been an incarnation of Providence. On occasions such as the great Dassehra Festival in October he feeds thousands of the poor people who gather for his blessings at Prashanti Nilayam. Sometimes he personally serves the dessert, placing a goodly portion onto the leaf plate of every one of those thousands. Then, too, the old and decrepit, the crippled and the blind, are given new festival clothes.

Apart from the important ceremonial occasion of Shivarātri, Sai Baba does not usually do spectacular materialisations before large audiences, but I saw him do it once to honour Dr. Modi. There could hardly have been a more deserving recipient.

Dr. Murugappa Chennaveerappa Modi is known throughout India and in medical circles abroad as an eye surgeon and opthalmologist, but to the six million blind of India he is much more than that. He is a hope for light in their darkness. They call him "our brother who gives sight". Son of a Bombay merchant, he became a medical practitioner in that city in 1940, specialising in eye surgery.

"Many of my patients had to sell a precious cow, or even their mud and straw house, in order to travel and have the treatment," he recalls, "so I decided to go to them."

In 1943 he gave up his private practice and began his now famous free treatment eye camps. With his headquarters in the Mysore town of Davangere, he ranges over an area of some 300,000 square miles with a population almost as large as that of the United States of America.

He usually sets up his mobile hospital in a school loaned by the grateful town authorities. Anybody in the district, rich or poor, may come and have their eye troubles examined and treated without any charge. Free hospitalisation is provided in the school building. The eye camp generally lasts for about two weeks, and in that time Dr. Modi treats thousands of cases. While he corrects squints and other optical troubles, the bulk of his operations are for cataracts. He has reached a high degree of dexterity in this and has been known to perform, with the help of trained assistants, over seven hundred cataract operations in one day. This production line pace enables him to handle large numbers and, apparently, efficiency does not suffer. His cataract operations are more than ninety-nine per cent successful. Since he began his crusade against blindness nearly twenty-five years ago, Dr. Modi's surgery has given back sight to well over one hundred thousand people. State and local health departments, philanthropic organisations and some wealthy individuals pay the expenses of the camps, but Dr. Modi accepts no fees for himself.

I met Modi when he was brought to Whitefield. He was there with Mr. Niak, the Collector, to take Sai Baba to Kolar. Baba had agreed to be present at the closing function of an eye camp just completed in this town, about thirty miles from Whitefield.

I was lucky enough to be invited to go with them. Also in the car were Raja Reddy and Seshagiri Rao, who lives at Whitefield and is a cousin of my Madras friend, G. Venkateshwara Rao. As we drove along in the hot sun of the early afternoon, Dr. Modi answered our questions about his work. He is a man in his late forties, solidly built, with a shining bald head and large gentle eyes. I noticed that there was a Western flavour about his manner and speech, and understood why when he told me that during the three-month monsoon season, when travel would be difficult for his patients, he goes abroad to America, England and other countries. This is to keep himself abreast of new techniques in eye surgery.

Outside the large school building where the eye hospital had been conducted, a crowd of about five thousand was waiting. We were conducted to the decorated platform. First the Collector made a short address, then Dr. Modi, who had been sitting near me at the side of the stage, went to the microphone. As he spoke in the local dialect, I could not understand much of what he said, but I picked up one point: he said that although he worked to cure physical blindness, we were all of us spiritually blind until our inner eyes were opened by a great teacher such as Sai Baba.

When he had finished, but before he could return to his seat, Baba stood up beside him and waved his theurgic hand in several swift circles. There was a flash of gold as between Baba's thumb and forefinger appeared a solid gold ring, set with a large ruby. This he slipped neatly and firmly onto the doctor's third finger. A deep hush passed over the crowd of watchers before they broke into delighted applause. The doctor seemed quite overcome with emotion when he sat down again, and gave me and others a close look at the beautiful ring. It fitted his finger as if measured for it.

Sai Baba usually begins his address with a *bhajan* song, sung solo in his divinely sweet voice; then he speaks for an hour or more and finishes by leading the crowd in more sacred songs and chants. His discourses, or sermons, delivered without notes but with superb fluency and powerful oratory, always hold his audiences in pin-drop silence. And so it was this day.

After a time Seshagiri Rao, who was our driver, slipped away. This was part of the escape strategy, for there always has to be a strategy to fit the place and the occasion. Otherwise Baba would be mobbed by the thousands who want to get close to him and touch him. It was predicted that this would be a particularly difficult exit. So, towards the end of Baba's address, on Raja's advice, I left too.

Right behind the stage was the school. I went through that, expecting to find Seshagiri Rao waiting in the car on the other side. But he was not there. I went around the corner to where we had left the car, and found him sitting at the steering wheel, with a small crowd waiting around him.

He explained that he would not move to the school doorway through which Baba would exit until the last moment. Baba's white car was easily identified, he said, and a big crowd would quickly form around the vehicle as soon as they spotted it. So we sat together waiting and talking about the wonders of Sai Baba.

Seshagiri Rao was wearing a ring identical to one his cousin, G. Venkateshwara, always wears. It is set with a big emerald surrounded by small diamonds, and through the emerald one can plainly see a silhouette of

Satya Sai Baba's head and shoulders. I asked him to tell me its origin, knowing there would be an interesting story behind it.

Baba, he said, produced the ring in his usual way, with a hand wave. But at first it did not have the Baba image in the emerald. So he said that, since he could buy such a piece for himself, what he really wanted was a ring showing Sai Baba's image. Hearing this, Swami took the ring back, held it in his hand for a moment, and then returned it. The unmistakable silhouette had appeared in the stone while Baba held it in his hand. Then, with another hand wave, Baba produced its twin, bearing the same Sai image, for G. Venkateshwara Rao.

We heard the sound of *bhajans* beginning, and took this as the start of our countdown for making a move. At the end of the second song we drove off in the wrong direction, to mislead the crowd, before doubling back and stopping outside the door of the school on the far side from the meeting. The singing ended; there was silence while the minutes passed, but Baba did not appear through the door as expected.

Then we were seen. Crowds began to race along the street towards us. Soon we were an island in a great sea of people pressing heavily against all sides of the car. Every window was a canvas of human faces and eyes, and inside the car it became hot, stifling and airless. As far as we could see in all directions there was a tight mass of people. When one is in the centre of such a mob one feels that it is not a number of separate individuals but one large unreasoning animal which could be led to do almost anything. It would not be safe to move off in case we hurt someone. We were trapped.

Just as I felt near to passing out for lack of air, a few policemen suddenly appeared and made a lane, through which walked Swami, cool, serene and smiling. Raja was right behind him. As soon as they had entered, a lane was cleared by the police in front of the car. Seshagiri Rao gunned the engine like one escaping from danger. But Baba, from the rear seat, called, "Slow! Slow!" He made us wind down the car windows while we snailed through the crowd, and he gave his blessings by hand and voice to the people on both sides.

Now the mob was no longer an animal; it was a collection of human beings warmed by a great vision. Some prostrated themselves on the ground, others ran beside the car, gleefully shouting: "Sai Baba, Sai Baba!" eyes and faces shining with the light of love and joy.

Mr. Niak had gone ahead in another car, and now we drove to his large house set in spacious grounds surrounded by high walls. When we passed through, the gate was shut behind us and locked, but it was not long before we heard a crowd shouting outside.

"They have put the children in front of the crowd; they think that will induce us to open the gate," the Collector commented.

Baba smiled gently. After a while, to our alarm, he gave orders for the gate to be opened. From a window I watched the mob pouring in like water through a burst dam. Swami went out to meet the flood. The Collector and others followed him, and soon, in the gathering twilight, I saw the crowd sitting in a quiet circle. Baba moved around so that all could see him closely, many could touch his robe or feet, some were able to have a word with him and a few received the sacred *vibhūti* from his hands.

From that day Dr. Modi became a part of the great Sai family. Early the following year Baba invited him to run one of his humanitarian eye camps at Prashānti Nílayam itself. People from miles around came for free treatment and many of the *āshram* residents acted as hospital assistants. Later the same year I observed the good doctor taking an active part in the Satya Sai World Conference at Bombay.

As June drew to a close at Brindāvanam, we began to feel that our days at that tranquil spot, where Baba somehow reminds one more than ever of Lord Krishna, were nearing their end. He had promised to take Iris and me with him to Prashānti Nílayam, but he did not say when that would be.

The gossip grapevine grew hot with rumours that he was about to leave. Knowing by now his manner of moving without warning, we planned the things we would take, and packed them ready for a swift departure. We were determined not to be caught on the hop a second time.

All places that the eye of heaven visits
Are to a wise man ports and happy havens.

Richard II, William Shakespeare

10

A PLACE APART

One evening, when Baba was out dining with a family of devotees in Bangalore, the story went around Brindavanam that he was leaving next morning for Puttaparthi. Everyone seemed quite certain on the point, so we gave the final touches to our packing.

Next morning, before breakfast, Baba walked into our room, looked with surprise at the waiting suitcases, and said, "What? Are you leaving?"

"We heard that you were going to Puttaparthi this morning, Swami, so we . . ."

"No, no," he interrupted, "but I'm going to Madras this morning, just for one night. Would you like to come?" He directed the question at me, alone. It was evidently to be a male party.

After breakfast we drove off: Raja at the wheel, two other males, Baba, and myself. A few miles from Whitefield we stopped at a service station for petrol, and before the tank could be filled, a crowd had gathered around the car. Among them was a beggar woman to whom Swami gave money. I have never seem him pass a beggar without giving alms. Even if one of them is beside the road in the country when the car is speeding along, Baba stops and passes out some practical expression of his sympathy and love to the unfortunate person.

Sitting in the back of the car, during this drive to Madras, were a youth of about sixteen and myself, with Baba between us. One never knows what will happen when driving along with Swami. Sometimes he sits silently for long periods, as if in abstraction, or perhaps relaxation: fellow passengers respect these periods, whatever they signify, and remain quiet. Sometimes he sings and asks all to join in; and mostly, some interesting incident takes place.

Once, for instance, as we passed slowly through the narrow street of a village a man dashed out in front of the car with a coconut in his hand. Our driver stopped while the man broke the coconut on the road in front of us. This is a Hindu worship ritual. Then he came to the side window to receive Swami's blessing before we continued on our way. On another occasion, we were driving through farmlands many miles from the *āshram*. The only people in sight were three workmen about a hundred yards away from the road. They were bent over their shovels with their backs towards us. Just as we were passing them, one stood up, placed his palms together in the Hindu gesture of greeting, and reverently bowed. The other two simply carried on with their work. How, I wondered, did this one particular labourer know? Did he see the car out of the corner of his eye and recognise it, or did he somehow feel the nearness of a great saint?

Today Baba was evidently in the mood to entertain the youth with some magic. Taking a green betel leaf, he cut from it with his thumbnail a small round disc which he marked with a symbol. Passing me the circle of leaf, he asked what the symbol was. It might have been a Sanskrit *mantram,* but I really had no idea. Without enlightening me he took it back and placed it on the youth's palm still holding it by his own fingertips. When he took his fingers away the disc of green leaf had vanished and, in the boy's palm, lay another disc of about the same size, but this one had an enamel front which bore a picture of the head of Vishnu. When I was given it to examine closely, I observed with interest that it was a green portrait on a white background, and the green was of exactly the same shade as the leaf had been. It was actually a pendant with a loop for attachment. Turning it over, I noted that there was a slight flaw in the metal backing.

Whether it was because of the flaw, or for some other reason, I do not know, but Baba held the pendant again in the boy's palm, leaving there this time a similar-sized one bearing the triple heads of the Hindu Trinity, Shiva, Vishnu, Brahmā. The colour of the second pendant was different, and there was no flaw in the metal backing. The youth was allowed to keep this one, while the first simply disappeared from Baba's fingers.

Looking back on my brief but marvellous time in Madras with Sai Baba on this visit, two things project from the wealth of impressions. One is the mysterious way in which his presence became known to the public. We arrived for a late lunch, had a short siesta, and then I took a look from an upstairs window of the Venkatamuni house where we were staying. The front garden was already nearly filled with people, hundreds sitting cross-legged on the ground waiting for a sight of the great man. No public announcement had been made; no publicity whatever had been given out.

In fact, our hosts themselves knew only a couple of hours before we arrived that we were coming, and they had merely telephoned a few close devotees to whom Swami wanted to talk for one reason or another.

This handful would probably tell a few friends who were also close disciples. But devotees are always careful not to publicise the news that Sai Baba is coming. The crowds swarm swiftly enough without such encouragement, and Swami seems to like a quiet beginning for his visits so that he can talk to the families who have loved him long and faithfully. Yet some telepathic whisper had gone through the city, and by evening the front and side gardens were packed with people patiently awaiting the appearance of the beloved figure.

The other thing that I was able to appreciate more than ever before was Baba's superhuman energy. From mid-afternoon until late into the night he was interviewing people, singly or in groups, moving among the large crowds, or going out to visit the homes of devotees who were either sick or needed him to come to them for some other reason.

The same constant activity went on the whole of the next day until about seven in the evening when we left for Whitefield. A few miles out of Madras, waiting by the roadside, was a carload of some of his most devoted followers who wanted one more sight of him, one more word, one more blessing from his hand. This he granted, and their eyes moistened with tears of love. Then we set off on our five-hour journey through the darkness, through the villages, through the straying buffaloes and nonchalant cows that infest the roads of India. We reached Brindāvanam after midnight to find a group of visitors there waiting to see Baba, even at that hour.

On subsequent tours I saw this same pattern of daily programmes, with the addition of *bhajan* sessions, public addresses and other big functions. We, his companions on the tour, would be permitted to drop out from time to time to take a few hours' rest while Swami carried on, or we would merely sit quietly in the car while he went into the homes of devotees, spending some time with them, bringing them joy, hope and spiritual food.

From morning till night, and usually to midnight or later, Baba is on the go, devoting himself to the needs and welfare of those who come to him or beg him to come to them – verbally or by the telepathy of prayer. He does the work of many ordinary human beings, yet I have never seen him really exhausted. Sometimes he may look a trifle tired, but he rapidly recovers full vigour. It is as if he drinks at the fountainhead of all energy.

Once when I asked Swami if he would do something for me, he answered, "Yes, of course. I'm your property; I have no rights." His life is a continual sacrifice and service to his devotees and, through them, to all men. For, when the divine pebble of love is thrown into the pond of human ignorance and sorrow, the waves circle outward until they reach the very edge.

A few days after our return from Madras came the hundred-mile drive from

Whitefield to Puttaparthi. Only my wife, Raja (driving) and myself were with Swami on this occasion. It was Iris's first visit to the *āshram* and along the route Baba pointed out various landmarks to her. He also gave her practice in a Hindi sacred song he was teaching her, but most of the time he was wrapped in serene silence.

As we entered Prashānti Nílayam my heart leapt to see all the residents, hundreds of them, lined up along the way, so that we drove through an avenue of smiling, joyful faces. At the big prayer hall we stopped, and lost Baba: he was sucked away into a maelstrom of people. But we were given a beaming welcome by friends like Mr. N. Kasturi, and soon found ourselves ensconced in my old room at the guesthouse.

I found that life in its externals had not changed much since my previous visit to the *āshram*. There was still the early bell, clanging one from dreams into the morning darkness to prepare for meditation in the prayer hall. Not all *āshram* residents go there; some meditate in their rooms, some choose other places, such as under the sacred banyan tree which Baba planted many years ago on the hill above the hospital. I preferred to go onto the high rocks where I could do some morning yogic exercises and watch the rising sun spread its magic light over the wild hills, filling the valleys with gold.

Later, the crowd gathers around the circular garden in front of the main building for their first visual contact with Baba as he comes onto the balcony to raise his hand in benediction. This is the day's first *darshan* (blessing by appearance). Soon after this, interviews begin: taking groups of anything from a dozen to twenty, he spends perhaps half-an-hour, sometimes an hour or more, with each group. In this way he manages to make close contact with an average of about one hundred and fifty people a day, more in busy periods.

Later in the morning there is an hour's *bhajan*. Baba often comes and sits in his high chair in the hall for part of this. During part of it he might walk among the people seated outside under the trees. Sometimes he spends most of the *bhajan* period at his group interviews in the rooms. The only thing one can be sure of is that he will never follow the same routine of action twice in succession.

When the second *bhajan* period of the day begins in the evening, Baba is usually still conducting interviews. Then, after some time, he comes out and walks down a path to feed his young elephant, Sai Gita. As soon as the elephant sees him, she approaches majestically, holding high in her trunk a garland of flowers made by some ladies of the *āshram*. When the two meet, Sai Gita places the garland over Baba's head and bows, bending her right foreleg. Baba pats her and feeds her with fruit from a basket which her young mahout has brought. After a while, he leaves her with the basket and walks around to have a word with people sitting by the side of the path. But all the while Sai Gita keeps her eye on him and turns so that her head is always facing towards her beloved Lord.

When her supper of fruit is finished she carries the empty basket back towards her stable. But if Baba calls her to stop, or to come to him, she obeys immediately. This pet elephant was presented to him when she was quite a baby by some devotees of the South. She has become a much loved feature of the *āshram,* trumpeting a loud salute when she spots Baba's red robe in the distance, or somehow senses his presence without seeing him. On occasions, richly caparisoned, she takes part in outdoor processions and important ceremonies at Prashānti Nílayam.

After the evening *bhajans* and its beautiful closing ritual of *aarati,* with camphor light and a hymn of worship, the crowd pours from the hall and from under the trees to the front of the building. Here all stand and wait for the evening *darshan.* Soon, the little red figure with the great dome of black hair is seen on the lighted balcony. There is a deep hush; his lips move silently, his hand moves in a gesture of upliftment. Something more subtle than the air around seems also to move upward gripping the heart and lifting it until the eyes are moist.

Then we all go to our suppers. But Baba, however, spends most of the evening seeing more people: *āshram* officials with administration problems and visitors with urgent personal problems.

Nor had the life at Prashānti Nílayam changed in its inner aspect since my last visit. When you pass through the gate you seem to enter a shining aura of peace and joy. Not that you entirely forget the world in some lotus-eating dream. But your sense of value changes; the world's problems and conflicts are seen as if through the wrong end of a telescope, tiny and very far away. Even the immediate problems of living at the *āshram* – the adjustment to certain discomforts, the struggle to secure some Western delicacies, such as bread, butter and cheese – seem very small. Always the important over-riding factor is the enveloping love radiated from the centre. What the famous "iron lung" millionaire of America, Fred Snite, said about Lourdes applies also to Prashānti Nílayam: "Here life is a prayer . . . . We are in a place apart from the world, a place half-way to heaven."

One of the most interesting features of life at the *āshram* is the people there, residents and visitors. A whole volume could be written on this subject alone. They come for such a variety of reasons. Some travel hundreds of miles, as people went to the Delphic Oracle of old to peep into the future. Others come for business reasons: to ask if they should sell a shop, start a factory, tender for a contract, look for a new job. Many come with serious health problems; some arrive as representatives of Sai Baba groups in other areas to invite Swami to grace some function with his presence; a few are there to ask him to their homes, perhaps to perform a marriage, or name a child, or bless a new house or, simply, for the indescribable joy of his company. Baba would need to be multi-bodied to satisfy all such requests.

An important point to note about Sai Baba, in both this body and the former one, is that he does not in the least resent being treated as a fortune teller, a soothsayer, a psychic investigator, a business adviser, or a universal physician. He regards all who come as his children: some are wanting a broken toy mended, some have an ear ache, some are just wanting a word of encouragement from the eternal parent. He tries to satisfy all at their own level and, by his powerful spiritual force, to raise that level towards the superhuman race that man must eventually become.

Lord Krishna classified those who came to him into four main divisions:

(1) those in distress;
(2) those desirous of worldly gain;
(3) those seeking spiritual knowledge and understanding; and
(4) those who have already attained a high degree of spiritual wisdom (i.e., the *jnānis*).

His task, Krishna said, was to give each what he asked for. His blessings were poured out on all men equally, but each could only receive according to his readiness, according to his position on the ladder of spiritual attainment. Sai Baba put the matter thus: the rays of the sun fall equally on all who are directly in their way. If someone is behind an obstacle, or in a room, he will receive only part of the illumination. Cultivating the higher spiritual yearnings is like coming out from the confinement of a room into the sun's full rays.

Now, five thousand years after Lord Krishna, those who approach Sai Baba fall into the same general classes, and, in like manner, he considers them all worthy of his help. He sheds his blessings on all, but of course their own limitations condition what they receive. If their present needs are for bodily health or material prosperity, that is what they get. Those in the higher grades, the *jnānis,* who are open to the sun's full illumination, are, as of old, much fewer in numbers than the others, but they do exist. With great joy, with a rare feeling of upliftment, I have met some of these – not only living a life of renunciation at the *āshram*, but also as householders.

When it became known that I was writing this book, one of the brightest lights of the *āshram*, a woman completely dedicated to the great Sai Baba mission, lent me the diary she had been keeping since her first visit to Puttaparthi in about 1950. It is an interesting document, giving a picture of life with Baba at Puttaparthi in the years before Prashānti Nílayam Ashram was built. From the diary I have learned a number of important things not generally known about Sai Baba.

For example, many people think that before the period when he began giving public discourses – that is, before he was about thirty-two years of age – Baba gave no spiritual instruction. It is true that in the first three decades of his life he was concerned mainly with *leelās* and *mahimās,* with phenomena such as the showing of visions, with astral travel, miraculous healing and other miracles; but the diary shows that he also gave spiritual teachings.

No doubt most of those who came out of curiosity to see the young Puttaparthi miracle man were in the kindergarten of the spiritual school. They needed the visual props of incredible wonders to sustain their faith. Or else, they simply desired superhuman help in curing diseases or solving material problems. When their curiosity was satisfied, or they got all the material benefits they could (or were, perhaps, disappointed in this), those incapable of receiving the deeper guidance drifted away.

But there were others who belonged to the higher grades in the school of life, those who were in search of the knowledge, understanding and happiness that the world cannot give. To these Sai Baba, right from the very beginning, gave personal instruction on right thinking, right feeling, right action. To these he gave individual spiritual disciplines.

Much of his teaching was done, as it is now, through stories, parables and homely analogies. All his teaching emphasised, as it does now, the need to actually live the life; emphasised that the mere spinning of fine phrases and fascinating webs of metaphysical speculation will get you nowhere. The pathway on which Baba has, from the start, led his disciples is chiefly the *bhakti mārga,* or the yoga of divine love.

This yoga, like all others, requires that we overcome our attachments to personal ambition, fame, pride, self-importance, and that we "flush out" the last hidden pockets of egoism lurking in the mind's dark corners. For this we must be prepared to suffer many austerities and a good deal of what may at first seem like personal injustice.

Another important point I learned from the diary was that when Baba appears to be hard on some of his followers, it is really a great compliment to them, and indeed a blessing in disguise. It does not mean, as some may think, that these disciples have lost his love and been cast into the outer darkness. On the contrary, it means that Baba has high regard for those he is putting through the grinding mill; he is training them for greater progress in the school of the spirit.

Sometimes in this way, and apparently for this purpose, he seems to test people to the highest level of their endurance. Even after their mettle has been tested and proved, he will if necessary put them through what he calls a 'polishing process'. This may bring a great deal of mental anguish until deeper understanding dawns on the initiate. Thus we found that many of Baba's long-term disciples helped us to perceive the hidden dimensions of the Master's mission and purpose. They made clearer to us the beneath-the-surface meaning of many of his actions and words.

As the days passed at the *āshram* many new, inspiring devotees came into the circle of our acquaintance. A number of them had deeply moving stories to tell about their miraculous and spiritual experiences with Sai Baba. I made notes of these, and gained permission from many of the narrators to use their names and other identifying particulars. These worthy people, many well known, stand as living witnesses to the truth of the strange facts I write. This may help some readers to accept what is, indeed, so far outside common everyday experience as to be well-nigh incredible.

Meanwhile, I must try to describe the special quality of our last interview with Swami before we left the *āshram* towards the end of August. Of course, at Prashānti Nílayam there had not been the same close personal contact that we had enjoyed at Brindavanam, and particularly at Horsley Hills. Life is on a different scale at the *āshram.* Crowds of visitors are constantly passing through, or gathering for some big religious festival or other special event.

During our stay there had been two occasions: Gūrū Pūrnimā Day in July – a festival to honour the great *gurus* – and the official inauguration of Prashānti Nílayam as a township. For the latter event, which took place on 5th August, many important officials attended from nearby towns such as Penukonda and Anantapur, and from the state capital. Hyderabad. Some of these visitors were Baba devotees, and some were not.

After the township inauguration ceremony Sai Baba provided a huge banquet for everyone. More than a thousand people sat down to a fine Indian dinner, while Swami moved tirelessly among the guests, making sure that every individual was well fed and happy.

Yet despite his busy life, we were really very fortunate in seeing quite a lot of the great master. I went with him on an official three-day tour to Anantapur, where I met and talked to a number of devotees who had known him since his early youth. He always called both Iris and myself to the interview room when he was seeing a group of visitors from abroad. So we sat at his feet among people from France, Italy, South America, Germany, Denmark and Persia. We saw him amaze and delight them with materialisations: the production of *vibhūti,* or sweets for us all to eat, or a jewel for one of the visitors. On all occasions we witnessed the most important miracle – every heart deeply stirred by the magic wand of selfless love.

We had many memorable sessions with Swami this way, and then, when there were only a few days of our sojourn left, he called us to him every day. These farewell gatherings, lasting sometimes up to a couple of hours, were enjoyed in the company of special *āshram* friends. Some like us were departing, and others remaining. Always Baba talked first on spiritual subjects, then on more general topics or personal problems that could be discussed in a group.

Present at the final interview were Mr. and Mrs. K. R. K. Bhat, in whose car we were being given a lift to Bangalore. Mr. Bhat is a retired divisional manager of the Life Insurance Corporation of India. He suffered a serious heart attack just before his retirement, and is now living most of the time at Prashānti Nílayam, being kept alive, as he says himself, "by the grace of Sai Baba". He and his wife were returning to Bangalore for a while to arrange some personal matters. But for a few days Mr. Bhat had been suffering pain on his left side in the heart region and, as doctors had previously forbidden him to drive the car, I volunteered to drive it for him.

After general conversation with the group of eight people, Baba took the various individuals who were departing into another room to speak privately with each. First there were the Maharani of Kutch and her daughter, Nanda. The Maharani was leaving for her home in Bombay, and Nanda was going part of the way with her, then returning to the *āshram* which has become her home.

Next, Iris and I were called. Immediately Swami was alone with us, he dropped all joking and teasing, and spoke very seriously in a voice of deep affection. He was like a mother seeing her children off to boarding school, except that he seemed to be the essence of all the mothers the earth has ever known. The stream of affection that flowed from him was a river carrying one off into an ocean of love. In that ocean one's physical body seemed to vanish, and all the hard lumps of separate self, of anxiety and worry and deep-lying fear, were melted away. For those exalted moments one touched the edge of the infinite and felt the ineffable joy of it.

Many of the Baba devotees have told me about their own personal experience of this deepest of the mysteries and miracles, where a man touches, and momentarily becomes one with, the Divine in man. But, like me, none has been able to describe it adequately, for it is far beyond the reach of words.

After giving us personal advice regarding our work and health and lives, and assuring us that there is never any need for fear or worry because he is always with us in our hearts, he waved his hand, this time in large vertical circles like a turning wheel. When his hand stopped it held a little silver container, an inch in height and over an inch in diameter. As he opened the lid a fragrant perfume pervaded the room. The container was full of light-grey *vibhūti* which proved to be as fragrant to the tongue as it was to the nose. Giving it to us, he said to take a little every day; it would bring great benefits and blessings to both body and soul.

The last persons to whom he spoke privately were Mr. and Mrs. Bhat. As it was an auspicious day for the devotees of Lord Subrahmaniam, their chief household god, Mrs.Bhat had brought a small bouquet of flowers and *tūlsi* leaves. These she placed at the feet of Sai Baba who has become to her the embodiment of Lord Subrahmaniam; the reason for this will be fully understood from her miraculous experience related in the next chapter.

Baba put a few of the flowers in her hair. Then, telling us all to wait for some *prasād* (gifts of packets of *vibhūti,* we thought), he went upstairs to his dining room, which is directly above the interview room. He took, we presume, the remainder of the bouquet with him, and we all stood waiting. Iris and I were standing by Mr. Bhat, on his left. Mrs. Bhat was to his right, while the rest of the group was on the other side of the room.

As we exchanged a word or two with Mr. Bhat, a very tall man, Iris saw what she took to be flakes of dried paint falling from the ceiling. I did not notice these 'flakes' until they were perhaps a foot and a half above Mr. Bhat's left shoulder, on which they came to rest. Then I observed that the 'flakes' were actually *tūlsi* leaves and a few flower petals.

I could see from Mr.Bhat's face that he immediately felt something miraculous in this event, but I looked for a natural explanation. It seemed, however, impossible to find one. The leaves and petals could not possibly have fallen off anything in the room, which was unfurnished except for one chair and a cupboard in a corner some distance from where we stood, and the walls of the room were bare.

Moreover, the leaves and petals could not have fallen from Mrs. Bhat's head because she is a very short woman, and was anyway on the right side of her husband, whereas they fell from a high level on his left side. Furthermore, there had been no leaves in her hair, only flowers, and these were still in place after the incident. Nor could the bits of foliage have blown in through the window: first, because there was no breeze, the air being quite still; second, because there are no *tūlsi* bushes anywhere near the window; and third, because if they had come in the window, they would not have been at the height where first seen by my wife, or even by me. I could think of absolutely no place from which they could have arrived by the normal forces of nature.

The Bhats had no doubt whatever that this was another of Swami's inscrutable works: that he had dropped some of the bouquet of leaves and petals from the room above, through the solid ceiling on to Mr. Bhat's shoulder – on his *left* side, where the pain had been nagging for days. Since the time of Lord Krishna *tūlsi* leaves have been associated with healing, and it is interesting that Mr. Bhat's pain almost immediately vanished.

Presently a messenger from Swami arrived with some packages of what the devotees call "emergency *vibhūti*" for those departing. This is wonderful stuff of a dark grey colour, and has been known to work great miracles in time of serious sickness or bad accidents.

However, after the touch of the leaves from above, Mr. Bhat needed nothing of this kind. He felt so well that he drove the car most of the way to Bangalore himself, letting me take the wheel for only a few miles, and then mainly to please me, I think. We stayed at his Bangalore house for about a week and every day he drove us somewhere, on one occasion to Whitefield where we collected the remnant of our luggage and saw Mr. and Mrs. M. S. Dixit. There was no return of Bhat's heart pain; it seemed to have been borne away by the healing beam which, as its signature, brought the miraculous fall of leaves and petals.

Not where the wheeling systems darken,
And our benumbed conceiving soars:
The drift of pinions, would we harken,
Beats at our own clay-shuttered doors.

Francis Thompson

11

DRIFT OF PINIONS

Though there is a multitude of Hindu gods, most Indians, and certainly the educated ones, understand that each god is really only a limited expression of the One Inexpressible Supreme Brahman. "God has a thousand heads," they say, and there should be no quarrel about the many different forms used to represent different aspects of that highest divinity which is ultimately formless. In fact, in the Hindu *pūjā* rooms, those sanctuaries set aside in homes for worship and prayers, you will mostly find statues and pictures of many divine beings, often including Jesus of Nazareth.

Yet each family usually has one special household deity who holds the place of highest honour. In the family of Mr. K. R. K. Bhat the traditional household god was Lord Subrahmaniam, but Mr. Bhat himself was inclined more to the worship of Lord Krishna. Perhaps for this reason, or perhaps because he was very busy as a top executive in the world of insurance, it was his young wife who carried out the daily ceremonial worship of Lord Subrahmaniam.

In 1943 Mrs. Bhat developed cancer of the uterus. Medical men advised an operation though there was no certainty that this would be successful. Mr. Bhat's widowed mother was staying with the young couple at the time, and she said to her son, "Lord Subrahmaniam cured your father of cancer without any operation; in the same way He will cure your wife."

The old lady's faith was so tremendously strong that the young couple agreed to forgo surgery and place themselves entirely in the hands of the household god. *Pūjās* to Lord Subrahmaniam were intensified, the religious practices became even more strict and devout than before, the prayers more fervent and prolonged. These *pūjās* were now carried out mainly by Mr. Bhat's mother, while the young wife remained in bed growing gradually thinner and weaker. This went on for about six months.

Then one night, while in a state of semi-sleep, the patient saw in the dim light from the moon a large cobra circling her bed. Alarmed, she switched on her bedside lamp and woke her mother-in-law who was sleeping in the same room, her husband being absent on a business trip.

No snake was found in the room. Yet, as soon as Mrs. Bhat switched off the light, she saw the cobra again, going around the bed. Almost immediately the snake took the form of Lord Subrahmaniam, as she knew Him by the picture hanging in the *pūjā* room. He seemed to be floating above her. Then, piercing her chest with His *velayudhan* (a kind of spear Subrahmaniam carries), He seemed to draw her away with Him.

Soon she found herself standing before Him on the peak of a high rocky hill. She knelt and touched His feet with her hands and forehead, and He began to talk to her. He asked her if she wanted to stay with Him or go back to the world. She understood this to mean a choice between life and death. Thinking of her husband and young children and their need of her, she told Lord Subrahmaniam that she wished to go back.

There was further conversation, and finally Lord Subrahmaniam said, "You are cured of your illness, and will soon grow strong. Throughout your life I will protect you; whenever you think of Me, I'll be there. Now go back."

"How?" she asked.

He pointed to a long, winding, narrow staircase that had opened up near their feet, and led downward. She began to descend – then there seemed to be a break in her consciousness and she found herself back in bed in her own room, awake. Immediately she woke her mother-in-law and told her about the vision. When her husband returned home she told him as well. But she regarded the experience as sacred, and did not make it known beyond the closest members of her family.

From that night onward she gained rapidly in strength and there were no more signs of the cancer. Soon she was up and carrying on her normal life. Only there was a difference. Now, in addition to her household duties and religious observances, she devoted herself to social welfare work among the poor and needy. God had given her back her life, and she was determined to use it fully in His service as best she knew how.

It was twenty years later that Mr. and Mrs. Bhat first heard of Satya Sai Baba and went to Prashānti Nílayam. To Mrs. Bhat he said, "I spoke to you long ago, twenty years ago."

Greatly puzzled, she replied, "No, Swamiji, this is my first visit."
"Yes, yes, but I came to you when you were living in Mysore," and he mentioned the name of the street and the city where she was living at the time of her cancer illness, when she had the vision of Subrahmaniam.

Then he took her a little way up the narrow winding stairs which lead to his rooms above and told her to look down. Immediately she was reminded of the staircase leading down from the heights on which she had been with Subrahmaniam: in fact, the two stairways seemed identical. She was more bewildered than ever.

To help her understanding, Swami now waved his hand and from the air produced a photograph of himself in the *Sômasūtra* (name of Subrahmaniam's chariot) with a cobra circling around Him. Now a light began to dawn on her. God can take any form, she thought. He had come to her twenty years before in the form she worshipped, Subrahmaniam. Now He was here before her in the form of Satya Sai Baba. She fell at His feet, weeping tears of joy.

Mr. C. Ramachandran of Kirkee, Poona, when I first met him at Prashānti Nílayam in 1967, was Deputy Chief Inspector of Military Explosives in the Ministry of Defence.

Some years earlier, he told me, he had had a lot of family worries, and as a result had taken to visiting the Sai Baba shrine at Shirdi, about a hundred and twenty miles from his home. This had brought him great peace of mind, and he had gradually become a devotee of Shirdi Baba.

Eventually he heard that this great saint had reincarnated at Puttaparthi and was known as Satya Sai Baba. Well, he thought, probably just another impostor, one of the many who have tried to make money by masquerading as the grand old Sai Baba reborn. A little later, however, he read in the newspapers an account of how Satya Sai Baba had relieved one of his followers of a bad stroke by taking it on himself, and then cured his own paralysis before a large crowd on a Gūrū Pūrnimā Day. This gave him the feeling that Puttaparthi Baba must at least be a genuine holy man, perhaps a real *mahātmā*.

When one of his family members brought a small photograph of Satya Sai Baba and put it in the *pūjā* room in his house, Ramachandran let it be. Two or three days later he noticed that some ash had formed on the photograph. He wiped it clean. But then, once, during the *pūjā* ceremony he saw the ash actually forming on the photograph. It appeared first like steam and turned into drops of milky liquid which ran down the glass and dried into grey ash.

Perhaps, he thought, this might be due to something peculiar in the glass, or in the cardboard backing, or the frame. As a chemist he tested these, but they were quite normal; however, he decided to change them all.

Nevertheless the ash continued to make its inexplicable appearance on the new glass and frame.

One day a young friend brought another photograph of Satya Sai. This was stuck onto cardboard without any glass front. With Ramachandran's permission, he put it among the other pictures in the *pūjā* room, and went off, but before he had reached the front gate, Ramachandran called him back. The young man's eyes widened as he saw the ash forming on the photograph he had just brought.

"I did not really trust your story before," he confessed, "but now I see it's true."

These events made Mr. Ramachandran decide to go to Prashānti Nílayam and see Satya Sai Baba. Some time after making this decision, he suddenly felt himself disgusted with the habit of cigarette smoking. One day, throwing away a cigarette, he vowed to himself that he would not smoke again until after he had had an interview with Sai Baba.

His holidays fell due about six weeks later, in June 1964, and he used the opportunity to make his first trip to the *āshram*. The discomforts and lack of facilities there upset him initially but he stayed on, and after some days found himself in an interview room, along with a few other people, waiting for the great man.

Presently Baba came in and, with his creative hand wave, produced *vibhūti*. He gave some of this to all present, except C. Ramachandran. The latter was very disappointed at being overlooked, and asked for some. Baba looked at him and said, "I gave you some not long ago."

Ramachandran was puzzled, and then he understood that Baba referred to the ash which had appeared on the photographs. Swami smiled gently and went on:

"Don't worry. I will give you a great deal, a very great deal. But don't go back to that bad old habit."

Ramachandran knew that he referred to the smoking habit. A thrill went through his nerves as he realised how much this great man seemed to know about his life and thoughts.

After that he made several visits to the *āshram*, and then towards the end of April 1965, he received at his home, in Poona, a telegram which read: "Satya Sai Baba arriving at your residence May 5th to perform *upanayanam* and give *Brahmôpadesham*."

Ramachandran was very startled. This referred to the sacred thread ceremony for his two sons, which was long overdue as his eldest son, Raja, was already seventeen and a half. Well, was Baba really coming? Such a thing had never been mooted, and Ramachandran felt he was not worthy of the great honour. Certainly, he had no idea whatever about the correct way to receive such a great and holy saint. First, however, he must check to see if the message was really a genuine one.

With the help of some of his office staff, he traced the telegram back to its origin. He found that it had been lodged at the main Poona post office and delivered to him from the suburban post office at Kirkee. The receiving clerk at the Poona office had reason to remember the sender of this telegram. He was, he said, a man with a small beard. He had driven up in a taxi, which he kept waiting while he wrote the telegram. When the clerk asked for his address, the bearded man replied that he was in transit and had no address in Poona. The clerk said that he must therefore write his permanent address on the form. After some hesitation the man wrote: "All India Sai Samaj, Madras." Then he drove off.

This Sai Samaj was founded some years ago by Swami Narasimha, who wrote the life of Sai Baba of Shirdi. The centre is dedicated primarily to the dissemination of the teachings of the old Shirdi saint. On investigation it was found that the bearded traveller was unknown to anyone at this place. So there Ramachandran's detective work reached a dead end.

He had been told that Swami was at Brindavanam and took the precaution of sending a telegram there asking for confirmation of the date of the intended visit. He repeated the same request in a further telegram to Mr. Kasturi at Prashānti Nílayam. No reply came from either of them.

Later he learned that Kasturi had never received the telegram. Ramachandran did not ask Baba about the one to him, judging by what had happened in the meantime that any answer that Baba might give, if he gave any, would be quite inscrutable.

"So I did not know what to expect on May 5th," Ramachandran told me, "but I thought it best to prepare everything for the ceremony, and say nothing to anyone about the possibility of Baba coming."

One problem, he said, was that he did not have enough ready cash for the function. But going to his bank to see what could be done, he found to his surprise that a sum of Rs. 468 had mysteriously appeared to the credit of his account. He was not able to trace the origin of this and, in fact, never succeeded in doing so; but it certainly was a great help to him. He decided to ask only his relatives and very close friends to come to the ceremony, which would mean providing lunch for about fifty people.

Some days before the function was due, friends, and even strangers, started asking him if it was true that Sai Baba was coming to his house. "All I could do," he told me, "was to give some non-committal answer and try to put them off."

Nevertheless, on the morning of 5th May people began arriving at an early hour to take up a position in Ramachandran's large garden. As the hot morning wore on, the crowd grew larger until there must have been about a thousand people sitting in neat rows awaiting the arrival of Sai Baba. All seemed quite certain that he was coming; the only point in doubt being how he would come, and from what direction. There was much discussion on these points.

Inside the house Ramachandran and his wife were working hard, and praying hard that everything would be in order when and if Swami arrived. There were flowers and decorations and all the necessary accoutrements for the ceremony. On a dais they placed their best armchair, covered it with a satin cloth and placed flowers on each arm. This was the seat of honour for Swami. The clock hands moved on, shadows in the garden shortened, but there were no signs of the *guru*'s arrival.

At about eleven in the morning Ramachandran entered his *pūjā* room, made a special prayer for guidance, and then conducted the sacred thread ceremony himself. Immediately afterwards he saw a little boy of about eight years, a complete stranger, among the people inside the house. The boy seemed to know the hostess, Mrs. Ramachandran, for he went to her and, saying that he was an orphan, asked for food. She gave him some but was surprised to see him eat only a few mouthfuls and walk away.

When she looked again for him he was gone. None saw him go but he could not be found. It was as if he had melted into the air. And who was he, anyway? He did not belong to the neighbourhood, and none of their friends had ever seen him before.

Soon after this it was observed that there was an imprint on the satin cover of Baba's chair as if someone had just been sitting there. Also the flowers on one arm were crushed as if a hand had rested on them. Yet no one could have sat on the chair in its prominent position on the dais without being seen. Besides, no one there in the house would have presumed to sit on the chair placed there, as all knew, for the great saint. The Indian followers of Sai Baba, with their strong feelings of veneration and *bhakti,* would never dream of doing such a thing, even if it could have been done unobserved.

Anyway, the conviction grew that Sai Baba had himself been present in the astral, or subtle, body and had purposely left these marks to let them know of his visit. This conviction was strengthened in Ramachandran's mind when his eldest son, Raja, confided something to him.

As part of the sacred thread ceremony a boy receives a *mantra* from the one performing the ritual, while both bow with a cloth covering their heads. In this case, of course, it was the father, Ramachandran, who gave the *mantra,* but Raja said that he had seen, while under the cloth, not his father's face but that of Sai Baba, which he knew well from photographs. Certainly, something had impressed Raja greatly for, after that day, his father said, the boy's character changed completely. He no longer wasted his time on frivolous pursuits, such as loitering in the bazaars, but concentrated fully on his studies.

After the ceremony came the lunch. But the wrong impression seemed to have got around that everyone present was to be fed. They began coming in from the garden in batches, filing past the chair to see the miraculous impressions on the satin and flowers, and then taking their places on the floor in the dining room.

Mr. and Mrs. Ramachandran had some extra supplies of food in case of emergency. Though they had planned for fifty, they "probably had enough for about a hundred," he told me. So they decided to just go on feeding the crowd until supplies ran out. But, incredibly, supplies did not run out, not until everyone had eaten his fill.

"We did not feed ten thousand, like Christ," said Mr. Ramachandran, "but there must have been at least one thousand; so the food was multiplied ten times. Without question it was one of Sai Baba's miracles."

Even after the lunch was over, there was no rest for the Ramachandran household. Those who went away talked to friends about the impressions on the chair, so others came to see and bow before the signs of the invisible presence. They continued coming throughout the whole afternoon and night, until about three the next morning.

Many of Baba's more devoted followers have experienced signs of his subtle presence: footprints in ash spread on the floor, a passing vision of his form, and other such manifestations. I myself saw, one evening during *pūjā* at Mr. Bhat's house in Bangalore, two indentations like foot marks appear in a cushion placed on the floor in front of an empty chair which is always left standing there as a symbol of Baba's presence.

But also many devotees tell of incidents where Baba came to them in a physical form other than his own, perhaps as a beggar, a *sādhū,* a workman, or even an animal. Frequently, those who see him have no idea that it is Baba until they get a sign later, or Baba may, on their next meeting, mention the incident, particularly if they have not treated the person or the animal well. Mr. Ramachandran is inclined to think that the orphan boy who appeared, asked for food, ate a few mouthfuls and disappeared, was one of those 'other form' manifestations which Sai Baba makes, although the latter has said nothing about this.

The above and other inscrutable events have brought Mr. Ramachandran close to Sai Baba, and he has received a great deal, just as Swami promised him at the first visit. For one thing, a stomach ulcer which had been resisting medical treatment completely vanished soon after that earliest interview. At a later meeting Baba materialised a *japamālā* for him, "clutching it out of the air above his shoulder height," as Ramachandran described it – the same manner in which I have seen Baba take several large items out of, perhaps, the fourth dimension. At the time Ramachandran told me his story at Prashānti Nílayam, he was extremely happy because Swami was giving him personal instructions in the use of the *japamālā,* and guiding him in his spiritual exercises. In fact, Sai Baba has brought a complete change into the tenor, outlook and meaning of this man's life, as he has done to so many others.

The Ramachandran story is not unique. Other devotees have had similar strange experiences. Many have, at times of importance or crisis, felt Baba's presence, caught glimpses of him, or been left with signs of an unseen visit. I have told Ramachandran's particular narrative here (actually only a part of his rich Sai Baba experiences) because the fact of his being a practical scientist with a responsible official position in the world may add some weight to his evidence for the sceptical mind.

Miss Leela Mudaliar is a lecturer in botany at Queen Mary College,

Madras University, but in her off-duty hours she acts as priestess in a small temple in Guindy, where she lives, on the outskirts of Madras. Back in 1943, when Leela was fourteen years old, that little temple did not exist and the events which led to its construction, and to this young scientist's dedicated service there, are about as inexplicable as one could imagine.

The first strange event was a prophecy some forty years earlier that the temple would be built where it now stands. In 1904 a wandering *siddhapūrūsha* (holy man with some miraculous powers) asked permission of Leela's grandfather to build a tomb for himself on a piece of land owned by the grandfather at Guindy. The latter gave permission and the holy man prophesied that to the right of his tomb there would be a temple to a great saint, and to the left an industrial estate.

The holy man, who was reputed to be a hundred and twenty five years of age at the time he entered the tomb, went into *mahāsamādhi* (permanently left the body) and was buried. His earlier prophecy had been written on palm leaf, and seen by many people, including Leela's father, Mr. M. J. Logananda Mudaliar. At this period, in the first years of this century, the land on which the tomb stood was surrounded by open country. Today, the little temple stands close by on the tomb's right and, to the left, an industrial estate, just as the prophet foretold half-a-century earlier.

But before the prophecy was fulfilled, some dark events were to take place on this piece of land. In the early 1940s a Gujarati *swāmi* put up a grass hut and settled down near the tomb of the holy man. But this *swāmi* was of the left-hand path. He soon became known in the district as a black magician who had broken up families and ruined several people's lives through his powers of sorcery (unclean *siddhis*).

Logananda Mudaliar, who was then owner of the land, ordered the Gujarati black magician to leave, but he flatly refused to do so. Several times this happened and, finally, in 1943, Mudaliar took a bailiff and went to his Guindy land. The sorcerer was not at home and so, in his absence, they proceeded to demolish his grass hut. Then, just as the demolition was about completed, the magician returned.

His rage was enormous. He fumed and shouted. Finally he put a curse of madness on Logananda Mudaliar. Looking at him with burning eyes, he said, "By tomorrow you will be a raging lunatic."

Logananda Mudaliar was not troubled: he thought himself immune from such black powers. He did not even bother to mention the incident to his wife or daughter, Leela. But the very next day the madness came upon him.

"He was utterly insane and violent," Leela said. "The Superintendent of the Mental Hospital in Madras was called, and said that my father must be taken to the hospital."

But evidently Logananda's wife was against this move; she decided to keep him at home for another day, hoping and praying that he might improve, even though she had great difficulty in holding him down during his fits of violence.

The madness had attacked him on a Friday; he was violently insane for two days, and then, during Saturday night or early Sunday morning, he had a dream or vision. In this, a young *swāmi* came to him and gave him a vessel containing water and *tūlsi* leaves, telling him to drink and he would be cured. This Logananda Mudaliar did, and the young *swāmi* disappeared.

When Logananda awoke next morning the madness had gone. He told his wife and daughter about the vision, describing the *swāmi* as "a young man dressed in a red robe, with thick hair that stood out from his head in a mop, like a woman's hair."

At the time of this event Satya Sai Baba, then a young man, was staying at the house of a devotee in Madras. Before lunch on the Sunday following Logananda Mudaliar's dream, Baba was being driven by car to another devotee's house. On the way he directed the car so that it passed near the Mudaliar home. When they arrived at the house, he asked his devotees to wait in the car as he had someone to see inside. Logananda was still resting in his room after his stormy mental sickness, and the young red-robed visitor was taken in to him by Leela and her mother.

As soon as the young man entered, Logananda recognised him as the healer of his dream. Sai Baba confirmed this in his opening words. "Last night I came to you and gave you *tūlsi* water. I will now make sure that you have no more madness."

With a wave of his hand he produced a protective talisman for Logananda to hang around his neck. The latter tried to prostrate himself before the astounding young *swāmi,* but found that his knee had gone out of joint. Baba, practical as well as miraculous, gave Logananda's foot a sharp tug, and the knee joint came right again.

"You are God!" Mudaliar declared, going down on his knees. He held Baba by the ankles and tried to lift him off the floor. Baba laughed and made him desist, patting him affectionately on the back.

Later, taking the wife aside, Baba told her to go to their plot of land at Guindy and look for some broken pieces of pottery on the surface. She must dig beneath these, and would find there the bodies of a goat and a hen. These carcasses must be removed as they were connected with the sorcery rites that had brought about the madness. Next, Baba phenomenally produced a lime and told her to put it under her husband's pillow, without his knowledge. Finally, with another handwave, the young visitor produced *vibhūti* and gave some to each of the family. As he was leaving, he told Logananda Mudaliar that he must come to Puttaparthi as soon as possible.

That day Leela and her mother went to the Guindy land, where they found and removed the dead animals as instructed. The next day Logananda left for Puttaparthi. Many strange and wonderful things happened to him there, and he came back more than ever convinced that Sai Baba was an incarnation of divinity.

He decided to build a house for Baba on his Guindy land. But before he could make much progress the form of Shirdi Baba appeared to him in a dream and ordered him to erect, instead of the house, a temple to Sai Baba and to install therein a staue of the Shirdi Sai body. On the day following the dream a letter arrived from Satya Sai with exactly the same instructions as given in the dream.

So the temple was built, Logananda selling three houses to raise the money. Meanwhile, a sculptor in Madras began having recurrent lucid dreams in which he was told that there was work for him to do at Guindy; that he must go to Guindy railway station. The dreams so impressed the sculptor that, finally, he took the train and alighted on the platform at Guindy. There he was accosted by a man who knew his name and said, "Please come with me."

Puzzled, the sculptor followed. The stranger led him to the site where the temple was under construction, and introduced him to Logananda Mudaliar as the artist who had come to do the statue of Shirdi Sai Baba. Then the stranger departed, and neither the sculptor nor Mudaliar ever saw him again.

The outcome of the incident was that the sculptor agreed to do the statue. He had never seen the old saint in his life, and had only a picture to guide him in the work. Strangely enough, though, there was no difficulty; some subtle, intelligent force seemed to direct his brain and hand.

The figure, in black granite, shows Shirdi Sai Baba sitting in characteristic posture, right leg resting horizontally across the left knee. Like Michelangelo's marble Moses in a little church in Rome, it gave me, personally, the immediate impression that it was alive.

On the day when Satya Sai installed it in the temple, with due rites and ceremonies, the several hundred people present thought that the figure had really come to life. It levitated, they say, about three feet above its pedestal, stayed suspended in air for a few seconds and then dropped into position again.

When the building was completed in 1947, Logananda left his home and took up residence in the temple to look after it and carry out the *pūjās* there. After he died, Leela took his place, living in her brother's house nearby, but sleeping and spending most of her time in the temple itself.

One Sunday morning my wife and I cycled over from the Theosophical Society Estate at Adyar to visit Leela at Guindy, about two miles distant. First she showed us over the grounds. We saw the tomb of the prophet, and those of Leela's father and mother. Then we went into the little temple itself. Here I felt a powerful atmosphere, a 'being-drawn-upward' feeling such as I have experienced at certain other spots on the earth: at Lourdes, in the cathedral of Chartres, and at Fatima in Portugal, for example. There is a strong impression of being brushed by the gentle, beneficent pinions of invisible worlds. And here there was an incident that served to confirm this impression.

Two flowers were before Shirdi Sai Baba's statue when Leela led us to it, accompanied by another visitor, an old friend of ours from Puttaparthi named Balbir Kaur, the Kanwarani of Ladhran in the Punjab. Leela presented a flower from the vase to each of the two ladies as a token of blessing from Sai Baba.

Soon after that we went to the far end of the temple. The ladies sat on a grass mat on the floor to talk. Leela had kindly provided me with a chair, but it was too far away for me to join in the conversation. So I drew it across the tiled floor to within a few feet of the grass mat. After about ten minutes of talk Balbir pointed to my feet and, in a surprised, mystified tone, said, "Look! See what's come!"

My feet were a few inches apart and midway between them on the polished tiles lay a lovely little orange-coloured flower. I knew for certain that this flower had not been there when I sat down, for I had noted specially the simple, plain tiles as I placed my chair in position. The floor had been completely bare. Furthermore, the flower could not have been dropped by any other visitor after I sat down, for no one had come near our group.

"Such flowers are not found anywhere in this district," commented Leela, the botanist, after examining it.

A young man, who also helped in the temple, drawn by our animated discussion, came across to our corner. When he was told what had taken place, he said to Leela, "Yes, I saw you give a flower to each of the ladies and not to the gentleman. Now one has come to him through the power of Sai Baba. What a gesture of grace!"

Leela, who has seen many miracles at the temple, agreed without surprise. We three visitors were filled with a strange joy, as if we had just seen Baba himself. The powers of other worlds seemed to find easy entrance to this sweet little sanctuary, with its rare purity and freedom from any taint of commercialisation or exploitation by priestcraft.

. . . Light and life to all He brings,
Risen with healing in His Wings.

Charles Wesley

12

MORE WONDER CURES

Who can possibly know the number of miracle-cures brought about by Sai Baba? There are no official bodies set up to investigate and compile statistics as there are, for instance, in connection with the miracles of Lourdes. But one is constantly hearing of the Sai cures wherever one moves among the devotees. They have been going on for years and are still going on. The means and methods Baba uses are many and varied, from sacred ash to surgical instruments which he materialises on the spot. But whatever his method, the marvellous medically inexplicable element is ever there.

In most of the following cases I have interviewed the ex-patients themselves, and people close around them. The other cases were investigated by medical men and various responsible witnesses, and reported to me or to the monthly magazine at Prashānti Nílayam.

Mr. T. N. Natarajan lives at Ernakulum, Kerala, and is very active in the Sai Baba movement in that area. His business is that of taxi owner, but anyone looking less like the typical taxi-man would be hard to find. Like so many of the Sai devotees, he is gentle and aglow with brotherly love. I have had long talks with him at Prashānti Nílayam about many things, including his miracle cure from Baba.

He told me that in 1957 he lost the sight of his left eye. First he went to his family doctor who sent him to an eye specialist in Bangalore. In that city he actually consulted two specialists (whose names he gave me) but both told him there was no hope of restoring the sight of the blind eye. Not only that, but probably the other eye would be affected in time, and he would lose the power of sight altogether. This was a grim, depressing verdict.

However, on the same day, hope came. Mr. Natarajan visited a cousin, saw a photograph of a man in a red robe with a black mop of hair and asked who it was. The cousin was a Sai Baba devotee, and the upshot was that Mr. Natarajan arrived in Madras to see Baba who was staying there at the home of Mr. Hanumantha Rao.

At the first interview, Mr. Natarajan proffered the letter he had brought from his devotee cousin, but Baba refused to take it, saying, "Don't worry, I know all about your case. I will cure you. But you must come to Puttaparthi for fifteen days."

So he returned to Ernakulum, made all the necessary arrangements, and went straight to Puttaparthi. There he was told to come to Baba each morning bringing a short string of jasmine flowers. Baba blessed this on each occasion and then tied it firmly on the patient's eyes. There it would stay for the day and the night. The next morning Baba would throw it away and put on the new jasmine floral string. This went on for about ten days.

Then one evening after *bhajan* Baba called Mr. Natarajan into a room, waved his hand and materialised a small bottle. From this he poured a few drops of liquid into the bad eye. The liquid stung and irritated the eye, but Baba soothed him by saying, "Never mind, you'll soon be cured." On the following day Baba again sent for him, and this time materialised what the Hindus call a *rūdrāksha,* a kind of talisman made from the berries of a tree growing in the Himalayas, used for bringing protection and other benefits. Baba handed this to him with instructions about how to employ it.

A few days later Mr. Natarajan returned to Ernakulum. The sight of his bad eye was very much better and it continued to improve. Within three months it was quite normal, and he has had no trouble in the ten years since then.

Here are two other cures which Baba performed.

An example of his power to exorcise evil spirits and cure madness was given me by Lilli Krishnan. She said that some years ago there came to the *āshram* a woman possessed of an evil spirit or demon. The woman had a wild look, used to scream, tear her hair, behave in a violent manner and eat all kinds of rubbish and dirt. Baba, by some means known only to himself, drove the demon out of her. "After his treatment there were no more signs of wildness or violence," Lilli said, "the woman became gentle, mild and sweet."

Dr. D. S. Chander, a dental surgeon of Bangalore who has been a devotee for twenty years, told me that in 1958 he was suffering some terrible pain caused by a stone in the gall bladder. His medical adviser said that a surgical operation was essential. Dr. Chander went to Baba who made the jocular remark, "You surgeons can only think of knives and forks." Then he took some *vibhūti* from the air and gave it to the dentist, telling him to take a little, dissolved in water, daily. In a short time the pain vanished, and no operation was necessary. In the ten years since then there has been no recurrence of the gall bladder trouble.

Despite Baba's joke about surgeons and their love of knives he has, on a number of occasions when he decided that tonsils or a tumour or something else must be removed, himself performed surgical operations. For this purpose he always materialises whatever surgical instruments he happens to require with a wave of the hand. Afterwards he makes them vanish. Many solid citizens of India have witnessed such events.

Yet notwithstanding the occasional surgery and phenomenal production of various types of medicines, Baba's most universal instrument of healing is his limitless supply of sacred ash. Through this wonderful medium the divine power flows to cure many kinds of complaints, and also to act as an incredible first-aid treatment for accidents.

A remarkable case* involving the use of *vibhūti* at a distance concerns a fourteen-year-old boy named Shiva Kumar who suffered from heart trouble. In November 1964, when Shiva Kumar was staying with his uncle, Dr. M. D. V. Raman, in Bombay, he developed cerebro-spinal meningitis, with partial paralysis of the left side, and loss of both sight and speech. On 30th November he became unconscious, and at 11.45 that morning, cyanosis intervened and the boy turned blue. The doctors gave him only a few hours to live.

But at noon he seemed to be making signs as if he wanted something. The people present interpreted his signs to mean that he would like a bath, and some of the *vibhūti* which had been brought by a friend from Puttaparthi that morning. They did as he requested, bathing him and applying the consecrated ash. Next he made signs that he wanted a photograph of Sai Baba. This was brought, and set in front of him. Then Shiva rubbed his paralysed left leg and arm with his good right hand.

Suddenly he got off the bed and walked, albeit falteringly and with assistance, into the family *pūjā* room. There he sat near the altar and seemed to go into a state of meditation. This went on for about two hours, then Shiva walked from the *pūjā* room, this time unaided, looked about, went over to a chair and sat in it.

Evidently his eyesight had returned; and then he spoke. He told those present that Sai Baba had appeared to him in a vision, saying that his life would be saved. Shiva had begged to have his sight and speech back too, and Baba had granted the prayer, telling him just what to do.

Soon afterwards Shiva was able to return to school and the studies he loved. When these facts were reported, over a year after the miracle cure took place, Shiva was still in the best of health.

At Prashānti Nílayam in 1967 I met Mr. Russi C. Patel, a Parsi of

*This story was first published in the magazine 'Sanathana Sarathi' (Timeless Charioteer), and checked by the editor, Mr. N. Kasturi, M.A., B.L., lately of the History Department, and ex-Principal at Mysore University.

Bombay, and his wife. From them I learned the story of their little daughter, Ketu.

At the age of two and a half years Ketu could not speak, walk or even stand. She had been given various kinds of medical treatment, including modern drugs and physiotherapy. But nothing seemed to have any effect. The source of the trouble was a mystery. Some thought it was a matter of mental retardation, others said that it was some unknown deep-seated nerve trouble.

This was the state of affairs in February 1965 when Mr. Patel decided to go to Puttaparthi and see Sai Baba. His wife, who was a very orthodox Parsi, was not in favour of the idea, thinking it a waste of time and money.

The Shivarātri festival was on when Mr. Patel arrived at the *āshram* and huge crowds were there. Although people urged him to seek an interview, he was different about doing so, especially as he felt that Baba knew all about his trouble and why he had come, without being told.

Several times he wrote a note, intending to hand it to Baba as the latter passed through the crowd near him, but each time, when he saw the little figure with the luminous face, full of the light of understanding, he decided that it was not necessary and tore the letter up. "When Baba wants me, he will call me," Patel said to his friends.

But the days passed and he was not called. Streams of people were going in to see the great saint, but not Patel. Then one morning, some days after the production of the *lingam,* it was announced that there would be no more personal interviews. However, Baba came onto the balcony and gave his blessings to all visiting devotees assembled there before they went home. Mr. Patel felt the great compassion pour onto the crowd and into his own heart.

Yet in the train on the homeward journey his faith and spirits sank to a low level. He thought of the days he had spent there and the chances of speaking to Baba he had missed. He thought of his poor little daughter still unable to stand or utter a word. He imagined his wife's reproaches about the time and money he had wasted. He arrived at the door of his home very depressed indeed.

When he opened the door, the first sight that met his gaze was little Ketu, who could not even stand when he left, walking down the hallway to meet him, calling out, "Daddy! Daddy!" He picked her up and embraced her; then he embraced his wife, while both of them wept with joy over the miracle that had somehow taken place.

On checking the facts with his wife, Mr. Patel found that Ketu had first begun to walk and speak on the day before he arrived home, just after Sai Baba had given his blessings from the balcony to the assembled devotees. Some time afterwards Mr. Patel took his wife and daughter to see Baba when the latter was on a visit to Bombay. In the midst of the many thousands that crowd around him in that metropolis, Sai Baba saw them and, in the words of Mr. Patel, "greeted the little girl as if she was an old friend returned after a long absence". He took her on his knee, materialised some *vibhūti,* and put it in her mouth. After that, her speech improved greatly and she began using longer words.

The next story concerns the friend who shared our experience in the Guindy temple, Balbir Kaur, the Kanwarani of Ladhran and grand-daughter of Raja Gurdit Singh, Netagariha of Patiala. This dark-eyed, soft-spoken Sikh woman looked about forty when I first met her in 1967 as a member of Baba's party at Horsley Hills. It was there that she told my wife and me the moving story of the "impossible" cure that had brought her to the feet of Satya Sai Baba. The case was confirmed by her daughter, the Maharani of Jind.

In April 1966, Balbir Kaur underwent an operation for an internal growth, and a test showed that it was a malignant cancer. She was not told this, but the report was given to her daughter who took it to a specialist in Bombay. In July Balbir had a bad haemorrhage and was taken from her home in the Punjab to Bombay and admitted to the Tata Memorial Hospital. The haemorrhage had been brought on by the growth of a cancer which, the Maharani of Jind said, "had come up as large as a horrible rose, the mother cancer having worked fast once released by the first operation".

The Maharani continued: "The doctors refused to touch her again, saying her case was hopeless and there was no chance of her coming through an operation. Sarcoma is the hardest and fastest-growing cancer, the operation for it the most aggressive and painful. However, with much begging and many tears on my part, the doctors at last agreed to operate."

So, on 2nd August, Balbir Kaur had her second major operation within a period of just over three months. She was on the table for more than four hours. Yet despite the fears of the doctors she still survived, coming back to dim consciousness to find six drainage tubes in her body. Attached to the tubes were electric suction machines drawing away the unwanted fluids. "With their horrible constant ticking," as her daughter described it, "they seemed to be also drawing the last of the life from Mother's frail body."

Twenty-one days after the operation, the drainage tubes were still in place. "The fast-growing cancer and the rot in the healing process, plus some faults in surgery, apparently caused the many leaks in the body. If one leak healed another place would open up," the Maharani told me. Balbir became so feeble that she seemed to be on the very edge of death. She was given glucose solution and a blood transfusion. But then there was a new leak of blood from one of the tubes. X-ray photography to find the cause of this revealed a hole in the ureter. The medical men decided that a third operation was essential in order to either repair the hole in the ureter or stop the left kidney functioning.

Balbir felt that she just could not endure any more major surgery. Her strength was at a low ebb; she had a bad cough and her mouth was so swollen as a reaction to antibiotics that she had to be fed through a nasal tube. To go through another operation before regaining some vitality would be her end, she knew.

By some fortunate stroke of destiny, just before coming to Bombay for the cancer surgery, she had been given by one of her relatives a photograph of Satya Sai Baba and the book on his life written by N. Kasturi. The portrait had somehow touched her deeply and, as she read the book, her faith in Sai Baba grew in strength.

In the Bombay hospital she had come to a fork in the road where both ways appeared quite hopeless. She could not continue to live with her system in its present hopeless condition, and yet on the other hand her chances of surviving the necessary surgery to put it right seemed very slim indeed. Her life, she felt, hung on a thin thread. Only a miracle could save her. She had begun earlier to pray to the new divine man of power she had found, Sai Baba. Now her prayers become more fervent and continued without ceasing while she was on the table being examined and X-rayed in preparation for the third operation, which was scheduled for the next day. Just before she came off the X-ray table at about 4 p.m., the leak from the ureter seemed to stop. But this was thought to be only temporary and plans for the operation were not changed.

That night she prayed with all her soul to Baba, asking him to heal her and spare her from the operation which she felt she could not survive. The leak continued to hold off through the night. Next day there was still no leaking and the doctors decided that the hole in the ureter must, by some mysterious means, have healed itself.

"They knew that I had been praying to Sai Baba," she told me, "and they were forced to agree that a miracle had happened. Instead of having the operation that day, I had the drainage tubes taken out and was on the road to recovery, thanks to Baba."

So the cancer had been cleared away, the rents and faults and leaks in her interior had healed up, and Balbir Kaur very soon regained sufficient strength to leave hospital and go home. Then her one desire was to go to Puttaparthi and see in the flesh the great saint who had saved her life. But people around her tried to persuade her not to go, saying that life at the *āshram* would be too uncomfortable for her.

Again she approached Sai Baba through prayer. "tell me what to do," she prayed. In a dream she saw him standing on the balcony at Prashānti Nílayam, where she had never been in her life. His words to her were distinct and clear: "Come to Puttaparthi."

When she arrived there she saw the building and balcony of her dream. Baba saw her and called her into a room alone. She had not given her name to anyone at the *āshram*. Yet he knew her immediately and told her all about the operations, about her nearness to death, and her cure.

She has now taken up her permanent abode at Prashānti Nílayam where Sai Baba, in his inimitable way, is teaching her the spiritual lessons she must learn in order to direct her life – the life she has through his grace – towards the right ends. The miracle of Balbir Kaur has been the means of revealing Sai Baba to many people, including her daughter, the Maharani of Jind, who has become an ardent Sai devotee.

In a back number of the *āshram* magazine I read a series of letters from H. N. Banerji who was at the time Professor of Physiology in the Medical College at Gwalior in central India. The letters were written to Y. V. Narayanayya, a scientist living at Prashānti Nílayam. The letters concerned Professor Banerji's niece, Mrs. Chatterji, a 38-year-old mother of seven children. The professor states that early in 1965 the doctors suspected cancer in Mrs. Chatterji's left breast. As soon as he came to know of this, he had her thoroughly examined at Gwalior and then at the All-India Institute of Medical Sciences, New Delhi. These examinations confirmed the original diagnosis of cancer.

At the All-India Institute an eminent surgeon, Professor B. N. Rao, F.R.C.S. (London), operated on Mrs. Chatterji. Then, in Professor Banerji's first letter to Mr. Narayanayya, dated 6th February 1965, from Gwalior, he wrote:

> The pathological report of the removed tissue shows a most virulent type of cancer – aplastic carcinoma. Dr. Ramalingaswami, the renowned pathologist of the Institute, has himself examined the tissue. This type of carcinoma is most fatal; *she has now hardly eight months or so of life.*

The letter concludes with a fervent request for the intercession and help of Satya Sai Baba.

The appeal for help reached Baba's ears. He 'produced' *vibhūti* and gave instructions for it to be sent to Professor Banerji.

The second letter from the professor was written on 20th February. He had, he said, received the packets of *vibhūti* and hurried to his niece's ward with them. The *vibhūti* was used as directed and, "by the grace of His Holiness, the temperature which was tormenting her for the last ten days, rising with severe rigour up to 106 and 107 degrees, with unbearable burning sensation and a severe sinking feeling, has disappeared today, and none of the painful symptoms has returned. What a miracle this alone is . . .". Eighteen days later, on 10th March, he wrote in the third letter:

> My niece is now much better. She has got over the anaemia, moves about, and is taking a practically normal diet. Further, the Cobalt 60 that caused so much set-back, is now being taken very satisfactorily. Cancer is most unpredictable according to medical science, but I am sure she will have a most flourishing life with the blessings of Bhagavan Sri Satya Sai Baba.

The professor's final letter to his friend, as published in the *āshram* magazine, was dated 23rd April. In this he says:

> My niece is by the grace of Sai Baba, doing well. She was to undergo an operation, ovariotomy, as a precautionary measure. But the doctors have dropped the idea, as the same is not warranted. I am very sure in my mind that my niece has been saved by the grace of Bhagavan Sai Baba. She was discharged a month ago, and left for Calcutta the same day with her husband. I offer my heartfelt thanks . . . .

A number of leading medical men and scientists were concerned in this case, including Mrs. Chatterji's own brother, a district medical officer, and her husband who is an electrical engineer. So the cure took place among a group of practical people who could not be called unreliable visionaries.

I noted, however, that Professor Banerji had written in February 1965 that medical opinion gave his niece "hardly eight months or so of life". At the time of his final letter, about two and a half months later, she was "doing well". But what happened after that? It was possible that the recovery was only temporary, and that the cancer had recurred because, as the professor said, it is a most unpredictable disease.

I decided to enquire, and wrote to Mr. Narayanayya at Prashanti Nilayam, whom I know personally. When my letter arrived, Professor H. N. Banerji was himself at the *āshram* on a visit. Soon afterwards, in February 1968, I received a letter from the professor in which he confirmed the medical details of the case as published in the magazine, stating:

> On a very crucial day I got an envelope from my friend (Mr. Narayanayya) which contained the *vibhūti* given personally by Baba to my friend. . . . Magic happened. Patient got round. She is doing well. She is being checked up by a specialist almost every month. Three years have rolled by and, by the grace of Bhagavan, she is doing fine. Medically, death sentence was pronounced, and very meagre hopes were given out. Miracles do happen, whether you call them so, or say it is nothing but Baba's grace and mercy.

The letter came from Patna, for just after the miraculous recovery of his niece he retired from the professorship at Gwalior Medical College and took up an appointment as head of the biochemistry division at the Rajendra Memorial Research Institute for Medical Sciences at Patna. He can, I consider, be judged a first-class witness to the miraculous Sai power being conveyed across India by a few packets of *vibhūti*.

Mr. P. S. Dikshit of Bombay is a producer of documentary films for the Maharashtra Government and a well-known singer of *bhajan* songs. I first heard of the remarkable healing in which he was concerned from the Maharani of Kutch and other Baba devotees; then later Mr. Dikshit gave me the facts himself.

His sister was suffering from trouble in the left breast, where there was a suspicious lump. Clinical tests at the Tata Memorial Hospital, Bombay, confirmed the presence of malignant cancer, and the doctors recommended that the breast be removed forthwith. The chief surgeon concerned agreed to operate a few days later, on the following Tuesday. Then his assistants, remembering that the Tuesday was a holiday, set the operation for Wednesday. With only a few days to spare, Mr. Dikshit tried to locate the whereabouts of Sai Baba in order to get his permission and protection. Finding on enquiry that Baba was on a visit to Anantapur in Andhra Pradesh, he and his sister took a train to that town.

Baba was staying at a house on the outskirts of Anantapur and, as it happened, I was there with his party on that occasion. Mr. Dikshit and his sister reached the house early one morning and waited on the glassed-in verandah for Baba to finish his bath. Although no one had informed him of their coming or the reason for their visit, when Baba came out he said to Dikshit: "I know - it's cancer in your sister's left breast. The operation was to be next Tuesday, before being changed to Wednesday. Actually, it will take place on Thursday. I shall be there and everything will be all right. Don't worry."

Then Swami produced some *vibhūti* in his usual miraculous way, gave some to the patient to eat, and rubbed the rest on Mr. Dikshit's left breast, massaging it well into the skin under the shirt. Finally he gave his breast a pat and said, "Now go!" They went.

They arrived back in Bombay on the Tuesday morning, and Mr. Dikshit took his sister for admission to the hospital on the Wednesday. The operation was scheduled, as Baba had predicted, for the next day, Thursday.

On Wednesday evening, while Mr. Dikshit was sitting on the edge of his bed just before retiring, a water-coloured liquid began to pour copiously from his left nostril. There was no pain, just the streaming fluid. Within two minutes it had wet his pyjamas so thoroughly that he had to change them. Both Dikshit and his wife were puzzled about this flow of liquid which started suddenly and stopped suddenly. He had no cold in the head and, anyway, why the flow from only *one* nostril, and in such quantity? However, they soon forgot the episode, for their thoughts were on the next day's cancer operation.

At 9 a.m. the next morning Dikshit's sister was taken in to the operating theatre. After about half-an-hour one of the doctors, a pathologist, came out and said to Dikshit, "We can't find the lump that was clearly shown in the X-ray. There is only watery liquid there. No signs of the cancer. We have drained off the liquid, and are freezing it for twenty-four hours to do a biopsy, just to make sure that all is clear."

On Friday morning Mr. Dikshit returned to the hospital for the results of the biopsy. The same pathologist came to him and reported, "All clear; no trace whatever of any cancer. Somehow, it vanished!"

The doctors concerned were very puzzled at this inexplicable disappearance of a maligant cancer that had shown its undoubted presence in all the scientific tests. But Mr. Dikshit was not puzzled; his heart was full of deep gratitude to the great doctor of doctors.

Meanwhile his sister's husband had arrived from Delhi in time for the scheduled operation. After what happened he made straight for Prashanti Nilayam, to which place Baba had returned, and waited before the prayer hall to express his heartfelt thanks. After a while Baba appeared on the balcony just above him and immediately called down with a smile, "Nothing there, eh, only water! Well, you can be happy that your wife is quite all right again."

A strange method, indeed, and a very rare one, to cure one person through another. But, as modern parapsychology is discovering, at deeper levels of mind and emotion individuals are closely interconnected. At the deepest level, spiritual philosophy teaches, there is no real division between us; we are all one. Even so, it may be asked, why did Baba adopt this unusual procedure? As many well seasoned devotees often remark, "Who can solve Baba's mysteries? We can only accept the benefits, and be grateful."

Less rare than the curing of one devotee through another is a great *sadgūrū*'s practice of curing devotees through his own body.

I had read of great *yogis* sometimes taking on themselves the *kārmic* complaints and accidents due to strike one of their followers. There are some examples of this in 'The Autobiography of a Yogi' by Paramhansa Yogananda, 'Life of Sai Baba' by Narasimha Swami, and other accounts of the miracle-working saints of India.

Satya Sai Baba has likewise drawn to himself and suffered physical pains on behalf of his devotees. N. Kasturi says in his book on Baba's life that, once, a doctor from near Madura wrote to him saying that he had been suffering pain and bleeding in an ear, but that the trouble had vanished suddenly in a miraculous manner. Mr. Kasturi said that the letter from the doctor reached him "just when Baba himself was 'free' from a slightly bleeding ear and some earache, which he had announced as having been 'taken over' from a devotee who was suffering the agony". Kasturi further states that, "Satya Sai Baba has taken upon himself, and suffered, mumps, typhoid fever, delivery pains and the scalding burns of his devotees". A striking example of this type of compassionate phenomenon was described to me by a number of witnesses who were present in the *āshram* at the time of the happening.

On the evening of 28th June 1963, Baba asked Mr. Kasturi to announce at the *āshram* that no more interviews would be granted for a week. Neither Kasturi nor anyone else understood or could guess the reason for this. But they soon found out. On Saturday 29th June at 6.30 a.m., Baba suddenly fell unconscious. Initially the devotees close around him thought that he had gone into a trance, as he had often done in the past when travelling in his subtle body to bring badly needed aid to some devotee somewhere. These trances had been known to last a few hours, but this time Swami remained unconscious for much longer.

His devotees became apprehensive and began to arrange for medical aid. In addition to a doctor at the *āshram* hospital, Dr. Prasannasimha Rao, Assistant Director of Medical Services of Mysore State, was called from Bangalore. He writes, after describing the symptoms fully,

> The differential diagnosis of such conditions . . . pinned me down to that of tuberculous meningitis, with perhaps a tuberculoma, silent for a long time. . . .

When the doctor tried to give the treatment that seemed indicated, Baba regained some awareness, it seemed, and refused the injections and other medical assistance. He stated later that the trouble would pass in five days' time.

During those five days he had four severe heart attacks, his left side was paralysed - stiff, useless, insensitive; the sight of his left eye and his speech were also badly affected.

On Thursday, 4th July, five days after the attack started, Swami became sufficiently clear and strong to announce that the clot in his brain had been dissolved, and there would be no more heart attacks. However, the left side of his body was still paralysed and his speech was thick and feeble. His followers believed that it would take several months for him to recoup his good health.

During the period of his suffering Baba had indicated to those attending him that one devotee at a distance was about to be affected by a stroke and heart attacks so severe that they would have killed him. So Baba had taken on the illness with all its symptoms of paralysis, heart seizures, high temperature, partial loss of eyesight, severe physical pains, and so on. His disciples understood and accepted this explanation.

But Gūrū Pūrnima, a religious festival day, was approaching and many visitors were congregating in the *āshram*. The visitors were very upset and dejected at stories they were hearing of Baba's condition. Not knowing the cause - or not believing it - they began to doubt. "If Baba is God in human form," they said to one another, "why is he also afflicted with physical ailments? Why does he not cure himself?"

On the evening of Gūrū Pūrnima Day, 6th July, came the final scene. Practically carried by several disciples, Baba came down the circular stairs from his bedroom to the crowded prayer hall below. The whole left side of his body was still paralysed and his speech was a feeble, scarcely intelligible mumble.

A doctor present described the scene thus: "His gait was the characteristic hemiplegic one, the paralytic left leg being dragged in a semi-circle, the toes scraping the floor. Seeing Baba in that condition, even the bravest wept aloud."

For a few minutes Swami sat in his chair on the dais before the assembled people, some five thousand inside and outside the hall. Silent, sorrowful, deeply moved they all were. Then Baba gestured for water. Some was brought in a tumbler, and Raja Reddy held it up to the twisted lips. Baba drank a few drops; then dipping his right fingertips into the water, he sprinkled a few drops onto his paralysed left hand and leg. Next he stroked his left hand with the right, and followed this by stroking his stiff left leg *with both hands.* The hearts of the watchers leapt at the sight, with dawning hope.

Mr. T. A. Ramantha Reddy, the government engineer whom I knew at Horsley Hills, was in one of the front rows and very close to Baba. He said, "In a second Swamiji's leg, eye, and all his left side became normal. It was a sight for the gods to see his sudden recovery, and the devotees present witnessed the greatness of his divine power . . .".

Mr. N. Kasturi describes it in this way: "He rose and we could hear his divine voice calling us, as was ever his wont . . . . He had begun his Gūrū Pūrnima discourse! People did not believe their eyes and ears. But when they realised that Baba was standing before them, speaking, they jumped about for joy, they danced, they shouted, they wept; some were so overcome with ecstatic gratitude that they laughed hysterically and ran wild among the crowd rushing in."

Baba was on his feet speaking for over an hour. Then he sang a number of *bhajan* songs, and finally climbed the stairs unaided. That night he ate his normal meal, and the following days saw him back in his usual vigorous, hearty health, carrying on a full programme of activities. The deadly stroke which had come at his bidding departed within the period he foretold, and left no tell-tale signs behind.

It is on record that during his former life at Shirdi, Baba took to himself, on behalf of close devotees, many diseases and accidents, as when he thrust his arm into the fire at the Shirdi mosque where he lived just at the moment when a child of a devotee fell into a blacksmith's fire elsewhere. Baba bore the burns and scars on his arm for a long time, but he stated that he had thereby saved the life of the child.

In the 'Gospel of Sai Baba', also called 'Baba's Charters and Sayings', he is quoted as stating that he would give up his very life if necessary to save a devotee who was completely surrendered to him. Many believe that that is how he died in 1918.

Even there shall come as a high crown of all
The end of Death, the death of Ignorance . . .

Sṛi Aurobindo

13

THE QUESTION OF SAVING FROM DEATH

There happened, in the latter part of 1953, an event almost as dramatic in its way as Christ's raising of Lazarus from the dead. I heard of it from a number of people, including the man most closely concerned, the Lazarus of the case, Mr. V. Radhakrishna. Then I finally had the facts carefully presented by Mr. Radhakrishna's daughter, Vijaya, who was an eyewitness, and who wrote down the details at the time of the happening in the diary she has always kept of her experiences with Sai Baba. While relating the experience to me she had her diary before her.

Mr. V. Radhakrishna, who is a factory owner and a well-known citizen in Kuppam, Andhra Pradesh, was about sixty years of age when, in 1953, he paid a visit to Puttaparthi. With him on this occasion went his wife, his daughter Vijaya and the latter's husband, Mr. K. S. Hemchand. Vijaya was about eighteen and had not been long married. Her father, she told me, was at the time suffering from gastric ulcers with various complications, He was really in a very bad way, and one of his reasons for visiting the *āshram* was the hope that he might get relief from his frightful suffering. He had known Baba for some time.

The great religious festival of Dassehra was on, and a good number of people were visiting Puttaparthi. Mr. Radhakrishna was given a room in the same building where Swami lived, and spent all his time on his bed there. Once, when Baba came to visit him, Radhakrishna said that he would prefer to die rather than go on suffering the way he was. Swami simply laughed at this, and made no promise of either healing him or letting him die.

One evening Radhakrishna went into a coma and his breathing was that of a dying man. Alarmed, the wife dashed off to see Swami. The latter came to the room, looked at the patient, said "Don't worry. Everything will be all right," and left. On the next day the patient was still unconscious. Mr. K. S. Hemchand, the son-in-law, brought a male nurse of the district who, after failing to find any pulse and making other examinations, gave as his opinion that Mr. Radhakrishna was so near death that there was no possibility of saving him.

About an hour after this the patient became very cold. The three anxious relatives heard what they thought was the death rattle in his throat and watched him turning blue and stiff. Vijaya and her mother went to see Baba who was at the time upstairs in his dining room. When they told him that Radhakrishna seemed to be dead, he laughed and walked away to his bedroom. Vijaya and her mother returned to the room of the "dead" man and waited. After a while, Swami came in and looked at the body, but went away again without saying or doing anything.

That was on the evening of the second day since Mr. Radhakrishna had become unconscious. The whole of the next night passed while the three stayed awake and anxiously watched for any signs of returning life. There were no signs. Yet they still had faith that Baba would somehow or other, in his own way, save Radhakrishna, for had he not said that everything would be all right?

On the morning of the third day the body was more than ever like a corpse: dark, cold, quite stiff and beginning to smell. Other people who came to see and sympathise told Mrs. Radhakrishna that she should have the corpse removed from the *āshram*. But she replied, "Not unless Swami orders it." Some even went to Baba and suggested that, as the man was dead and the body smelling of decomposition, it should either be sent back to Kuppam or cremated at Puttaparthi. Swami simply replied, "We'll see."

When Mrs. Radhakrishna went upstairs again to tell Baba what people were saying to her, and ask him what she must do, he answered, "Do not listen to them, and have no fear; I am here." Then he said that he would come down to see her husband soon.

She went downstairs again and waited, with her daughter and son-in-law, by the body. The minutes dragged by – an hour passed – but Swami did not come. Then, when they were beginning to despair entirely, the door opened and there stood Baba with his red robe, copious hair, and shining smile. It was then about half past two in the afternoon of the third day. Mrs. Radhakrishna went towards Baba and burst into tears. Vijaya too began to cry. They were like Martha and Mary, the sisters of Lazarus, weeping before their Lord who, they thought, had come too late.

Gently Baba asked the tearful women and sorrowful Mr. Hemchand to leave the room. As they left, he closed the door behind them. They do not know – no man knows – what happened in that room where there were only Swami and the "dead" man.

But after a few minutes Baba opened the door and beckoned the waiting ones in. There, on the bed, Radhakrishna was looking up at them and smiling. Amazingly the stiffness of death had vanished and his natural colour was returning. Baba went over, stroked the patient's head and said to him, "Talk to them; they're worried."

"Why worried?" asked Radhakrishna, puzzled. "I'm all right. You are here."

Swami turned to the wife: "I have given your husband back to you," he said. "Now get him a hot drink."

When she brought it, Swami himself fed it to Radhakrishna slowly with a spoon. For another half-hour he remained there, strengthening the man he had "raised". Then he blessed the whole family, placing his hand on Mrs. Radhakrishna's head, and left the room.

Next day the patient was strong enough to walk to *bhajan*. On the third day he wrote a seven-page letter to one of his daughters who was abroad in Italy. The family stayed a few more days at Prashānti Nílayam, then, with Baba's permission, returned to their home in Kuppam. The bad gastric ulcers and complications had vanished for ever.

When I spoke to Mr. Radhakrishna himself about the experience I asked if he had any memories at all of the time he was unconscious and to all appearances dead. He replied, "No, when I became conscious again I thought at first that it was just the same day. Later they told me it had been three days I was unconscious, that I was 'dead' and actually starting to stink. But Swami can do anything he wishes. He is God."

When is a person dead? Does any man know? Some who have seemed dead by all medical tests have in fact returned to their bodies – often, unfortunately, after being placed in their tombs, as evidence of movements by "corpses" seen later has proved. When Jesus received word that Lazarus was dead, he said to his disciples, "Our friend Lazarus sleepeth; but I go that I may awake him out of sleep."

Sai Baba himself, during the early years at Shirdi, once left his body for three days. He asked a close disciple to guard the body, saying, "I am going to Allah. If I do not return after three days, then get my body buried at that place," indicating a sacred *neem* tree. An inquest was held. Officials declared Sai Baba dead and ordered the corpse to be buried. But the disciple, with the help of some others, stoutly opposed the order, and would not surrender the body. Then at the end of the third day Sai Baba returned to his tall Shirdi physique and lived in it for another thirty-two years.

When Mr. N. Kasturi a few years ago was writing something about the incident of Mr. Radhakrishna being raised from the dead, Baba told him to put the word "dead" in inverted commas. So maybe we should say here that Mr. Radhakrishna was very near to death, more than half-way through death's door, when Baba called him back to life. Perhaps the same could be said of Lazarus.

Some people Baba saves from serious illnesses, or from the threshold of death. Others he does not. Why does he use his miraculous healing power for some and not for others? Why does he not cure all, save all from death? Many people ask these questions.

In the same way one might ask why Christ did not cure all the sickness around him in his day. And why was Lazarus the only one he called back from the tomb? Did Jesus, and did Sai Baba later, make a special effort against the power of death for a greatly loved family of close devotees? Maybe, but, I think there is more to it than that.

When Jesus was informed that Lazarus was sick he made the enigmatic remark, "This sickness is not unto death, but for the glory of God, that the Son of God might be glorified thereby." So, what would normally, under ordinary conditions, be a death-dealing disease may be an occasion for the glorification of God through the works of a God-man. Then, too, there is the profound and complex question of *karma*. To what extent is the specific ailment or the approach of death *kārmic*, and how far should the God-man interfere with the patient's *karma*?

There are two cases within the same family; one where it seems the claims of *karma* could be put aside, so to speak; and the other where it is wiser not to interfere.

Once when Mr. G. Venkatamuni's mother, nearly eighty years old, was so close to death that all relatives had been warned of her imminent end, his wife Sushila took a *japamālā* given her by Sai Baba and placed it on the old lady's breast. Baba had told Sushila that the *japamālā* could be used in emergency as a healing charm.

The patient immediately began to show marked signs of improvement. This happened about ten o'clock one evening and when next morning a number of close relatives arrived, summoned to bid the old lady a last farewell, she asked in a puzzled tone why they had all come. She was soon hale and hearty again, and lived several years more.

Later, however, when one of G. Venkatamuni's sons, an epileptic, took very ill and seemed to be dying, Sushila decided to use the Sai Baba *japamālā* to try to save the boy. She went to bring it from where it was lying among other things in a case in the family *pūjā* room; but she came back without it, telling her husband in a distressed and bewildered tone that she could not get hold of the *japamālā*. She had tried to pick it up several times, but each time it had somehow eluded her hand. She could not explain this strange thing, an object seeming to avoid her grasp. What could it mean? Talking it over, husband and wife could only decide that, for some reason, Baba did not want the charm used on this occasion.

The boy died. Soon afterwards the parents called to see Baba. They had often listened to his wise words on the true nature of death, yet they were but human, and wore long sad faces. Moreover, they were a little hurt to find that Baba himself was far from mournful; in fact, he was cheerful and smiling.

He said to them, "You must not sorrow over the boy. I have just seen him again, and he is very happy 'over there'. He had just a little *karma* to work out here on earth, and when he had completed that he was ready to go. It was much better, much happier for him to go."

Then the parents understood that they had really only been sorry for themselves in their loss, and they were comforted to know that the boy they loved, who seemed dead, was in fact alive and well beyond his suffering physical body. Mr. and Mrs. Venkatamuni's faith in Sai Baba did not for a moment waver, but there are some devotees whose belief is shaken when someone near and dear dies. Several have told me of this, saying the situation is often aggravated by sceptical relatives who say, "Well, why didn't Sai Baba save *him*?" Even the faith of deeply devoted and highly intelligent followers can suffer an eclipse in sufficiently tragic circumstances.

For instance, Mr. V. Hanumantha Rao, mentioned earlier, had a sick son who had developed polio at the age of about six months. To make matters worse the boy was an only child.

Mr. and Mrs. Hanumantha Rao met Sai Baba when their son was about four years old. The young, lovable Swami became like one of the family; but he puzzled the couple by often referring to their child as "my boy", and he always called the little fellow "Shiva" although his name was actually Ishvari Prasad Dattatreya. Swami would often say to them, "Shiva is the rope that brought us together, and holds us so."

The parents did not understand this and many of the young Swami's sayings, but he performed uplifting miracles in their presence, and they had great hopes that he would cure their son.

The boy was very happy when Baba was present but his health grew worse. Polio affected the brain; there were frequent fits and after a few years little "Shiva" died. And with his death the rope was broken. The bereaved parents stopped seeing Sai Baba. No doubt they felt that he had somehow failed them.

Yet the time they had spent with him, his elevating spiritual influence, his silent and his spoken teachings, had had a profound effect upon them. Soon after the death of his beloved son, Mr. Hanumantha Rao devoted a large part of his fortune to establishing and maintaining in Madras an orthopaedic centre for children crippled with polio. The centre, one of the few of its kind in India, is named after the little boy, Ishvari Prasad Dattatreya, to whom it is a memorial. The children there are given medical, surgical and rehabilitation treatment and a regular education. It lies just across the Adyar river from the Theosophical Society headquarters, and I have several times called there to see Mr. Hanumantha Rao. I have watched the joy that lights the faces of the young cripples when the old retired transport commissioner walks into wards or classrooms. Also I have seen them in wheelchairs or held up by frames and crutches saluting with deep reverence the bust of little Ishvari Prasad, which stands in the hospital entrance. They feel that, in a certain way, he died for them; that it is his spirit which has brought them modern scientific help in their sufferings and the hope of a happier life.

When this couple had triumphed over their great sorrow and turned it to a worthy and constructive end, a veil seemed to fall from their eyes. They saw how wrong they had been in blaming Sai Baba for not keeping their boy alive. As Mr. Hanumantha Rao said to me, "There must be suffering in the world; it belongs to the nature of things here because man brings it on himself." They understand that the Divine One cannot lift all the *karma* from man's shoulders, and also that much good can, in fact, come out of what seems to be evil from our limited viewpoint.

So, Mr. and Mrs. Hanumantha Rao returned to the one who for them is the focus of divinity on earth today, and they are among his most deeply devoted disciples. In their home they keep a special bedroom set aside for Sai Baba. The room is never given to anyone else and their constant prayer is that Baba will grace it whenever possible with his presence.

My wife and I have several times been at the Hanumantha Rao home, one of a small group there, when Sai Baba paid a visit. It is a special joy to watch him there. As in former years he seems to be one of the family - happy, carefree, boyish, full of fun. It is as if he is the son, yet at the same time the father and mother and god of this gentle, sweet old couple. The soul of the child that led them, the rope that drew them towards the light, is, I feel, somehow still there though unseen.

In a number of cases where Sai Baba has not cured or saved - has not performed the outer miracle - I have noted a similar *inner* and really much more important miracle. He has perhaps cured the desire to be cured and brought acceptance; he has healed the soul wounds of loss, and lifted minds and hearts to a better understanding of life. He has brought a new and broader vision about suffering and death.

It is the same pattern now as it was long ago at Shirdi. Then and there he healed and saved the lives of many. Some he did not save. One of these was the daughter of his great devotee H. S. Dixit. So people murmured, "If Sai Baba could not save Dixit's daughter at Shirdi, what is the good of a *sadgūrū*?"

On this point the profound Sai Baba apostle, B. V. Narasimha, writes: "One might as well say when dear ones die, 'What is the good of God?' Faith is not a guarantee that there will be no death or evil in the world nor pains in life. But, as in the case of Dixit, intense faith makes the devotee brace himself up against all inevitable calamities and learn more and more of God's scheme for our life. Life is not intended to be a bed of roses and a treasure house of wealth. . . . Faith enables the devotee to see what life is, and what God's plan is, and improve his own attitude to life."

In this, as in his former incarnation, Sai Baba has sometimes said that to cure a certain person, to save from death, or to remove some inborn physical blemish, would be to interfere unduly with the person's *karma*. And in such cases he has left the person concerned to bear that cross.

From all this we might conclude that some diseases are *kārmic* and some are not. Some are the result of our own actions (most likely in a former life) and are part of the great moral law of compensation. We must expiate our past misdeeds by bearing the consequences and learning thereby. On the other hand, some afflictions – diseases, accidents, and so on – are only to a limited degree, if at all, brought about by our own actions. And with such we do not need to suffer long in order to learn some specific lesson from our own past mistake.

Likewise with regard to death. Generally, I think, the time of death is not strictly pre-ordained; there are several points, let us say, along your lifeline when you could meet death, but it is not an absolute *kārmic* necessity that you should die at the first or second of those points. Nevertheless, in man's present state, death is essential to the pattern of life, and in the end every man must die. Though Lazarus was called back from the tomb, some years later he died. And so must any man whose life Sai Baba saves. When that final point comes at which it is best to die, at which it is unwise and detrimental to the soul to prolong life, then what enlightened saint would interfere? The Illuminati, the God-men, the great yogis know when that right time is for those who come to them – as, of course, they do for themselves. When the ancient writings say that the yogi conquers death, they do not mean that he lives for ever. They mean he himself decides the right time for him to depart this earth, and then he goes, leaving his body, consciously, of his own volition.

But, as mankind is today we cannot expect Sai Baba, or any other God-powered man, to dissolve away the whole heavy cloud of man's *kārmic* sins, curing all diseases, making all the cripples walk, cleansing all the lepers, opening the eyes of all the millions of blind that exist in India alone. The most he can do is lift a little of man's heavy *karma* here and there and point the way.

There the When is an eternal Now,
The Where an eternal Here.

The Dream of Rāvana

14

ETERNAL HERE AND NOW

Mr. N. Kasturi has written of the following incident:

At about 1.30 p.m. on June 21st 1959, Baba's close disciples were alarmed because his temperature shot up suddenly to 104.5 degrees. About five minutes later the thermometer registered a fall to 99 degrees. This was a mystery to them, and Baba did not at the time enlighten them.

However, that evening he was having dinner with a number of his devotees on a terrace in the moonlight. Among them was a young man from Madras who had been for some time staying with Baba, but was leaving the next day. Suddenly Swami said to him: "When you go to your mother tomorrow, tell her that she should be more careful about fire."

This aroused considerable curiosity and some anxiety. So Baba told them that the lady's sāri had caught fire that morning in Madras while she was in her *pūjā* room but that the flames had been extinguished in time. The sāri was ruined but she was unharmed.

After dinner one of the devotees thought of putting through a trunk call to Madras. Baba agreed, and it was done. The lady came to the telephone herself and gave the enquirers more details of the accident. Then Baba spoke to her, and the listening devotees heard him laugh and say, "Oh, no, I did not burn my hands. I just had an increase in temperature for a short while."

Some years later I had first-hand confirmation of this story from Mr. G. Venkatamuni whose wife, Sushila, was the person concerned. Yes, her sāri had caught fire while she was in the *pūjā* room, he said; in a moment she was enveloped in flames. Panic seized her, but she had long been a devotee, and the first words that sprang to her lips were, "Sai Baba". Immediately the flames died away and Sushila, knowing from experience the power of Baba at any distance, felt quite sure that he had somehow come to her aid in the crisis.

Forgetting for a moment that he had not come to her in his physical body she had asked him on the telephone if he had burned his hands. Yet this is not such a foolish question as might at first sight appear. Psychic research workers have found many case histories of astral travel where a shock to the astral body has caused effects, such as wounds, burns and bruises, on the physical body. This is brought about by the occult law of reciprocity. Baba's sudden rise in temperature seems to have been a mild example of this.

Throughout the 1940s, and for most of the 1950s, Baba often went into a trance during his out-of-the-body journeys. Suddenly and unexpectedly he would become unconscious, and those near him would know that he was away, probably with some devotee at a distant place. On returning, he might or might not tell those around him something of what happened.

On occasions there would be reciprocal effects on Baba's physical body indicative of what he was doing. Sometimes, for instance, a few words of what he was saying at the distant place would issue from his physical lips. At other times *vibhūti* would emanate from his body. This latter was usually when he had gone to be present at the death of a devotee. Mr. Kasturi says, "On such occasions, symbolic of death, destruction and the end of the temporary and the evanescent, sacred *vibhūti* issues from the mouth of the body that Baba leaves behind in order to proceed to the deathbed."

Kasturi then gives an example. At about 5.20 p.m. on 15th November 1958, Baba was reading a letter aloud to some people around him, when suddenly he exclaimed, "Ha!" and fell to the floor. The body was quiet for ten minutes, then it appeared to cough. Puffs of *vibhūti* were coming from the mouth, shooting out, Kasturi says, "to a distance of more than a foot and a half".

At 5.35 p.m., having been unconscious for fifteen minutes, he resumed the reading where he had left off, quite naturally and showing no signs of exhaustion. When requested, he told the devotees where he had been: Dehra Dun in the Himalayas. There, he said, the mother of a doctor, well known in the *āshram*, had just passed away. Baba had gone to give her help at the time of transition, which was 5.30 p.m. He also remarked that the doctor, her son, was present at the woman's death in Dehra Dun, and that people were singing *bhajan* songs in the room there. He further described how the old lady had at the end announced to everybody, "This is my last breath", and then expired.

Two days later, on 17th November, a letter came to Baba from the doctor whose mother had died. He wrote,

My mother drew her last breath on Saturday, at 5.30 p.m. We were doing *bhajan* during her last hours as per her wish. She was remembering you constantly.

Here is another example of Baba's knowledge of things at a distance and his power to intervene. In the early 1960s, when Mr. K. R. K. Bhat was a divisional manager of the Life Insurance Corporation of India, there was a case of bribery and corruption among his subordinates. This was in connection with an important promotion and some anonymous letters had set an official enquiry in motion.

It was found that several people were involved in the plot but the main culprit seemed to be Mr. Bhat's male stenographer who, however, tried to protect himself by shifting the responsibility onto his chief. He stated to the enquiry officer that he had simply carried out Mr. Bhat's instructions in all that he did.

It began to look as if Bhat, although completely innocent, would become involved, it being a question of one man's word against that of another. Bhat could think of no way in which to establish his innocence, and he began to be very worried. If he were found guilty of involvement in such an affair, the effects would be drastic to his career.

Finally, the whole matter hinged on whether Bhat had or had not received personally in his office, and signed for, a certain registered letter. The stenographer stated that his chief had done so, whereas Bhat knew for certain that he had not. It should have been easy to check with the appropriate post office and find out whose signature had been given for the letter on the known date. But the postmaster stated that he could not assist because it had happened too long ago. The records, he said, were kept only six months, and then destroyed. The relevant letter had been received more than six months before.

At this point Baba began appearing in dreams to Mr. Bhat, who was a devotee. In a dream vision Baba assured Bhat that the records were, in fact, still at the post office. They had not been destroyed as stated. In the end the postmaster was forced to admit that this was true. He made the excuse that his predecessor had let the old records pile up, and that there were so many, in fact, over three years' accumulation, that he had neither the time nor the facilities to destroy them. He maintained, however, that as the mass of documents were not in any order but all in a jumbled heap, it would be quite impossible to find the one little paper so important to Mr. Bhat. There was absolutely no point in making the attempt, he said, as it would be like looking for a needle in a haystack.

That night Swami appeared again in a dream to his devotee, Mr. Bhat, saying that a man should be appointed to search at the post office, and that the relevant document would be quickly found. Following this, Bhat at last persuaded the postal authorities to attempt what he wanted. A clerk was put on to begin a search through the great stack of papers. Quite at random he picked out a bundle and began going through it.

"Miracle of miracles," said Mr. Bhat, "there was the document I needed so badly, right in the first bundle." It showed conclusively that the stenographer had signed for the vital registered letter on behalf of his boss. This cleared the latter of suspicion. The stenographer and several other men were found guilty of corrupt practices, and the Corporation administered appropriate penalties. Sai Baba's all-seeing eye and intervention from afar had saved his devotee from injustice.

"Not only is he above the limitations of space but, of time too," Mr. Bhat declared. "When we were at Prashānti Nílayam early in 1965, Swami told my wife privately that I should retire or take long leave, but must somehow stop work and be away from the office by June 1st that year.

"He did not say why, but I had learned by this time to follow Swami's advice. However, it was quite impossible for me to clear up all my business affairs, train my successor, and hand over by June 1st. I could manage it, I found, by July 1st, so I decided that that must suffice. I would be a month later than Swami had intimated, but I hoped that would be all right. I was wrong.

"On June 4th I had my first heart attack. Baba had obviously foreseen it and given me the warning. The strain of work had brought it on, no doubt, and if I had taken his advice I could have avoided it. Well, through his grace I am still alive and able to do many things that the specialists say I must not do."

Many other people have told me that Baba has foreseen events of importance in their future. Not only dangers to health and limb, but many things that loom large in their daily lives - births, marriages, new jobs, business opportunities and examination results, even to the precise marks that will be obtained.

Here is an amusing example of his precognitive power. Mr G. K. Damodar Rao, a retired judge, was at the time in question Governor of the Lions Clubs for several districts of southern India. He was about to leave for Chicago to attend an international convention of Lions Clubs there. When he called at Prashānti Nílayam and told Sai Baba, the latter asked him to take a parcel, containing *vibhūti* and other items, to a group of Sai Baba devotees in California. Damodar Rao was delighted at the prospect of delivering the parcel, not only for the joy of doing something for Baba, but also because he looked forward to seeing his devotee friends in California.

But the difficulty was that the Indian Government would allow him only enough foreign exchange to travel to Chicago and back by the shortest route, that is, across the Atlantic. He found it was quite impossible to obtain officially the necessary dollars to make the extra journey from Chicago to the west coast of America.

Reluctantly and sadly he told Swami that the hard facts of foreign exchange control and geography made the mission to California quite impossible. Swami was silent for a moment, then said, "Nevertheless you *will* go to California, so don't worry, just take the parcel." In Chicago, Damodar Rao called a number of times at the office of the airline company by which he was travelling to enquire whether there was any way in which he could possibly make his return journey across America and the Pacific; but there was none.

The girl of whom he used to enquire frequently in the Chicago office got to know him and, noticing the image of Sai Baba on his ring, asked him about it. He told her that it was his *guru* and that, furthermore, his *guru* has said that he, Damodar Rao, would go to California - so there had to be some way in which it could be done.

"I'm very sorry to disappoint you and your *guru*," she replied with apparent regret, "but there's just no way that I can do it. I would help you if I could."

Then one morning she greeted him joyously, "Your *guru* was right!" she cried. "You are going to California."

When, with a leaping heart, he asked her *how*, she informed him that there had been a strike of pilots in the airline by which he was to travel back, and that now she would have to re-route his return to India by another airline. In this way she could send him via the Pacific, and he would be able to make a stopover at Los Angeles.

Thus, as Baba had foretold confidently weeks earlier, the parcel was duly delivered to the Californian Sai Family. I was myself at Prashānti Nílayam when Damodar Rao came there straight after his return from America. He was still highly elated when he told the story, all hearers shared his joy in the telling. No one doubted but that Baba had foreseen the strike, and the manner in which it would affect Damodar Rao's movements.

Through the years since Sai Baba's following first began at Shirdi last century there have been numerous reports of him appearing in a materialised form at places far away from where his body actually was at the time. He may make the appearance in his own form or in some other, such as an old friend or relative, a beggar, a workman, a *sādhū* or holy man.

Sometimes, it seems, he creates a temporary *māyā*, or illusion, of the form. Sometimes it may be that he "overshadows" a real living person or animal, making them do what he requires, and himself noting the response or reaction from the devotee concerned. Then he tells the devotee about it at a later date. Or he may at the time make some remark to people where he actually is, physically, at the time which gives a clue as to what has happened at a distance. Then this is confirmed later.

One example took place when H. S. Dixit received a letter at Shirdi to say that one of his brothers at Nagpur was ill. He told Baba about it, saying regretfully, "I am of no service to him." Baba replied "*I* am of service."

Dixit could not make out why he said this, and what he meant. But he found out some time later, for just at that moment at Nagpur, a *sādhū* arrived and used the very words of Baba, "I am of service". The *sādhū* cured the brother of his illness. And Dixit realised that across a thousand miles Baba saw what went on, and did what was necessary.

That may, perhaps, have been a real *sādhū* "overshadowed" by Baba, but one that appeared to a devotee in more recent years in Delhi seems more like an illusive creation, a temporary form taken by Satya Sai Baba.

This story was told to me by Mrs. Kamala Sarathi, wife of the late Mr. R. P. Sarathi who was at the time of the event Additional Secretary of Defence under V. K. Krishna Menon, the Indian Minister for Defence. The incident concerns a man named V. S. Chidambaram, a violinist who was Kamala's music master. Not being herself too sure of all the details, Kamala kindly wrote on my behalf from Madras, where she now lives, to her old music master in Delhi. He replied giving a full account of the event, and Kamala passed on the letter to me.

It happened in Delhi back in 1950 at the time when both Kamala and her music master, Chidambaram, had been devotees of Sai Baba for about two to three years. Both had visited Puttaparthi some five or six times and Chidambaram was at that period living in a room in Sarathi's house in Delhi.

One morning the music master, then a man of about forty-five, was riding his cycle along Minto Road between New Delhi and Old Delhi. He had been out teaching some pupils, and was due back home to give a violin lesson to Kamala at eleven o'clock that morning.

As he cycled along he was turning over a problem in his mind. It used to cost him a lot to travel all the way to Puttaparthi and, although he had some beautiful and wonderful experiences there, he began to wonder if he could really afford the journey. He writes: "I was just thinking whether Baba was a real incarnation of God and whether it was worth spending so much money in going to Puttaparthi to see him."

It was then that an old *sādhū* came cycling fast behind him and caught him up. The music master noted that the holy man was wearing a robe and had a cloth tied around his head, just like the pictures of Shirdi Sai Baba. The old *sādhū* stopped, and Chidambaram did likewise, offering his salutations. The *sādhū* remarked that he would like to speak alone and privately to the music master and, as the street was busy and noisy, suggested they go to a quiet spot. Chidambaram, realising that he would be late for Kamala's lesson, made some protest, but the *sādhū* said it was only a question of ten minutes.

The music master says, "I had the feeling that this *sādhū* was like Shirdi Sai Baba, and so I consented to go with him." After walking some distance down a side road, pushing their bicycles, they came to an old tomb. The *sādhū* sat on this, putting one leg over the other in the manner of Shirdi Sai Baba. The music master, after making customary gestures of respect and reverence, sat on the ground before the holy man.

Sādhū (after about a minute's silence): "Who do you think I am?"

Chidambaram: "You seem to be like Shirdi Sai Baba."

Sādhū: "All right. See my hand." He held his palm before Chidambaram. The palm became like a mirror in which was reflected in radiant colours the figure of Sai Baba of Puttaparthi sitting in a chair and smiling. The music master gazed at the vision in awe.

Then the *sādhū* unbuttoned his robe and undershirt to expose his chest. There again Chidambaram saw a vision of Puttaparthi Sai Baba. This time he was "sitting with a garland around him, shining and blissful".

The music master was completely overcome. He began to tremble and "shed tears of joy". Then the *sādhū* rubbed his back as Satya Sai Baba so often does for devotees in distress, smeared him with *vibhūti* and fed him with some candy. Both of these were materialised from the air in Satya Sai Baba's inimitable way.

Assuring the music master that the two Sai Babas are one, the *sādhū* said, "Don't lose heart under any circumstances. It is because of my love for you that I have come. Now let us go."

As they walked away Chidambaram begged the *sādhū*, whom he now believed was the Sai Baba he knew and adored, to come with him to the Sarathi home. But the holy man would not do so. Chidambaram writes, "I watched him cycle off up the quiet side road. In two minutes both he and the bicycle had completely vanished." The music master could not himself ride, being too overcome with emotions, and so, he says, "Loading my bicycle onto a *tongā* I went home."

Kamala told me, "He was very late, and I was wondering what had happened. Then he arrived in the *tongā*, and in such a state too! I thought he was ill. When he could speak coherently, he told me all about the experience. Since then he has had no doubts, and is very devoted to Sai Baba."

This story concerns Mr. V. Radhakrishna of Kuppam, whom Baba seems determined to keep on this earth as long as possible. In 1960, seven years after he had been raised from the dead, Radhakrishna was again sick, and was suffering a good deal of pain.

He told me: "One night the doctor gave me a morphine injection and I went off to sleep. But it seems that I got up later and wandered about in a state of unconsciousness. I don't remember anything about it, but I must have fallen down the well near the house. The well was open, about ten feet in diameter and some fifty feet deep, with about thirty feet of water in it. The sides are of smooth stone, and there are no ledges, or anything whatever to hold on to, or stand on."

His daughter, Vijaya, who was present at Kuppam at the time of the accident, takes up the story from her diary notes.

"My mother awoke at about 3 a.m. and saw that Father was missing from his bed, so she went to search for him. Outside she called his name and presently she heard a voice shout, 'I'm in the well.' She ran over and looked down with an electric torch. There he was. He seemed to be standing in the water, about up to his waist in it, but she knew that there was nothing there for him to stand on. She called down to him but he did not reply, just remained there in the water.

"She rushed inside and awoke my two brothers and myself. So we went over, but did not know how to get him out. There was a stone slab across the top of the well with a gap on either side, through one of which he must have fallen. My eldest brother, Krishna Kumar, tried to reach my father from the slab, but Father was too far down for this. We must have been making a lot of noise because the Chief of Police suddenly appeared on the scene. He told us later that he just happened to be passing that way from the railway to his office when he heard us. It was not his usual nightly route home, and he does not know why he went that way. Incidentally, he was a friend of our family.

"With ropes and a pulley and a basket they finally fished my father out. I'm not sure exactly how, because I kept back out of the way. But it did seem to me at the time that Krishna Kumar had superhuman strength in pulling my father up. Yet now I believe that he was helped by a force from below. Well, you know what I mean. . . .

"My father seemed half-conscious when they got him out. He was taken into the house and put on his bed. We sent for the doctor. Then as we waited, we heard Father say, 'When will I see you again, Baba?' just as if Sai Baba was standing there in the room. No doubt he was, though we could not see him.

"When the doctor came and examined Father, he would not believe about his being in the well, but the Chief of Police was still there and confirmed our unlikely story. The doctor said there was no shock and, in fact, the patient was much better than he had been before his misadventure. There was no need for any treatment or medicine, he said, just a cup of strong coffee was all Father needed."

Radhakrishna himself told me: "I knew that it was all Baba's work, keeping me up in the water, so on the same day I hired a car and we drove to Puttaparthi. As soon as we arrived, Baba greeted us from the balcony. Then, laughing, he called down, 'My shoulders are aching with holding you up so long last night, Radhakrishna!" Earlier that morning Baba had told other devotees that he had been "away" during the night helping Radhakrishna who was in trouble.

What can one say? Was Baba at Kuppam in subtle form, seen only by Radhakrishna in another state of consciousness? And was he employing his tremendous psychokinetic power, an attribute of the psyche as yet only glimpsed by parapsychology, to hold Radhakrishna's body above the waterline in the well?

Today in India, at many different points, some psychokinetic force is operating frequently in association with the name of Sai Baba. Its most usual manifestation is in the production of *vibhūti* on holy pictures, mainly on photographs of Baba but also on pictures of gods and *avatārs* in the same shrine rooms. The ash may be sticking to the glass on the *outside*, or it may be *under* the glass of the pictures. It may come as a small patch that gradually grows until, like a layer of hoarfrost, it almost covers the entire picture. Or, on the other hand, it may appear all at once, practically smothering the picture in a moment.

Dr. D. S. Chander, the dental surgeon of Bangalore, is one of many who have experienced this strange phenomenon. He told me that *vibhūti* suddenly appeared on all the pictures of his shrine room; then, after about a month, it completely vanished. He felt uneasy about its disappearance as if, perhaps, the divine grace were withdrawn because he had done something wrong or left undone something which he ought to have done.

His wife often assisted him in the surgery, and it was his custom to ring a bell when he needed her for something. One morning, when he rang the bell, his wife happened at the moment to be putting flowers in the shrine room. All the pictures there were clear, she said, with no traces of ash on them. She was sure of this because after the sudden disappearance of the ash, she always looked hopefully for any signs that it might be returning.

Leaving the flowers, she went off quickly to the surgery to see what her husband needed and, when she returned a few minutes later, all the pictures in the shrine room were again covered with *vibhūti*. She hurried back to tell her husband and, as she passed through the sitting room, she saw that there, too, Baba's photographs had patches of ash on them.

Most of the *vibhūti* vanished again after a month or two. But a little remained to keep the doctor happy, and was still there when I paid him a visit.

My wife and I have been taken to see various houses in various cities where this strange phenomenon is taking place. I noted that when the ash is on top of the glass it adheres tightly to the surface, although some falls off and collects on the bottom of the frames.

A woman in one home told us, "At first it came on the *outside* of the glass, and some people said that we must have put it on ourselves for publicity or something. So then it began forming underneath, between the glass and the picture."

I examined some of the pictures where the ash was *under* the glass. The backs, in most cases, were securely glued on and certainly looked as if they had been undisturbed for a long time. Apart from that, these people and all the others we met in connection with the ash phenomena were not the types to indulge in imposture. They were devout, religious people, filled, it seemed to me, not with egotism and spiritual pride, but with humility, veneration and awe regarding the benevolent power that had left its mark in their homes.

In some houses various things appear in addition to the ash: other powders used in ritualistic worship, drops of *amrita*, tiny statues of Hindu gods, flowers, and sometimes garlands placed around the pictures.

The dynamic psychokinetic force associated with the name of Sai Baba is working in other incredible ways. Here is an example.

Mr. K. E. Kulkarni of Poona used to visit the local Shirdi Baba temple of the city every Thursday. On one occasion he had taken with him to the temple some pamphlets and photographs of Satya Sai Baba. In the bag he had six pamphlets in Hindi, six in English and about the same number of photographs of Satya Sai.

He started giving these out to worshippers in the temple. This drew a crowd of about a hundred people around him. They all wanted the Hindi pamphlets and the photographs; apparently, none could read English. Kulkarni began to distribute the few he had, and was about to say regretfully that he would bring more next week for those people who were disappointed.

Then, putting his hand in the bag for the last pamphlet, he was completely stunned to find it not empty but half full. Looking in he saw a big bundle of Hindi pamphlets and another bundle of photographs. As it turned out, there was exactly the number needed to go round. Everyone was satisfied and not a single copy of a Hindi pamphlet or photograph was left over. Only the six English pamphlets remained in the bag. These had not been in demand, and none had been miraculously added to their number.

Other psychic happenings reported from here and there include automatic writing, and written messages seen by clairvoyants either in *rangôli* powder or on plain walls and ceilings. These messages purport to be from Sai Baba. The people closely concerned with such phenomena (at least the ones I have personally met) seem sincere and high-minded. They describe enthusiastically how the messages are used to help the sick, to give ethical training in action and habit, to assist people in distress concerning their personal relationships, their jobs, and so on. So the power at work seems to be a good, compassionate one.

There is, of course, a danger in communication phenomena. For one thing, as occultists know, the lower astral plane contains plenty of impostors, pretenders and worse, ever ready to seize a chance of communicating with this world. Therefore psychic forces not so good, not so benevolent, might easily begin to manifest themselves under the guise of the great spiritual name. Thus people may be fooled and misled. And the eventual result would be to foster man's pride, egotism and lower desires rather than his higher spiritual aspirations.

There were indications that greed and desire for notoriety were already being stirred among followers when a notice appeared in the *āshram* magazine, under the direction of Baba. The notice said: "Some persons misuse the name Baba, and announce that Baba is in communication with them, giving them messages, answering questions and granting interviews, their object being to gain money or fame." The notice goes on to say that such phenomena have to be explained either as the manifestation of spirits or as sheer fakes by cranks or crooks: "It is the duty of devotees to stop all such trickery by wise counsel and firm denial."

Baba makes it clear that recipients must judge the genuineness of any psychic happenings for themselves, but they should never use them as a means of drawing a crowd around for publicity, fame or making money.

Into my heart's night
Along a narrow way
I groped; and lo! the light,
An infinite land of day.

Rumi

15

THE SAME, BUT DIFFERENT

The people whose experiences have been given in the foregoing chapters are highly respected citizens, many of them holding important positions in the life of modern India.

However, the truth which they come forward to attest is difficult for the modern mind to accept, particularly in the Western world. It is not merely that their attestations reveal more things in heaven and earth than are known to the widely embraced materialistic philosophy, but that these things frequently seem to contradict the laws of science and common experience as we understand them. More specifically, it is that there is a man living in India today who can take objects, and many types of objects, out of nowhere; not just *seem* to take them, like a conjurer on the stage, but *actually* take them; and that he is doing this kind of thing daily, wherever he happens to be. They further attest that this man can read minds, not only when you are near him, but that he can be with you wherever you are, knowing what you are thinking and doing and planning to do; that he can either be invisibly nearby, or take some appropriate form in order to be there, to guide and protect and teach. Furthermore, their testimony states that he can see into the future, perform surgical operations with "materialised" instruments, cure many deadly diseases by miraculous means and – far above all else – lead his devotees towards the spiritual goal of life.

Millions of men believe, or perhaps half believe, such things about Christ and Krishna. "But then, the reader may say, "that was all long ago. This is the age of science, not of miracles. You ask me to believe that a living man is doing such things now, and has been doing them constantly for the past twenty-five years?"

My witnesses do not ask anyone to believe anything, they merely state what they have seen and known. And I, who was myself conditioned by the modern sceptical mental climate, certainly do not expect or hope that any blown-in-the-glass doubter will accept such things, unless like Saint Thomas, he sees and hears and feels for himself.

Nevertheless, there are millions who will never have the good fortune to sit physically at Sai Baba's feet, either at Prashānti Nílayam or wherever else in the world he may go in the years ahead. Therefore, for the sake of the many among them who can believe even though they have not seen, whose faith and hope and understanding may benefit thereby, I bring further witnesses to the stand. Among those whose stories are given in the next few chapters are leading men of science, business, statecraft. They are a few of the many devotees well known to large sections of the public in and beyond India. Into their lives has come the same miraculous Sai power, but for each its manifestation is different, unique.

One afternoon my wife and I were sitting in a room in Madras talking to a woman who had come down from the north of India and was on her way to Prashānti Nílayam to attend the festival of Shivarātri. She has known Sai Baba since the late 1940s and is one of his truest, purest and most sincere *bhaktas*, or devotees. She has not given me permission to use her name, so I will call her Mrs. B. Among others in the room that day was Dr. C. T. K. Chari, who is Professor of Philosophy at Madras Christian College, a member of the London Society for Psychical Research, and a well-known name in parapsychology circles throughout the world. Mrs. B. was persuaded to tell us a number of her miraculous experiences with Sai Baba, and I relate two or three of them here.

She said that in 1952 her son, Jawahar, who was then about five years old, contracted some disease with a high fever and delirium. Her husband is a medical man but was absent at the time, and she called in another doctor. At first he thought it was malaria and was treating the child for that. But on the sixth day of high fever the doctor decided that he had been wrong in his diagnosis. He now thought it was typhoid; the next day he would do a blood test to make sure.

Mrs. B. had then been a follower of Sai Baba for several years. She had seen him perform miracles, but although she often prayed to him as her *sadgūrū*, she was still not sure of the extent of his powers, and was inclined to test him. Now, very worried about her son's health, she began to pray earnestly to Baba, asking his help.

After a while, noting that Jawahar looked somewhat better, she took his temperature and found that it had dropped several degrees. Moreover, he was no longer delirious. Was her prayer being answered, or was this just happening naturally? She longed to know, but how could she? Then, feeling sure that Baba would help her in her doubts and questions, she thought of a way to test the matter. Mentally she spoke to Baba: "If his temperature is exactly 98.4 degrees tomorrow morning, I will believe that it is your work." Next morning she took the temperature and found it exactly 98.4 degrees. When the doctor came later in the morning, he declared that the boy was quite all right and that there was no need to do the blood test he had planned.

Mrs. B. learned some time later that on the night when she was praying fervently to him, Sai Baba was staying at the Venkatagiri Palace. While sitting in a room there with a number of devotees, he suddenly went into a trance. After a while he returned to his body and told those present, among them the Kumaraja (prince) of Venkatagiri, that a devotee (naming Mrs. B.) had been in trouble, her son being sick, and that he (Baba) had been to help her. "Now Jawahar is all right again," Baba remarked.

The Kumaraja was curious to see this boy whom Baba had "flown off" to help, and some weeks later when Mrs. B., the boy Jawahar, and the prince were all visiting Puttaparthi at the same time, Baba was able to satisfy the latter's curiosity.

A couple of years later the same boy was the victim of an accident, was badly cut about, and contracted sceptic fever at an awkward period when Mrs. B.'s husband was again absent. It was difficult for her to obtain the medicaments urgently needed. Her prayers to Sai Baba seemed this time to work a miraculous charm over circumstances, enabling her to obtain what was required, and the boy soon recovered. Again she thought it might all be coincidence . . . until she heard from her sister, Lilli, in the south.

Mrs. B., who was still living hundreds of miles away to the north, had not written to Lilli, or to anyone else, about the boy's accident. Yet not long after it happened, when Lilli was in Puttaparthi, she heard the story from the lips of Sai Baba himself. He told her all the details of the accident, saying that he had been there. His words to her suggested that it was Mrs. B.'s sincerity and earnest prayers that forged the link and brought the timely help. So although Mrs. B.'s mind used to doubt and question things, at deeper levels her faith and devotion were very strong indeed.

When Mrs. B. had finished telling her stories, Dr. Chari remarked that he had heard her relate these supernormal events not long after they occurred, and several times later to various people. He has known her for many years. Her descriptions, he said, had not varied in detail since the first telling; no additions, no embroidery, which he, speaking as an experienced investigator of psychic phenomena, declared to be remarkable.

"She's a first-class witness," he assured me.

"Have you, yourself, witnessed Baba materialise anything?" I asked him.

"Yes, I have, *vibhūti* on several occasions," he replied, and added, "you're at liberty to use my name if it's of any value to you."

Whereupon an ironical gentleman in the company jested, "You'll be thrown out of the S.P.R. for that."

Dr. D. K. Banerjee is a Doctor of Science and Professor of Organic Chemistry at the Indian Institute of Science in Bangalore. His wife is the daughter of a Professor of Physics. Both are Bengalis, and both were brought up without any formal religion.

My wife and I called to see them one afternoon at their home in the pleasant grounds of the Institute and found them quite willing to talk about miraculous experiences with Sai Baba. In fact, we talked of little else for some four hours, while tea came and went, the sun sank in the west, and darkness fell over the lawns and gardens.

Dr. Banerjee told me that he had been brought up on Vedanta philosophy. This does not make a religion of science. But it does take a scientific attitude towards religion. It certainly does not predispose the mind towards such things as miracles or the idea of divine incarnation. However the doctor admits that he did have one spiritual hero. That was his uncle, Soham Swami, who became famous as a holy man of mighty physical strength and used to wrestle with wild tigers. Later, as a young man, Banerjee read some of his uncle's spiritual books. Nevertheless, he was still very much of a Vedantist and a cautious scientist when he first heard of Sai Baba.

In November 1961, mainly out of curiosity, he paid a visit to Puttaparthi. After all, when a scientist hears repeatedly of things that appear to spurn the laws of physics and chemistry he should make it his business to find out about them for himself. With Dr. Banerjee on that first occasion went Professor Iyer of the same department at the Institute, and an officer of the Indian Air Force who, incidentally, was a champion parachute jumper.

The inexplicable experiences which the doctor had then and in many subsequent contacts with Baba cover a number of different types of miraculous phenomena, such as visions, healing, the production of articles from an invisible dimension, and the conversion of one object into another before the eyes of the beholder. In relating some of his many experiences here I shall sort them out into groups, although they were to some extent intermixed.

The first of Dr. Banerjee's strange visions was to do with Lord Krishna. Although millions of Indians worship Krishna as a divine incarnation, Banerjee had always thought of him as a voluptuary, a playboy. In fact it was his custom to nickname any loose-living libertine "Krishna of the Kali Yūga".

While sitting in the room with Baba on his first visit to the *āshram*, Banerjee saw Baba's face becoming transfigured into the face of Lord Krishna. This happened three times, momentarily each time. He was puzzled. But there was more to come.

Though the nephew of Soham Swami does not wrestle with tigers, he believes in keeping physically fit. Every morning early he makes use of the parklands around his house for exercising. At about five on the morning after his return from Puttaparthi, while he was limbering up on the lawn, a vision of Krishna suddenly appeared before him. Then the little dark-blue figure seemed to come towards Banerjee and merge right into him. For some days the doctor felt that he was "possessed" by the one he had always regarded as the prototype of rakes. But it did not make him feel like a Mr. Hyde. In fact, the effect was quite the opposite. He seemed to gain complete and absolute control of his senses and desires. It was the most wonderful inner experience he had ever known. "It made me feel like a king," he said.

In this elevated state he made another journey to the *āshram* to tell Baba, and try to find out what was happening. Baba just smiled and said nothing; then he placed one hand on Banerjee's head and the other on the small of his back, holding them there for a while. After that the obsession vanished and the professor came back to normal.

But the experience made Banerjee realise how mistaken he had been about the character and significance of Lord Krishna, the divine cowboy, the great king and statesman, the timeless charioteer who spoke the golden words of the 'Bhagavad Gítā' to Arjuna, and to all mankind. Baba had taught his new devotee an important lesson in the understanding of God.

The second vision, also a transfiguration, is mixed with a materialisation phenomenon. It took place at Brindāvanam, Whitefield, where Dr. Banerjee and family had gone to see Baba. Suddenly, as the doctor sat in the room looking at the unique Sai head, it changed into the head of Shiva with the waters of the Ganges falling onto Shiva's matted hair. Again it was but a momentary vision. After some time Baba produced a locket and, holding it in his palm, showed it to Banerjee's son, asking, "What is that?" "It looks like Shiva," the boy replied. Baba said nothing but after a moment held it up again and asked the same question. This time the boy replied, "It looks like Shirdi Baba." The father felt annoyed that his son apparently could not distinguish between the forms of Shiva and Shirdi Baba.

Satya Sai gave the locket to the boy, and when later Dr. Banerjee examined it he observed that it had a picture of Shirdi Baba on one side, and on the other the illustration of Shiva with the matted hair onto which the waters of the Ganges were falling, really like the transfiguration he had just witnessed.

Materialisations began at Banerjee's first visit. Apart from the *vibhūti* produced for all of the party, Baba took from the air for Dr. Banerjee a gold medal. The professor showed this to my wife and me when we visited him. On one side is Shirdi Sai Baba with "Shri Sai Baba" written in Sanskrit, while on the other is an open hand showing the palm and "*Aum*" in Sanskrit blended with the inscription "*abhayam*" in Telegu and some Tamil script meaning "When I am there, what is the fear?"

However, for sceptics on the watch for sleight of hand tricks, perhaps the most evidential phenomenon is one seen by Dr. Banerjee soon after he met Sai Baba. At this stage he was himself still a bit suspicious, not being quite sure whether the productions were extremely clever stage magic or genuine miracles.

On this occasion, besides Banerjee, there were two women and three children present. Baba stirred the air in the usual way, turned his hand up, and opened it to show ash covering his palm like a thin layer of powder. Now, before their watching eyes, keeping his palm steadily upturned, he stroked a finger across the powdering of ash. As he did so there appeared on his palm five large circular sweets, one for each person present. The professor said that these confections were made mainly from cheese, and belonged to a type of sweet not well known in India, being found only in certain parts of Bengal, the Banerjees' own state.

Mrs. Banerjee, her husband says, is the "handyman" around the place. Her practical capabilities range from driving in a nail to repairing an internal combustion engine. She was brought up without any formal religion and had never opened a book on spiritual subjects when she met Sai Baba.

At her first interview Baba blessed her by placing his hand above her head. Afterwards her husband saw a streak of *vibhūti* along the line parting her hair. Strangely, within a few days he saw his wife reading books containing Baba's discourses, and then later, other spiritual literature as well.

Some time afterwards Baba remarked on this new interest in reading and again blessed her. In doing so he placed his hand again above her head, but a bit higher this time, and those watching saw *vibhūti* shower from his palm to cover the whole crown. Her interest in spiritual writings strengthened, deepened, and like her husband she has become a close devotee of Sai Baba.

Dr. Banerjee told me about three miracle cures of which he had had personal acquaintance. The first, which concerned himself, was a minor one but still amazing. In travelling by train to Penukonda *en route* to Prashānti Nílayam, he had jammed his little finger in the carriage window. It was black and swollen and very painful.

After arriving at the *āshram*, he was sitting with a crowd in front of the prayer hall waiting for a sight of Baba. Presently the heart-stirring figure appeared, walking in his accustomed way along the narrow aisle between the sitting people. Banerjee was in a front row and, when Baba reached this spot, he stopped. But instead of looking at Banerjee, he turned his back and, leaning over, spoke to someone in the opposite row. As he bent forward the back edge of his robe stroked and covered the doctor's hands, resting in front of him as he sat cross-legged on the ground. Then, after a moment, Baba moved on without saying a word to Banerjee.

Shortly afterwards the doctor noticed that the throbbing pain in his finger had practically subsided. Looking at it, he saw with amazement that all the blackness and swelling had completely vanished. The damaged finger was in fact now quite normal, healed by the touch of the Master's robe.

Another cure concerns the champion parachute jumper who accompanied Dr. Banerjee on his first visit to Prashānti Nílayam in 1961. This Air Force officer was suffering from a long-standing 'incurable' disease and, for this reason, although married, was not able to have children.

Baba produced some *vibhūti* and gave it to the officer to take internally, saying that he would be cured and would have a healthy son. Whether it was through the *vibhūti* or the presence and will of the great healer, or both combined, the impossible did happen. The 'incurable' disease was cured and, as Baba promised, the champion parachutist later had a son of sound health.

The third cure is equally 'unscientific', yet the worthy scientist of Bangalore tells of it without turning a hair, in fact, with obvious delight. The son of a friend, a wealthy manufacturer of chemicals, was suffering from asthma. At least, it seemed like asthma to the family doctor.

But when Dr. Banerjee took the boy to Prashānti Nílayam into the presence of Sai Baba, the latter remarked that it was not asthma at all but a fault in bone structure that caused difficulty in respiration. Then Baba waved the magic hand again and brought from the Sai Stores, as he sometimes calls his mysterious source of supply, a gold locket carrying the picture of Shirdi Sai. Baba said that the boy must wear this as a talisman around his neck, and that there would be no respiration trouble. From that day, Banerjee said, the boy had no more signs of the "asthma". After a time the locket began coming off its chain and, when Baba was told of this, he said that it had served its purpose and there was no longer any need to wear it. It could now be kept in a box.

When a scientist has repeated experience, over a number of years, of phenomena outside the laws and theories of modern science, what should he do? Turn his back on it, making scornful, self-protective noises, or admit that science has merely gathered a few pebbles and shells beside the vast unexplored ocean of the unknown?

Dr. Banerjee has, along with some of the greatest of his scientific brethren, taken the second course. He is now a devoted follower of Sai Baba and loses no opportunity of travelling often on his motor scooter, over the hundred bumpy miles to Puttaparthi or the twelve to Whitefield if Baba is there.

In these places or his own home, which Baba sometimes visits for a meal or a talk, the old Vedantist hears not infrequently, and not without delight, from the lips of Sai Baba what he describes as "the very gist of Vedantic philosophy".

Dr. Y. J. Rao, Head of the Geology Department, Osmania University, Hyderabad, was an appropriate person to witness the transmutation of solid rock to another substance, with a valuable spiritual lesson thrown in, for good measure.

One day at Puttaparthi Baba picked up a rough piece of broken granite and, handing it to Dr. Rao, asked him what it contained. The geologist mentioned a few of the minerals in the rock.

Baba: "I don't mean those; something deeper."
Dr. Rao: "Well, molecules, atoms, electrons, protons. . ."
Baba: "No, no; deeper still!"
Dr. Rao: "I don't know, Swami."

Baba took the lump of granite from the geologist and, holding it up with his fingers, blew on it. It was never out of Dr. Rao's sight, yet when Baba gave it back to him its shape had completely changed. Instead of being an irregular chunk it was a statue of Lord Krishna playing his flute. The geologist noted also a difference in colour and a slight change in the structure of the substance.

Baba: "You see? Beyond your molecules and atoms, God is in the rock. And God is sweetness and joy. Break off the foot and taste it."

Dr. Rao found no difficulty in breaking off the 'granite' foot of the little statue. Putting it in his mouth as directed, he found that it was sugar candy. The whole of the idol, created instantly out of the piece of granite, was now made of candy.

From this Dr. Rao learned, he said, something beyond words and far beyond modern science; in fact, beyond the limits of the rational mind of men today. He is a great enough scientist and man to realise that science gives but the first word: the last word is known only to the great Spiritual Scientist.

The Raja of Venkatagiri is a prince of the old school. He was educated in England, mixed in international social circles, hunted big game and played polo. He has a palace at Venkatagiri in his old royal state and another in the city of Madras. He is a largely built man, with a princely demeanour, and the manners and speech of an English gentleman. Yet in religious matters he has the reputation of being a very orthodox Hindu, and his wife, the Rani, is still in *purdah*.

I have met the Raja at several Sai Baba gatherings, and he has called at our residence in Adyar to tell me of his strange and wonderful Sai experiences. I believe his reason for doing this was to orientate me correctly, as he saw it, towards the miracles. Through the years he and members of his family have experienced many of these. Here are some examples.

The Raja's second son was one of a party of men driving by car from Madras to Puttaparthi on one occasion. Not far from Chittoor in Andhra

Pradesh they stopped to have a picnic by the roadside. After they had eaten the main course, Baba asked what fruit they would like for a dessert. They proved to be a very difficult party: one asked for a mango, another for an apple, a third for an orange, and the fourth for a juicy pear.

"You'll find them all on that tree over there," Baba said, pointing to a wild tree growing nearby.

Full of excitement, because they had learned that anything was possible with Baba, they went. Sure enough on one branch of that wild tree hung the fruits they had named: a mango, an apple, an orange and a pear. They plucked them and declared that the flavours were of rare excellence.

Once at Puttaparthi, before the hospital was established, a visitor was suffering from acute appendicitis. There was no surgeon for many miles. One of the Raja's sons was among the dozen people present when Baba waved his hand, materialised a surgical knife, and went into the room where the patient was groaning.

No one was actually in the room to see Baba perform the operation, but he showed them the removed appendix and the incision which had already healed to a small scar. As usual he had used *vibhūti* and the divine power it represents as both anaesthetic and instant healer of the surgical wounds.

The Raja has himself seen a good many of the divine miracles. One that impressed him very much took place at Venkatagiri in 1950, not long after he had met Sai Baba. It was one of the earliest visits of the young twenty-four-year-old Swami to Venkatagiri.

A party of between twenty and thirty people left the palace in a fleet of cars for a drive in the country. Baba, who had never been in the area before, asked the Raja to stop by any patch of sand they might happen to see. A few miles further on they came to a dry, sandy riverbed. Here they stopped, and all sat on the sand around the young Swami. After talking for a while, he rolled his sleeve up to his elbow and thrust his arm deep into the sand before him. "Then," the Raja told me, "we all heard a strange sawing sound – at least that's what it seemed like. I asked Baba what the sound was, and he replied enigmatically that the goods were being manufactured in Kailāsa."

Kailāsa, incidentally, is the abode of Shiva, the god associated with yoga, yogic powers and divine grace bestowed on mortals. Many of the Sai disciples believe that Baba is himself an incarnation of the Shiva-Shakti aspect of divinity.

As the young God-man withdrew his arm from the sand there was a great flash of blue light that spread to a circle of some ten feet in radius. Then they all saw that Baba was holding in his hand something about eight inches in height and made of pure white *sphatika*. It proved to be a statue of Rāma, one of the *avatārs*, together with his consort, Sítā. After everyone had seen this "gift from Kailāsa", Baba handed it to the veiled Rani of Venkatagiri telling her to wrap it in silk and leave it thus covered until the following day.

When it was unwrapped the day after, the white stone had turned blue. The little statue now stands in the Raja's shrine room, still the colour, he says, of the blue light that flashed forth at the moment it was drawn from the sands.

The Raja, like so many other Indians, has seen miraculous phenomena produced here and there by ceremonial magic, by the *tāntric* and other occult arts.

"But," he said emphatically, "the Sai Baba miracles are on an entirely different level, and the word 'miracle' is really inadequate. It could be misleading to some people."

"What other word can one use?" I asked.

"I don't know. But you must at least call them 'divine miracles'," he replied.

Like other close devotees, the Raja and his family regard Sai Baba as an *avatār* of divinty.

Dr. A. Ranga Rao, M.B.B.S., M.S. (O.P.H.) (U.S.A.), F.I.C.S., is one of the leading eye surgeons of Madras. For some years, at an early stage in his career, he was serving the community at Bhimavaram as a general medical practitioner, and was haunted by the dream of becoming some day a surgeon of renown.

He believes that the fulfilment of this dream had its beginnings on a day when he went to attend an old man who was a devotee of Shirdi Sai Baba, one who had seen Shirdi Sai in flesh and blood and had built a temple to him. The doctor was so affected by the saintliness and devotion of that old man that he himself began to pray to Lord Shirdi Sai, and became his devotee.

From that day Sai remained in his heart. "As the years rolled by," he said, "Sai got more and more deep-rooted in me. I walked through life with a smiling face. In 1954 I was asked to join the University of Iowa, U.S.A., for higher studies. . . . By his grace I qualified for the degrees, and returned an A class surgeon. I began practising as an eye surgeon at Bhimavaram itself."

One day a woman came to his clinic complaining of dimness of vision. She was suffering from cataract, with the complicating factors of rheumatism and iritis. The surgeon told her and her relatives that she was not a fit case for operation. Then she said, "I am a devotee of Satya Sai Baba at Puttaparthi. He directed me to come to Bhimavaram, saying, 'At Bhimavaram there is an eye surgeon who has been my devotee for many years. Go to him and tell him that I want him to operate on you. He will do it, and you will have your sight restored'. " Baba had gone on to tell her exactly who this devotee was, showing in the telling that he knew details of Dr. Ranga Rao's past.

The doctor was perplexed and amazed. The woman told him that Satya Sai was a reincarnation of Shirdi Sai and, because of Baba's words to her, Ranga Rao felt faith in the truth of this statement. He performed the operation against his professional judgement. It was successful and the lady regained her sight immediately.

The surgeon wanted to go at once to Puttaparthi, see the deity in real human form and prostrate himself before him. Some months later he had the opportunity to move to Madras and begin practice as an eye surgeon there. Within a few days of taking up residence he heard that Satya Sai Baba was visiting the city and staying at No. 3 Surya Rao Road (the Venkatamuni house). He drove there, but felt desperate when he saw the huge crowd. Then a young man unknown to him (it was Ishwara, the eldest son of the house) accosted him: "Are you Dr. Ranga Rao? Baba wants you to come in, with your family. He is on the first floor."

With beating heart the doctor climbed the stairs and immediately fell at Baba's feet. The little saffron-robed figure patted him on the back and lifted him up.

"Doctor," Baba said, "I have been with you and you have been with me for ages. It was I who brought you to Madras. I am with you always. You do not have to worry any more. . ." It was, the doctor said, a "soul-touching experience" that made him happy beyond words.

From then on the surgeon had, within his clinic, many rare experiences. It sometimes seemed as if his hand was being guided when he was performing difficult operations. If the patient was a devotee whom Baba had sent, he (the patient) would sometimes see Baba himself there. One said, as Ranga Rao was operating, "Baba! You have come, I see your face. Your fingers are moving. You are doing the operation yourself."

At the same time the surgeon felt a peculiar phenomenon, as if other fingers were moving within his, doing all the work. "It was over in a few minutes. . .it was a miracle. My ego fled," the doctor said, "I knelt down to the doer of all things. I sobbed at heart, for I could not see the Lord's face and garments as clearly as my patient was able to."

But later Dr. Ranga Rao was able to see as well as feel the presence of the surgeon of surgeons. Let him tell it in his own words.

"Baba directed another patient, Chaganlal of Shanti Kuteer, Royapuram, to me for cataract operation. He had fixed the time too – 10.30 a.m. This very patient had been refused operation by many surgeons, including myself. He was a very complicated case. His blood pressure was as high as 200; his heart was very dilated; he was a heavy diabetic; his liver was cirrhotic; he had a hernia on both sides; so that any eye surgeon worth his salt would close his clinic and take a holiday if asked to operate on this patient. But. . .he was admitted. Preparations were being made in the theatre. I was in my office, nervous, moody, fearful of the loss of the patient and my reputation.

"Suddenly, I felt Baba catching my hand and asking me to come up with him to the operating room. I followed him, seeing clearly his saffron robe gliding softly up the stairs before me. I washed and scrubbed my hands in the routine way; put on gown and gloves. The patient was on the table.

"But his blood pressure went up. His heart was throbbing. He was feeling suffocated. It appeared as though he would die on the table itself. Such fear had never before overpowered me. I felt helpless. I yelled, 'Sai Ram, Sai Ram!' [This is a *mantram* used by many Sai devotees.] My assistants too joined the chorus, 'Sai Ram, Sai Ram!' The patient also repeated 'Sai Ram, Sai Ram!'

"To the astonishment of everyone in the theatre, and to my own surprise, the white apron I wore became saffron in colour. My gloved fingers were no longer mine. Sai, the mighty surgeon, had manifested himself in me, and he was performing the operation. In a few seconds it was over, the finishing touches were given by the Master's hand and he left. The surgeon's gown was white again. It was exactly at this time that Baba informed the devotees around him at Prashānti Nílayam: 'Chaganlal's operation is over'! "

When at thy love a lamp we light,
Our barn of being is ablaze,
And of that inward glow so bright
A wisp of smoke to heaven we raise.

Iraqi (A Persian Mystic Poet)

16

A WORD FROM THE WEST

Pilgrims of the spiritual search from all parts of the globe have found their way to the Abode of Great Peace hidden in the wild hills. Some have just managed to pay a flying visit: Baba has filled them with wonder and joy, and almost always found the way into the deep recesses of their hearts. Others have been able to remain months with the man of power and love, and so have gone through a "deep sea change"; their lives are never quite the same again.

As the years pass, what was at first a trickle from the far-off places is increasing to a steady stream. That stream is being fed from America (with emphasis on California), Australia, Europe, Africa, the Far East and South-East Asia. People as a rule do not come so far merely out of idle curiosity. They come with big personal problems, or seeking the path to enlightenment. They come with hope and at least a little faith, or they would not be there at all.

Who can describe his inner glow when his personal lamp has been lit at the flame of Baba's love? For as the old Persian poet says, when a man's "barn of being is ablaze", all he can give out are a few smoke signals. These, rising heavenward, tell a little, but only a little, of the story. They represent the limits of verbal communication, and so the "wisps of smoke", the stories, the experiences told, usually deal with the outer miracles and scarcely touch the great, glowing, inward miracle.

It is interesting to know a little of the reactions of those Westerners who have been brought up within narrower spiritual horizons than those of Hinduism, and of Sai Baba in particular. Here I can mention only a few whom I know personally, and who have spent a fair length of time with Sai Baba.

Earlier in the book I spoke of Miss Gabriella Steyer who was living at the *āshram* when I first met Swami. She stayed there for many months, and when I visited Prashānti Nílayam the first time she told me about many wonderful miracles she had personally witnessed. She had had a very rich experience of these outward signs of power and grace. As always, though, the most important factor was Baba's love; this was the magnet that held her to the discomforts and austerities of *āshram* life month after month. Gabriella finally had to tear herself away and return to her own country and profession; but I doubt if her life could ever be the same again after it had once been kindled by the great flame. There were many outer signs of the inner glow.

Two others we met in our early Sai days, who have since become our close friends, are Bob and Markell Raymer of Pacific Palisades, California. Bob, an aircraft pilot, was the red-haired American who kindly went in search of Baba for me on my first visit.

Before coming to rest at Prashānti Nílayam this couple had, like us, conducted their own "search in secret India", visiting many *āshrams* and meeting some great yogis. They had gained some spiritual nourishment here and there, but it seems that they have now found their *sadgūrū* and the true glory. Of their inner experiences I cannot speak here, though in confidence I have been told of some. Their outer experiences include a good range of phenomena of the type described in these pages. They have often watched the magic hand stir the air or dig into the sand to produce some charming personal gift, or some confection for the enjoyment of all in the magic circle. And they have seen the same hand transmute one substance to another. Once Baba idly rolled in his fingers a scrap of paper while Bob sat near him as one of a group. Unexpectedly he told Bob to open his mouth, and popped the roll of paper into it. But there was no taste of paper; the roll had changed to a delicious piece of candy.

Like many Westerners, the Raymers have learned that Baba's miracles are genuine, varied, of daily occurrence, and yet always unexpected. They have come to accept them as part of his divine nature.

Soon after our initial meeting, the Raymers returned to America, but since then they have flown back on a number of visits to Baba, and they went with him from India on a tour in East Africa in 1968. Just before that I saw them at the Satya Sai Conference in Bombay, following which they, with my wife and myself, travelled for a while with Swami. It was during this pleasant period that I had the opportunity of learning what sincere Sai devotees, and serious *sādhakas* (searchers on the spiritual path), they really are.

But among the non-Indian followers of Sai Baba, one of the best-known names is Madame Indra Devi, the internationally famous yoga teacher and authoress of several books on yoga.

Once when she was on a visit to the Theosophical Society headquarters at Adyar, my wife and I told her some of our experiences with Baba. This was apparently the first time she had heard his name but she at once sensed intuitively his great importance. Immediately she seemed to have no doubt whatever that this was one man in India she must see at no matter what cost in time and trouble. She was scheduled to fly to Saigon for a lecture engagement, and had originally intended returning to her Yoga Foundation in Southern California directly from Vietnam. But now she changed her mind and came back to India in order to meet Sai Baba.

After a mountain of difficulties, because Baba was touring and his movements were uncertain, she finally made the contact at Prashānti Nílayam, reaching there in the hammering heat of an Indian summer. She seems to have recognised his great spiritual stature from that first meeting, and straight away became a fervent and very active devotee.

At that time she was just starting on her mission to teach and encourage meditation throughout the world. Baba gave his blessings to this work, her mission of "light in darkness". Since then, Indra Devi has made the long journey from California to India several times a year to spend a period with Baba at Prashanti Nilayam and other places. I will leave her, as a writer herself, to tell whatever she wishes of her own spiritual and miraculous experiences. Of the various materialisations Baba has performed for her, and which she has described to me, there are two I would like to record here, for their interest as well as their evidential value, coming from a witness of world renown.

One is this: in front of Indra Devi and a party of American visitors, Baba "took" for her, from his "land of nowhere", a long, bulky *japamālā*, a string of 108 large pearls. She was wearing it when a little later I saw her at Adyar in company with one of the Americans who had witnessed its production.

A good many people have seen Baba change one object to another or one substance to another openly, without shield or covering before their gaze. I myself saw this, for instance, when at Horsley Hills he turned a piece of hard rock into sugar candy. The second incident in connection with Indra Devi's experience concerns a dramatic example of this type of transmutation through *sankalpa*, or divine will. It also involves some mind reading.

One day Baba materialised for her an ornate ring, set with a large spray of colourful stones. Indra Devi told me that she has no liking for jewellery, particularly the striking, decorative type worn so well by dark-skinned Indian women. She herself is a Russian-born American citizen whose name, Indra Devi, derives from an association with India earlier in her life. She has a very pale skin.

Anyway she was not happy about the ring. It was a gift from Baba and she felt she should wear it for that reason, but it did not suit her and she did not like it. The dilemma worried her a good deal for a day and a night, she said. Then she found herself invited to another group interview and, wearing Baba's disturbing gift on her finger, she waited with several other people for his arrival.

Soon after he entered the room he asked her to hand him the ring, making a remark from which she was sure he was fully aware of her dilemma. Then, holding the ring between his thumb and forefinger, with the display of stones uppermost, and in full view, he blew several times on the stones as if blowing out a match. Suddenly, as all watched, the spray of brightly coloured stones merged into a single, sparkling diamond. Baba handed the ring with its solitaire diamond back to her. It was now something which she could wear happily and constantly.

Here is the story, in condensed form, of how one man of the Western world came to Sai Baba and of how it affected his life.

Mr. Alf Tidemand-Johannessen of Oslo, Norway, arrived in India with nothing but the proverbial typewriter and his own ability, grit, energy and ambition to make a fortune. Within twelve years, that is, by 1962, he had built up one of the largest ship agency companies in India, handling more ships each year than any other individual company. His was India's pioneer company in grain discharging. It handled more than half of the grain ships bringing enormous quantities of food to India to avoid large-scale starvation there. His big success did not pass unnoticed. Into certain minds entered jealousy, envy, and schemes for getting control of his business. Certain key men on his executive staff were soon actively engaged behind the scenes in misusing their powers to divert the company's assets into their own pockets.

"When I found out that malpractices were taking place," Alf Tidemand told me, "I knew that I would have to face a furious battle with a ruthless enemy. As soon as I took steps to seal the leakages, the executives concerned terminated their services and started a competing company. Their aim was to take away all my business."

As part of their scheme his enemies sent anonymous letters to Income Tax, Reserve Bank and Customs authorities, indicating that the Tidemand Company was abusing the laws and regulations of the country. Apparently, it is customary for such authorities to take action on anonymous letters: they soon discovered who the senders were, and then months of investigations followed during which Alf had to provide documents covering all the past years to prove that the allegations against him were false.

Naturally, his business clients were disturbed at the sudden exodus of his key staff and the rumours that were floating around. To add fuel to the fire, his scheming enemies sent letters to all his clients informing them that his company was in trouble with the Government. All this put tremendous restrictions on his business operations, and things looked very black indeed.

Nevertheless, because of his past integrity, Alf's clients did not immediately desert him, and the new competing company established by his defecting executives was not doing well. So then they made their next move, a move that is apparently not uncommon in the concrete jungles of modern India. They engaged a black magician to work against him.

Alf said, "I could handle the other assaults, but was not prepared for this attack from occult black science; nor did I at the time have the slightest idea that such methods were being used. Even if I had known, I would have laughed at it as pure superstition."

But Alf's lawyer in Bombay, who was working on the company's problems, soon caught a whiff of the black magic. He had known similar cases before. Being a good friend and knowing Tidemand's innocence and integrity, the lawyer took him along to a Parsi priest who lived in an old temple in Bombay. The priest, who was clairvoyant and had other powers, confirmed that strong dark forces were being used against Alf Tidemand. The latter kept in regular touch with the old Parsi priest and, he says, "By many strange methods he began piloting me and my business through the troubled waters stirred up by the black magician."

The magician, himself, now came out of hiding. Discovering that counter forces were being played successfully against him, he decided to strike directly and boldly. He turned up at Alf's office and, by various methods well known to students of sorcery, tried to gain dominion over his intended victim. But Tidemand had been warned of this possibility by the Parsi priest, and immediately suspected the evil-eyed old Indian who, by clever ruses, had gained admittance to his private office.

Alf managed to avoid the initial traps, and then manoeuvred the sorcerer into his car, planning to take him along to the old Parsi priest. On the way, perhaps recognising Tidemand's strength and also his liberality, the magician decided to change masters. He admitted involuntarily that he had been employed by Alf's enemies to destroy him, his family and company. But he had changed his mind, he said, and would work for Tidemand if the latter paid him reasonably well. He would see to it that Alf's enemies were completely annihilated.

"Black magicians are very powerful," he announced, and added meaningfully, "they can even kill a child in its mother's womb." Alf had just received that very morning a cable from Norway informing him that his wife had lost her child in its seventh month. This must be more than coincidence, he thought.

At the temple the Parsi priest immediately recognised the sorcerer for what he was and chased him away, threatening to report him to the police. He warned Alf to have nothing whatever to do with this man of unclean powers.

Soon after that Alf Tidemand was taken by a business friend, his taxation expert, to Shirdi. There he had "the feeling that God had opened a door to let me feel His greatness for a blessed moment, during which the great weight fell from my shoulders and my troubles evaporated". He learned that the old Parsi priest who was helping him was a devotee of Shirdi Sai Baba, and he began to understand that it was really the Sai power that was guiding him through the reefs and shoals of strange, difficult waters.

Soon the black magician gave up the unequal struggle; the Government authorities decided that the accusations were false and baseless and all the intrigues of Alf's underhand enemies fell to the ground. The difficulties that had threatened to destroy him were completely overcome, and the troubled year came to an end.

Early in 1963 the Tidemand Company was getting back on its feet and beginning to prosper again. Though the struggle had taken a toll of Alf's strength, it had also shown him a light. This light, and a power that brought peace and refreshment to his mind and spirit, were at the village of Shirdi over which the spirit of old Sai Baba seemed to brood. It was only a few hours' car journey from Bombay and Alf paid regular visits there during the next three years.

On 26th February 1966 he was at Shirdi with the friend who first took him there and the Parsi priest, whom he now addressed as "father". In front of the temple a short man in a blue shirt walked up to Alf and asked, "Have you ever met Sri Satya Sai Baba?" Alf replied that he had not, and the man went on, "You must see him. He is coming to Bombay on 14th March. If there is any God on this earth, he is God." Then he gave *vibhūti* from a silver container to each of the party, and to Alf he gave a small locket with a picture of Satya Sai in a blue shirt.

"Don't forget to see him in Bombay on the fourteenth of next month," he repeated, and went away. Later, as they were about to leave Shirdi, they again saw the man, by the side of the road. He greeted them, and repeated again the advice to Alf, that he should see Satya Sai on 14th March.

The Norwegian was at this period in the middle of another deep problem. Because of his wife's bad health she could not live in India, and really needed him with her and the children in Norway. He felt that he must somehow sell his business and return there. But how could he find a good buyer?

He had built the business on his own personal integrity and efficiency. He knew that it depended very much on the good will felt towards him personally in the shipping world. Potential buyers would think that with Tidemand himself gone, the business might not be worth much. He had faced many mountainous obstacles in his life, and this was one of the biggest.

He had learned that the Sai power was very great. If, in fact, Satya Sai was a reincarnation of Shirdi Sai, and was a divine *avatār*, as people said, he could solve this or any other problem. Alf decided that he must have an interview with this man if he should come to Bombay as predicted by the character in the blue shirt. Deciding such a thing and achieving it are, however, two different things. Most people have to work hard and overcome obstacles to reach Sai Baba. Some have to go through the labours of Hercules; Alf was one of these.

Certainly Satya Sai was in Bombay by 14th March, just as Blue Shirt had foretold. Day after day for many hours the Norwegian sat cross-legged in the broiling sun with the big crowds outside the place where Baba was staying; first the Gwalior Palace and then the house of Mr. Savant, the Food Minister of the Maharashtra Government. Or he sat with even bigger crowds in the stadium listening to Baba lecture in Telegu, with a translation into Hindu by Dr. B. Ramakrishna Rao. Alf understood neither of these languages.

During this time he saw the little figure of Satya Sai, with his shining robe and black dome of hair, walking among the people signing photographs, blessing objects presented for his touch, producing *vibhūti* here and there. The big blond Norwegian was favoured with a nod, a friendly smile, a greeting now and again, but there were no signs of the longed-for interview.

Being one of the very few Europeans in the crowds, Alf was becoming well known among the Sai following. He was invited to homes of devotees and heard wonderful stories about Baba's love, grace and miraculous powers. This was all very inspiring, but it did not solve his problem. After four days of trying and getting nowhere, he almost decided to give up.

It was then that a strange man with a curved nose and black beard said to him, "Would you like to meet Sai Baba?" The stranger said that he could arrange an appointment, and Alf decided to take a sporting chance with him.

There was still much to go through. Under the direction of this bearded stranger Alf had to buy grass for a cow, give something to beggars, visit a temple and touch the floor with his forehead before an image there, buy garlands of flowers and *kankans* (circlets) of *mŏgrā* flowers. Perhaps all this ritual helped, or maybe the stranger knew the right people near Baba. Anyway, on the morning of 18th March, Alf went for his first appointment. Stepping out of the car in front of Mr. Savant's house, he took off his shoes and, with a garland and *kankans* in his hand, began to climb the steps. Suddenly he looked up and there stood Baba as if waiting for him.

"I am so happy to see you," Baba said with simple friendliness. Usually Swami will not let people place garlands on him; he merely takes the garland in his hand and places it aside. But now, before the ministers and V.I.P.'s who had gathered in the entrance, he permitted the tall Norwegian to garland him.

"Please come up," he said, patting Alf on the back. The latter soon found himself on the first floor of the huge house occupied by the Food Minister. There, sitting on the carpet with about twenty people, he heard Swami give a discourse, again in Telegu with Hindi translation. Every so often during his talk, Baba paused to perform a materialisation miracle.

In one pause he materialised *vibhūti*, in another a small locket with a picture of Shirdi Sai Baba. These were for Alf, who writes that "they were taken out of the air in front of the ministers, who all consider this to be a normal procedure for him". Then the Master went on teaching, mainly in parables, which were later translated into English for Tidemand. Came another pause in which he autographed a photograph for one of the women and materialised for her a locket of Vishnu. Then he got up and put a *vibhūti* mark on everyone's forehead. During the talk he had been playing with Alf's *kankans*. Now, he gave the big Norwegian another friendly pat and a few encouraging words before leaving the room.

Although Alf had at last gained regular access to the house where Swami was staying, the long-awaited private interview and the solution to his big problem still seemed difficult to obtain. But other things happened. Urged on by the man with the curved nose, who also seemed to Alf to have a precognitive nose for Baba's movements, he even had the temerity to invite the great Master to his top-floor apartment. The latter graciously accepted and came with a small group of close devotees on 24th March, ten long days after Alf had first sighted him at the Gwalior Palace.

Elaborate arrangements had been made under the direction and supervision of that curved precognitive nose. These included lavish floral decorations, a children's band, a young woman (she was supposed to be, and probably was, a virgin) to blow a conch shell and wash Baba's feet on his arrival. She blew the shell successfully, but Swami would not permit the feet-washing ritual. He was more interested in some sick people who had been brought than the display and splendour of the decorations. But he listened to the children's music with pleasure and 'took' *vibhūti* for each and a nine-stoned ring for the leader out of the fresh sea breeze stirring the flowers in the roof garden. Most important of all, he invited Alf to come to him for a private interview on the following morning.

During this hard-earned climactic interview, Alf Tidemand discovered, as many have done before and since, that Sai Baba already knew his problems and his past.

"I have been thinking about selling my business," Alf said.

"I have been thinking about the same thing," Swami answered.

Then the Norwegian began to explain the difficulties.

"Do not worry," Swami told him. "I will help you find a reliable buyer and obtain a good price." He went on to say that it was now right for Alf to get away from life in the Bombay business circles with all it entailed, and settle down in Norway with his family. In this way his wife's health would improve. Perhaps, to infuse more confidence and dispel any doubts in the mind of the worried shipping man, Baba said, "Do you remember the black magician? I helped you then."

In his notes on this interview, the turning point of his life, Alf writes: "He gave me convincing evidence of his divine powers, and I was made to understand the purpose of my life. I knew that all the prayers I had made to God during my lifetime, and all the help I had got as a result of those prayers, were known to Baba. I knew too that though there had been many obstacles in the final stage of reaching him, many tests to my faith and courage, he had really *called* me to him through strange and miraculous ways. The man in the blue shirt at Shirdi, for instance, who was he? I had found on enquiry that none of Sai Baba's closest devotees, not even Mr. N. Kasturi, knew that Baba would be coming to Bombay on 14th March.

"Swamiji seemed to know too that I had long been searching for a living spiritual teacher, and at this first interview he said: 'You need not look for a *guru* any more. From now on I will guide you.' At the end Baba materialised for me a locket with his picture, some sweets to eat and some *vibhūti*.

"The next day the manager of the Bombay branch of one of the largest companies in India phoned me to say he had heard I might be interested to sell my company. He would like to talk to me about it.

"During the negotiations that followed I was in regular touch with Swami, seeing him often. And in my early morning meditations, which Swamiji had told me to observe with regularity, I received amazing inspiration for solving the complex problems in connection with the proposed selling contract, for which there was no sample precedent of any kind available. After some months of difficult negotiations, helped by the ever-present guiding hand of Baba, a very favourable contract materialised for the sale of my shipping agency business in India."

Alf Tidemand returned to his wife and family in Oslo. His early dream had come true: he had made his fortune. But something much more important had happened to him in India. He had found his *sadgūrū*, his spiritual guide and mentor, who brought meaning to the chaos and emptiness of life lived only at the material level.

Talking to him recently, learning something of his eventful and sometimes heroic saga, I came to the conclusion that my friend, Alf Tidemand-Johannessen, will always have hard problems to solve because he is of the type whose spiritual muscles grow through solving such problems. He is essentially a man of action, but in the future, his *karma* will, I feel, be *nishkāma karma*, action without greed for the fruits of action. It will be action that, in some way in keeping with his own *dharma*, will help to spread the glory of God and His message of light for this age. All this through the grace of Sai Baba.

I might have to speak of laws and forces not recognised by reason or physical science.

Sri Aurobindo

17

TWO PRE-EMINENT DEVOTEES

A man who had quite a distinguished career in public life was the late Dr. B. Ramakrishna Rao, who died in September 1967. The obituary notices in the press at the time stated that he had held several important positions in public affairs and administration. He was, for instance, during the early 1950s, Chief Minister of the old Hyderabad State and, as such, helped create the modern state of Andhra Pradesh in 1956. In later years he held office as Governor of two different Indian states, Kerala and Uttar Pradesh. The newspapers, however, did not mention what to Dr. Ramakrishna Rao himself was by far the most important factor in his life, his discipleship of Sai Baba.

The little doctor, as we often called him because of his diminutive stature, was a first-class linguist and often acted as interpreter for Sai Baba. It was in this capacity that I first met him in Mr. G. Venkateshwara Rao's house in Madras. On that occasion he, Mr. Alf Tidemand-Johannessen, my wife and I were sitting on the carpet with Baba while the last was giving some advice to the Norwegian, who was shortly leaving India. The little doctor was acting as interpreter when necessary.

That was in my early acquaintance with Baba, who knew telepathically that I still half doubted the genuineness of his miraculous productions. In his gracious and understanding way he seemed to make use of this opportunity, as of many others, to help remove some of my doubts.

It was a hot night and he wore half sleeves so that his forearm from the elbow was bare. My knee as we sat cross-legged on the floor was practically touching his, and for much of the time he let his right hand rest on my knee instead of his own. I could thus see beyond all question that his hand was empty as it lay loosely, palm exposed, below my eyes; and it was from this position that the hand went out to wave before our noses like a magic wand and produce from the air a number of things, including the usual *vibhūti* for all of us, and a large nine-stone ring for Alf Tidemand-Johannessen.

I developed an admiration and affection for the little Gandhi-capped doctor who, while distinguished and cultured, had true humility. Fortunately I was able to have a good talk with him about a month before he died when we were neighbours in the *āshram* guest house. That was in August 1967, and Dr. Ramakrishna Rao was present in Prashānti Nílayam at the time for its official inauguration as a township. I had heard a good many bits and scraps of stories concerning his miraculous experiences with Sai Baba, and I took this opportunity to get the facts from his own lips. He knew, of course, that I wanted the information for publication and he had no objections to that, or to the use of his name, so very well known in India if not, perhaps, abroad.

Here is one remarkable story that he told me. In 1961, when he was Governor of Uttar Pradesh, he and his wife were travelling by fast train from Bareilly to Nainital in the Himalayas. They were the only occupants of their first-class carriage and the train had no corridor by which anyone could enter or leave their compartment.

At about 11 p.m. the Governor noticed some sparks coming from the electric fan. These rapidly increased in volume until he and his wife grew quite alarmed, thinking the compartment would catch fire any minute. He looked for a cord or bell by which he could sound the alarm and stop the train, but could find none. It began to look as if the Governor and his lady might be burned to death before anyone learned of their plight. There was nothing they could do but pray, which they did, wholeheartedly.

Then there was a knock on one of the outer doors. Very surprising this was, because the doors simply led to the open air through which the train was roaring at a good speed. The doctor walked over and opened the door. In from the dark night stepped a man dressed in the khaki uniform of an electric wireman. Without a word this man went to work on the faulty fan from which the sparks were now flying "like chaff from a threshing floor".

About a quarter of an hour later the electrician said to them, "There's no danger now. You can go to bed and sleep." With this he sat down on the floor near the door.

The Governor's wife lay down on her bed and closed her eyes. But she kept half opening them to watch the man by the door because, as she told her husband later, she thought that anyone who risked his life to walk along the running board of a fast-moving train was probably a burglar who, when they were both asleep, would rob them. The Governor himself, with no such suspicions, was deeply engrossed in a book.

Suddenly he was startled to feel the touch of the workman's hand and hear his voice asking quietly if the doctor would mind closing the carriage door after him, because he was now leaving. The little doctor was astonished that the electrician did not wait until the next station before leaving, but before he could say anything the khaki-clad figure had opened the door, and the night air was whistling into the carriage. Dr. Ramakrishna Rao jumped up, and stepped to the open doorway in time to see the man stand a moment on the running board, then vanish into the darkness.

It was all rather mystifying. How in the first place did he *know* that the fan was giving trouble? How did he get to the carriage, and why did he choose to leave and make his way along the running board of this swaying, fast-moving express when he could have easily waited until the next stop? He either liked living dangerously or he was simply crazy, but in either case he must also be clairvoyant to know about the fault in the electric fan. With a mental shrug the little doctor lay down to sleep.

About a month after this incident the Governor was again travelling, this time by the aeroplane that was kept for his official use. With him on this occasion, besides his wife and the pilot, were his A.D.C., his personal assistant, and the pilot's wife. They were flying from Kanpur to Benares.

Above Benares the Governor noticed that they seemed to be circling a very long time over the airfield before landing. He asked if there was anything amiss and was informed that the under-carriage was stuck: the wheels would not come down. Furthermore, they were now almost out of petrol. With Dr. Ramakrishna Rao's agreement, the pilot decided to attempt a crash landing on the grass of the airfield. He signalled the ground to this effect. The fire engines were brought out, and everything made ready for the attempt. All knew, of course, that it was a highly dangerous operation, and both the little doctor and his wife sent fervent prayers to their *Gurudev*, Sai Baba, for his much-needed protection.

Perhaps the A.D.C. was praying too, for he also was a devotee of Sai Baba. Like the doctor he wore on his hand a talisman, a ring that had been materialised by Baba. The pilot knew this and, as a last resort before trying a crash landing, asked the A.D.C. to try his hand at working the lever for releasing the jammed undercarriage. The A.D.C. placed his hand on the lever and pressed as directed. The undercarriage came down without any difficulty. They were able to make a normal landing.

The next day Mrs. Ramakrishna Rao, knowing that Baba was at Bangalore in the south, telephoned him from Benares in order to thank him for his grace and protection which, she believed, had saved them from their perilous predicament in the plane. She found, not at all to her surprise, that he knew all about the event, and mentioned details.

Then he remarked, "But you have said nothing about the train incident."

"What train incident, Swami?" she asked, for it had slipped from her mind.

"Why, when the fan was almost on fire and you thought I was a thief," Baba laughed.

Dr. Ramakrishna Rao was sure the train story could not have reached Baba in the ordinary way because neither he nor his wife had talked to anyone about it. They had refrained from mentioning it on the following morning, not wanting to upset any of their staff; then the incident had faded into the background of their busy lives.

Nothing superhuman that Sai Baba did could ever surprise the little doctor; he had through the years seen and experienced so much. For example, when he was Governor of Kerala, and was entertaining Baba and some devotees at the guest house in Trivandrum in 1962, his wife had arranged a dinner party one evening for sixty people. But when Baba is around, crowds have a habit of multiplying their size, and about a hundred and fifty people turned up. It was impossible to obtain extra food at the time. Mrs. Ramakrishna Rao became very worried, and asked Baba what she should do about it.

"Feed them all," Baba told her. "There will be enough, don't worry."

So the extra places were set and the whole crowd sat down. Baba moved among the guests and servers, blessing the food, seeing that all were happy and turning the meal, as always, into a banquet. No one went short because of the extra ninety mouths to be fed. Somehow Baba increased the food, and there was enough for all.

I knew that it was on this visit to the south that one of the dramatic miracles described in N. Kasturi's book took place. A number of Baba's disciples were walking with him on the sands of Kanyakumari where three seas meet and play around the southernmost tip of India. Suddenly a kingly wave swept high up the beach around Baba's feet and, on receding, it left about his ankles a magnificent necklace, 108 fine pearls on a thread of gold.

I have spoken to a number of men, including Dr. Sitaramiah, who were present and witnessed the arrival of this treasure from the deep, and I asked Dr. Ramakrishna Rao if he had been there as well. He replied that, unfortunately, official duties had taken him elsewhere that day. In fact, he was meeting Dr. S. Radhakrishnan who had just become President of India. But, he said, a number of his friends and acquaintances, including the Chief of Security Police, were with Baba on the beach and saw it happen. They described the event to him on the following day and he was shown the pearl necklace. Baba later gave this to an old devotee whom the doctor knew.

It was while he was still Governor of Uttar Pradesh that Dr. B. Ramakrishna Rao saw the miraculous events that moved him most deeply.

In the summer of 1961 Sai Baba, with a party of devotees, was touring in the north, and decided to visit the famous temple of Badrinath high in the Himalayas. Dr. Ramakrishna joined the party at Hardwar on the Ganges for the 182-mile mountain trek to Badrinath. The devotees say that the object of Sai Baba's journey was not only to take them to this holy place, but to reinfuse it with spiritual efficacy. It was established some twelve hundred years ago by Adi Shankara, one of the foremost spiritual leaders of all time. He it was who brought the 'Upanishads' into the light of day from where they had been collecting dust for centuries in caves and monasteries. At Joshimath he wrote his celebrated commentaries on the 'Upanishads', the 'Bhagavad-Gítā' and the 'Brahma Sūtras', thus making these spiritual classics accessible and intelligible to a wider and ever-widening audience.

Adi Shankara not only travelled all over India and taught the people, but he organised and established centres in the north, south, east and west which he hoped would remain as beacons of light to carry on his work after he had gone. Badrinath was one of those spiritual power points.

But in the course of twelve centuries – albeit millions of devout pilgrims had brought their adoration and veneration there – the power was certain to run down, the life was bound to ebb from the ancient form. Even though a particular priestly caste may not be corrupt, it has most of the human weaknesses, and cannot maintain the high level set by a God-man such as Adi Shankara. The only thing that can recharge the spiritual battery of such a place is the presence and power of another God-man.

However, there appeared to be an obstacle in the way. By tradition, the doctor told me, the only persons ever permitted inside the temple *sanctum sanctorum* to perform *pūjā* were the members of a special sect of Kerala Brahmins. This caste of priests had held the position and exclusive rights since the days of Adi Shankara. The request of Dr. B. Ramakrishna Rao, the Governor of their state, counted for nought; they had heard of Sai Baba, the miracle worker who some said was a divine *Avatār*, a God-man, but they could not make an exception even for him. God himself in human form would not be allowed to enter here, for what human eyes can read the credentials of divinity?

"No matter," Baba said, "let them keep to their traditions."

However, before some two hundred people outside the temple he materialised a statue of Vishnu. This was about ten inches high and was, it is said, a replica of the big idol within the temple. With another wave of his hand he produced a silver tray on which he placed the little Vishnu idol. Then in the same way he created a thousand-petalled lotus of gold. Everyone gasped at its beauty; and while they were wondering what it was for, Baba waved his hand again to produce a *Shivalingam*. This, some three or four inches in height and made of a beautiful crystal material, he placed in the centre of the golden lotus.

With the idol, lotus and *lingam* on the silver tray, Baba and his followers came away from the temple to the guest house where they were staying. There, while they all sang *bhajan* songs, Baba carried the *lingam* around and showed it to everyone, pointing out the beauty of the material, and the form of an eye which was mysteriously incorporated inside it.

Then Baba materialised a silver vessel full of holy water, 108 *bilva* leaves of gold, which fell in a shower from his hand onto the tray, and a heap of *thumbi* flowers with the dew still fresh upon them. These are described as "tiny bits of fragrant fluff, plucked from a hundred little tropical plants".

All of these were materials for ritualistic worship. Baba performed *abhisheka* (sacred ceremonial bath) and then, in his presence, N. Kasturi writes, "The *pūjā* was performed, on behalf of all present, by Dr. B. Ramakrishna Rao, appropriate *mantrams* being recited by the devotees".

Afterwards Baba handed all the materialised items to the Governor's lady, Mrs. Ramakrishna Rao, instructing her to take good care of them, because she would be held responsible if anything was lost. The poor woman felt very apprehensive about such a responsibility, as well she might. She locked the precious articles in a cupboard in her bedroom and kept the key on her person.

Some time later Baba asked her to bring the *lingam*. Unlocking the cupboard, she found that it was missing; everything else was there, but the *lingam* had vanished. In great consternation she hurried to Baba and reported the loss.

At first he scolded her for not taking proper care, but then he laughed and said he was only teasing her. He explained to all present that he had sent the *lingam* back to the place from where it had been apported by his power, to the base of the idol in the temple. This "*netralingam* from Kailāsa", as he called it, had been placed in a secret niche in the holy of holies long ago by Adi Shankara himself. There it had rested through the long centuries until that day, 17th June 1961, when he had brought it out to consecrate it anew and recharge it with spiritual potency. So the work he came for was done in spite of the hampering traditions of the place.

Baba later asked for the other articles in the cupboard. He distributed the 108 gold leaves among the two hundred or more people around him and, as usual, there were enough for all. Mrs. Ramakrishna Rao was then greatly rewarded for those few moments of anguish she had suffered at the disappearance of the *lingam*. She was presented with the materialised idol of Vishnu, the golden lotus, and the silver tray on which they both stood.

The doctor told me that these sacred objects were still in his *pūjā* room in Hyderabad where the regular family worship was held.

It may be surprising to many people – though, in fact, it should not be – to find that a scientist of the calibre of Dr. S. Bhagavantam, M.Sc., Ph.D., D.Sc., is a devoted follower of an adept in that field of high transcendental magic which science tends to scorn. Dr. Bhagavantam, formerly Director of the All-India Institute of Science, holds the prominent position of Scientific Advisor to the Ministry of Defence in Delhi, and is well known in scientific circles outside India.

When I met him at Prashānti Nílayam he was occupying a room furnished only with two bedrolls and a few cushions on the floor. Like all good Indians, he was quite happy to use the tiled floor as bedstead, chair and table. With him in the same room was one of his sons, Dr. S. Balakrishna, Assistant Director of the National Geophysical Research Institute of India. Both were visiting the *āshram* for a few days.

I sat on the floor with these two cultured scientists and charming gentlemen, anxious to hear of their experiences with Sai Baba. Outside the open door and windows the July sun gleamed on the sandy soil, white buildings and rocky hills. Inside Dr. Bhagavantam spoke in his quiet, friendly, concise way, while his son confirmed many of the strange events which he too had witnessed. Dr. Balakrishna has had some wonderful experiences of his own with Baba, but here we are concerned with the remarkable reports from his eminent father.

At Dr. Bhagavantam's first meeting with Sai Baba, which was in the year 1959, they went for a walk on the sands of the Chitrāvati river. Others were present, but Bhagavantam was walking by the side of Baba. After a while Swami asked him to select a place on the sands for sitting down. When the doctor hesitated, Baba insisted, explaining that only in this way could Bhagavantam's scientific mind be quite sure that Baba had not led him to a spot where an object had been "planted" in the sands.

After the scientist had chosen an area and the party was seated on the sands, Baba began to tease the doctor a little; he made fun of the complacent "all-knowing" attitude of many men of science, and deplored their ignorance of or indifference to the ancient wisdom to be found in the great Hindu scriptures.

The doctor's pride was stung. He retorted that not all scientists were of this materialistic outlook. He himself, as an example, had a family tradition of Sanskrit learning and a deep interest in the spiritual classics of India.

Then, in an endeavour to establish the *bona fides* of his scientific colleagues, he told Baba that when Oppenheimer, after exploding the first atom bomb, was asked by the press representatives what his reactions were, he replied by quoting a verse from the 'Bhagavad-Gítā', thus showing that he was a student of that great work. "Would *you* like a copy of the 'Bhagavad-Gítā'?" Baba asked him suddenly, scooping up a handful of sand as he spoke. "Here it is," he continued, "hold out your hands."

Bhagavantam cupped his hands to catch the sand as Baba dropped it into them. But when it reached the scientist's waiting palms, it was no longer the golden sand of the Chitrāvati. It was a red-covered book. Opening it in stunned silence, the doctor found that it was a copy of the 'Bhagavad-Gítā' printed in Telegu script. Baba remarked that he could have presented the doctor with one printed in Sanskrit, but as the latter read Sanskrit script with some difficulty, Baba had given him one in Telegu, Bhagavantam's native tongue. Bhagavantam had not mentioned his limited proficiency in Sanskrit; this was something that Baba just knew.

As soon as he could, Bhagavantam examined this miraculously produced volume closely. It appeared to be quite new and was well printed, but *where*? The names of printer and publisher, always given in the normal way, were nowhere to be found.

One day in 1960 Sai Baba was visiting the great scientist's home in Bangalore. At this time Dr. Bhagavantam was Director of the All-India Institute of Science in that city. He had known Sai Baba for about a year and was struggling to make the incredible phenomena he had witnessed fit in with his scientific training.

He said on one occasion at a public meeting: "I was a fairly lost person at that time for all this was in utter contradiction to the laws of physics for which I stood and still stand . . . . Having learned the laws of physics in my youth, and having taught others for many, many years thereafter, about the inviolability of such laws - at least so far as any known human situation is concerned - and having put them into practice with such a belief in them, I naturally found myself in a dilemma. . . ."

One of Dr. Bhagavantam's sons, at this time a boy of about eleven years, seemed to be mentally retarded. Some medical men had recommeded as treatment the piercing of the lumbar region of the spine to remove cerebrospinal fluid, and so relieve pressure on the brain. Others had been against such treatment, saying that it would only make the boy worse. Dr. Bhagavantam had decided not to have it done.

Baba, who loves and understands children, saw the boy and asked a sympathetic question about him. The scientist began to talk about his son's case, and then Baba took over the narration and himself related all that had happened, including the medical debate about the advisability of a lumbar puncture. He went on to say that this would in fact do no harm, but on the contrary would help the boy, making him appreciably better as time went on. Then, casually, as if it were nothing at all, he said that he would himself do the puncture, then and there.

The scientist was startled. Doubt and fear agitated his mind. He began to wonder about things like professional qualifications for such an operation, but before he could utter a word, Baba had waved his hand and materialised some *vibhūti*. Uncovering the boy's back, he rubbed this sacred ash on the lumbar region. Next, with another handwave, he took from the air a hollow surgical needle, about four inches long.

The father felt himself in the presence of a power so far beyond his understanding that he could say nothing; he just waited, watched and hoped for the best. The boy seemed to be semi-conscious, apparently anaesthetised by Baba's *vibhūti*. Without hesitation Baba inserted the needle, showing that he knew the precise spot at which such insertions must be made. To the watching father the needle seemed to go right in out of sight, and he began to worry about how it would be recovered.

Meanwhile Baba was massaging the back and removing the fluid that came out through the needle; he seemed to take away about one cubic centimetre of this fluid, the scientist said. Then, massaging more strongly, or in a different way, Baba brought the needle out of the boy's back. He held it in the air as if handing it to some invisible nurse. Immediately it vanished.

"Have you a surgical dressing?" Baba then asked the watching, spellbound people in the room: Bhagavantam, another of his sons called Ramakrishna, and a friend named Shastri who was a Sanskrit pundit.

Young Ramakrishna replied, saying that by telephoning the Institute he could get a dressing within ten minutes.

"Too long!" Baba laughed, waving his hand again and took a dressing of the right type, as if from a trained assistant in another dimension. Carefully he arranged it on the boy's back, and then brought him around to full consciousness. The patient seemed to suffer no pain or discomfort, either during or after the operation.

"And is he any better?" I asked the good doctor.

"Yes, his condition has improved, though not remarkably," he replied cautiously, "but who knows what he would have been like without the operation? Swami says that he will go on improving as he grows older."

Dr. Bhagavantam has seen Baba produce many things by his magical handwave. These include medicines in bottles and other packs, properly sealed, but without any name of the maker marked on them. He has seen Baba change one stone or decorative figure, set in jewellery, to another of an entirely different character, simply by stroking his finger across the face of it. The relevant item of jewellery did not for a moment disappear from view during such operations.

Once he saw Baba produce *amrita* in a container which the physicist estimated from his experience of capacities would hold enough for about fifty people, each receiving the spoonful which Baba doled out. In fact, though, Baba fed about five hundred people with the ambrosial liquid, which apparently was miraculously increased to ten times its original volume.

On another occasion the doctor was sitting with a group of devotees around Baba on a beach in southern India. The talk turned to the various names by which the ocean had been known in Indian mythology. Someone mentioned the name "*Ratnākara*", which means, he said, "Lord of Diamonds or Precious Stones". "In that case," Baba remarked playfully, "the ocean should produce some diamonds for us." Putting his hand in the water, he took out a sparkling diamond necklace.

Everybody was enthralled at the sight of this circlet of large stones, and someone asked Baba to wear it. Bhagavantam could see plainly that it would not go over Baba's head, being too small and apparently without a clasp for opening the necklace. But such problems did not bother the miracle man; he simply pulled it outward with both hands as one would stretch a rubber ring. It increased to the right size, yet there were no gaps between the stones. Then, to please his devotees, Baba put this diamond garland from "*Ratnākara*" over his head and wore it on his neck for a short time.

Dr. Bhagavantam has also had his own personal experience of Sai Baba's faculty of knowing what is taking place thousands of miles away, without benefit of telegraph or radio.

When Dr. S. Balakrishna, Bhagavantam's son, moved into a new house in Hyderabad, Baba agreed to go there and perform a house-blessing ceremony. The auspicious day for the ritual was named by Baba, and he promised to come on that day. Dr. Bhagavantam was himself away on a government mission to Moscow, but he was scheduled to be back in Hyderabad on the morning of the day of the ceremony, which was to take place in the afternoon.

However, engine trouble in the aeroplane by which he was returning developed somewhere near Tashkent, and he was forced to spend the night in that city. This was the night before the ceremony and Baba, who was at Balakrishna's house in Hyderabad, informed the family that there was engine trouble and that Dr. Bhagavantam was spending the night at Tashkent, but would be flying on to Delhi the following day. No one else in the area knew that there had been any trouble with the plane or that Bhagavantam was at Tashkent. No word of this had come through ordinary channels. But Baba had his own way of knowing, and also of foreseeing that the fault would be righted by the following day.

In the afternoon of the auspicious day, as pre-arranged, Sai Baba carried out the house-blessing ceremony. During this he produced in his usual miraculous manner a beautiful statuette of Shirdi Sai Baba which the two scientists informed me is about three inches in height and seems to be of solid gold. Baba said it was to be kept in the shrine room of the Hyderabad house where it was materialised. And there it is still.

All felt sorry that the head of the family, Dr. Bhagavantam, could not be present at the important ceremony, and that evening they talked about where he might perhaps be spending his time. Was he back in Delhi? they asked Baba. Yes, the latter told them, and he was at that moment in the office of the Minister of Defence, New Delhi.

Then Baba booked a telephone call to the Minister's office, making it a personal call to the Scientific Adviser, Dr. Bhagavantam. At that period, I am told, there was always a considerable delay for a trunk call over such a long distance. But Baba's call came through in a few minutes.

Dr. Bhagavantam was at the office, as Swami had stated. He was closeted with the Minister, and in the middle of an important conference. The Minister had, in fact, given strict instructions to his staff that he was not to be interrupted no matter who telephoned or called to see him. Nevertheless, and no one knows why, one of the secretaries *did* interrupt him to say that there was a telephone call from Hyderabad for Dr. Bhagavantam. With the Minister's concurrence, the doctor left the room and took the call; then Swami's sweet voice was in his ear, telling him that all had gone well at the house blessing. Baba elated him further by saying that he would remain in Hyderabad with the family until Bhagavantam returned on the morrow. With joy in his heart and renewed spirit, the scientist went back to discuss his country's defence problems with the Minister responsible in those days, V. K. Krishna Menon.

When I asked Dr. S. Bhagavantam if I could use his name in support of the incredible things he had told me, he promptly answered, "Yes, I'll stand behind every word of it."

The earlier dilemma, the conflict between his scientific training and the evidence of his senses, has been resolved. He says, "In our laboratories we scientists may swear by reason, but we know that every time we have added a little to what we know, we have known of the existence of many other things, the true nature of which we do not know. In this process we become aware of further large areas, to understand which we have to struggle more. Thus, while adding to knowledge, we add more to our ignorance too. What we know is becoming a smaller and smaller fraction of what we do not know." He goes on to say, "Sai Baba transcends the laws of physics and chemistry, and when he transcends a law, that fact becomes a new law. He is a law unto himself."

Once, in Madras, addressing an audience of some 20,000 people who had come to hear Sai Baba's message, the worthy doctor said, *inter alia*, "Scientists are aware that knowledge is not the same as wisdom. Wisdom has to be got from Bhagavān [Sai Baba], and the like of Him, who come among us from time to time for this express purpose. . . .

"He is a phenomenon. He is transcendental. He is divine. He is an Incarnation. He is our nearest kith and kin; turn to Him for the eternal message. That alone can save us."

Flake of the world fire, spark of Divinity,
Lift up thy mind and thy heart into glory.
Sun in the darkness, recover thy lustre.

Sri Aurobindo

18

REALITY AND SIGNIFICANCE OF THE MIRACULOUS

The wealth of miraculous things that my own eyes have witnessed assures my acceptance of things of similar nature about which I have heard. This acceptance is aided by my knowledge of the integrity, intelligence and high moral character of the many witnesses. However, although to many eminent community leaders and to thousands of ordinary folk like myself the Sai miracles are indisputable facts, the eye-witnesses represent only a small fraction of mankind. So what about the millions beyond the orbit of those who have been fortunate enough to *see* for themselves? What about the masses of materialists and atheists, conditioned by the superficial philosophy of modern technological progress? Is there the slightest likelihood that they may credit the truth of the incredible events described in these pages?

Nearly a hundred years ago, when a Theosophist, A. P. Sinnett, Editor of British India's 'Pioneer', was trying to convince the Western public through his writings that similar miraculous phenomena were taking place, a great Himalayan Adept wrote to him: "None but those who see for themselves will ever believe, do what you may. . .. But so long as men doubt there will be curiosity and enquiry."

The human mind by its nature regards anything outside a commonly accepted framework of rationality as impossible and rejects it. A materialisation phenomenon, for example, is so foreign to everyday experience that, even after watching it happen, it is not easy for one to believe that it really took place. One seems to have been in some odd way out of space and time. When one is back in the normal dimensions of space and time, the reality of a miracle seems to vanish. It goes as the reality of a dream goes on waking.

"Did the miracle really happen?" the thinking mind asks. But the glittering jewel, which came from nowhere, lies in the hand; the taste of the candy, which a moment ago was granite or paper, is undeniably on the tongue. The effects are apparent; the comprehensible causes are missing, and they are not to be found by our rationalistic thinking.

Of course the apport, the transport of a material object without any known material agency, is well known to spiritualists and other occult circles of the West. I myself have witnessed them there. The theory behind them is that the object, which is already in existence somewhere, is dematerialised and brought in that state by psychic force to the circle where it is rematerialised.

Baba has said that some of his "productions" are apports. In this regard the observation of one Sai devotee is suggestive. A well-known Indian princess told me that she was once sitting close in front of Baba while he stood above her on a daïs, waving his hand to 'produce' something. She was able to look for anything happening beneath the down-turned palm. First she saw a small luminous cloud appear there; this condensed quickly to form a small shining object over which Baba's hand closed. The object proved to be a gold ring.

The old, gold ten-dollar piece which Baba 'produced' for me at Horsley Hills was no doubt an apport. But, what of the interesting phenomenon he performed for Dr. V. K. Gokak, Vice-Chancellor of Bangalore University? On an early visit to Dr. Gokak's home Baba saw on the wall for the first time a portrait of an Indian saint, Shri Panta Maharaj of Balekundri, and asked about its presence there.

The Vice-Chancellor replied to Baba that the saint had been his father's *guru*, and that he, himself, held the holy man in great reverence.

> Baba: "Have you a smaller portrait of him to carry when you're travelling?"
> Dr. Gokak: "No."
> Baba: "Would you like one?"
> Dr. Gokak: "Yes, Swami, very much."

Baba waved his hand, for a little longer than usual, remarking, "He is coming." Turning the palm up, he handed the doctor a small enamel pendant. It bore a miniature replica of the saint's portrait.

Apports are perhaps better known to all classes in India than to those in the West. The former government minister, great educationalist and well-known writer, Dr. K. M. Munshi, states in his excellent 'Bhavan's Journal' that he has seen apports 'produced' by a man sitting near him on the sofa of his own drawing room. First there was "*kūmkūm*" (red powder) on a tray, another time flowers, a third time *prasād*, and a fourth time currency notes.

Munshi goes on to say that he thinks the sacred ash materialised by Baba and used for curing ailments and evoking faith must amount to a pound in weight per day, and is not apported, but "produced in some other even more mysterious way". It seems obvious that the sweets made while you watch from age-old solid rock, and many other phenomena performed by Sai Baba, cannot be apports.

But whether objects are 'transported', created on the spot by divine will, or materialised in some other way, what amount of evidence, what number of attestations from people of intelligence and integrity, does it take to convince those who have never seen such things?

Of course, within India itself there are large numbers of people who have no difficulty whatsoever in accepting the reality of miracles. Beneath the surface of life the miraculous has always been going on in that country. There have always been men who could perform some supernormal feat or another, create a perfume from the air, read a sealed letter, crack a tumbler from a distance, heal with a touch, drink strong acid with impunity, levitate, and so on. These things are part of the fabric of the common culture. They are accepted not only by the masses but by thinkers and thought leaders, of the status of Dr. K. M. Munshi, for instance. On this subject I have spoken to many of the well-educated and highly cultured; most of them have seen some examples during their lives of miraculous phenomena, quite apart from the Sai Baba miracles. The possibility of *siddhis* is so basic to the Indian heritage that even those who have never seen anything of the kind are ready to believe in the miraculous.

Yet, for this very reason, it seems to me, some of the intelligent are inclined to miss the main point of the Sai Baba miracles. I have heard them say: "Advanced yogis are able to perform miracles, but so what? What is the value in such things?"

Some go further and say that miracles should not be performed, that they are an obstacle to spiritual progress. They quote statements from their scriptures and yogic texts to support this view. But if we examine such statements properly we find that the warnings about the perils of performing miracles are given to disciples, to those at an intermediate stage on the spiritual path. Patanjali, for instance, points out that, at some level of training in yoga, latent supernormal powers of various kinds are liable to make their appearance. That is to say, the disciple will find that he has the power to perform certain "miracles".

But there are several grave dangers inherent in this. It may stir his pride and egotism. He may start using it for selfish purposes. It may make him think that he has reached his goal. Instead of understanding that these psychic and psychokinetic powers are mere by-products, he may consider them the final product or, at least, a sign that he has reached a high level of spirituality. But psychic powers are not in themselves a sign of spirituality. Thus the pupil enamoured of such powers, will be led astray and make no further progress towards life's true goal.

Baba himself, while in his former body at Shirdi, often gave warnings to his devotees on this matter. He pointed out that the acquirement of supernormal powers often takes a disciple, who has not reached the highest levels, farther away from the main object of his spiritual disciplines, which is the realisation of God. To one of his devotees who had just developed clairvoyance, for instance, Baba said, "Why are you gazing at the strumpet's performance? It does not behove us to dally with a strumpet!"

The man's wife, who was present, thought that Baba was referring to some fleshly concubine, but the devotee himself understood that his *sadgūrū*, Baba, was giving him a timely warning, lest he be carried away by the charms and seductions of his newly acquired powers.

Such dangers, and such warnings, apply only to *chélās*, pupils on the path, not to those who have reached the final goal - not to a fully God-realised man, a God-man or *avatār*. There is no desire for earthly gain, no pride, no egotism, no self-glory in the miracles of a Christ, a Krishna, a Sai Baba. Therefore there is no danger, neither to the performer of the miracle nor to the recipient of its benefits.

However, though the recipient can suffer no ill effects from divine miracles, he may not always obtain all the good effects potentially there. To every such miracle there is a spiritual string, so to speak. If the receiver fails to perceive the string he has lost a golden opportunity. He may perhaps have gained a golden jewel, or he may have been blessed by merciful healing, helped in a practical problem or saved from some deadly peril. These are important things, no doubt, but small compared with what he might have gained.

If he continues to dodge the spiritual string, he will in time become surfeited with miraculous phenomena. They will no longer impress or delight him. Moreover, they will not continue to serve him; and when the point is reached where the miraculous powers of the God-man work no more that materialist's way, where he no longer gets the worldly benefit he expects, he will drop away from the God-man's following. As Captain James Cook, when he discovered the east coast of Australia, sailed past and missed the narrow inlet to the fine harbour where Sydney stands, so such a one will miss the narrow way to the divine harbour for which all human ships are searching. And how long must he wait, how many years, how many lifetimes, for such another opening?

What, then is the significance of the divine miracle, the high, transcendental magic that works never for the benefit of the performer, but always for mankind? Some of its purposes are obvious, some more hidden.

As the great Himalayan Adept suggested to Sinnett, miracles do tend to lead men towards investigation and enquiry into the deepest mysteries of the universe. Colonel H. S. Olcott, after seeing a stream of miraculous phenomena during the final quarter of last century, wrote: "For my part I can say that the great range of marvels of educated will potency which I saw made it easy for me to understand the Oriental theories of spiritual science."

This effect – helping the understanding of "spiritual science" – the miraculous will have on minds that are open, alive and anxious to explore the deeper strata of existence. Though the wonders in themselves are subordinate to and less important than the spiritual truths behind them, they are signs more powerful than words to guide men towards those truths, which at their deepest levels cannot be expressed by either wonders or words. For men are in general apathetic, and need something spectacular to shake them out of their inertia. B. V. Narasimha Swami wrote: "One common feature in the lives of both Sai and Jesus is that people always had to be convinced of the divine nature of the two, only through the miracles they performed. Miracles are a concession that divinity allows for human blindness."

Concerning words, spoken or written, men nod or shake their heads, agreeing, disagreeing, debating, comparing. . .for there are many who have spoken wise words. But if, as they say in journalism, one picture is worth a thousand words, one miracle is worth many thousands.

When the Almighty ordered Moses to lead the people of Israel out of Egypt, Moses protested that the people would not believe he was sent by God, and would not accept him as their leader. So the Almighty told him to throw his staff on the ground. Obeying, Moses saw the staff become a serpent. Then the Lord ordered him to pick up the serpent by its tail, and doing so he found the serpent was a staff again. This was the first of the many miracles that Moses was able to perform through the power of God. The purpose of such marvels was not only to make the Israelites – and Pharoah – realise that Moses was a divine messenger, but also to overcome the many tremendous obstacles in the long journey from bondage in Egypt to freedom in the promised land. Like all the immortal stories of man's pilgrimage, this one has deeper meanings too. It teaches among other things that miraculous powers have a value in freeing man from the bondage of the flesh, leading him through the many obstacles of life and his own vain mental strivings to the promised land of spiritual freedom and liberation.

So, beginning with the nucleus of disciples around him, the God-man uses miracles to help them grasp the truth about his divine nature, and also to help them overcome blockages in their spiritual progress. The nucleus of disciples grows to a large following, and gradually – as the religious history of the past shows – the good news, the gospel, spreads until millions become his followers. Thereby the heavy *karma* of mankind is lifted a little, and more and more souls are brought from darkness towards the light.

But it is wise to remember that the greatest miracles are not always the obvious ones. In the presence of the man of divinity our awakening spiritual perception beholds a demonstration of the most stupendous miracle in the very existence of such a man. We, who are ourselves bond slaves to desire, see one who is master of earthly desire. We, who are always centred in our little, separate, self-important selves, see one who is centred in the Self of all mankind, all life. We, who struggle on through sorrow and passing joys, see the embodiment of eternal joy. We, who constantly confuse love with lust, possessiveness, self-love, feel from the great one the nectarine flow of a love that is divine, universal, embracing all life. Yet at the same time this love is not vague and impersonal; it is very personal, focused on each devotee's innermost heart. And in it there is no taint of egotism.

If our feet are on even the beginning of the spiritual path, we know that these great qualities are goals towards which we ourselves are struggling in life's pilgrimage. But often such goals have seemed a long way off. We have wondered sometimes if we could ever reach them, if any human being ever really came to them. Perhaps, after all, we ponder, they are no more than a beautiful dream of the heart. But now before us in the flesh is one who has scaled the spiritual Everest. An ideal, a dream, has thus become an actual, living reality in time. Human nature, we thus see, *can* indeed be changed, the lower animal self of man *can* be completely transmuted into a higher Self.

Here lies, perhaps, the deepest significance of divine miracles; they demonstrate the God-like potentialities, the "flake of the world fire", in each human being. They build our faith, and help us to work with new zeal towards the production of a divine edition of ourselves. And this is accomplished not only through the great inspiration of the living example before us, but also through the silent, transforming ray that emanates from the Divine One and unbeknown to us reaches to our depths. By his very nature of pure love the divine *avatār* calls all men to him, and the many who come he guides along the razor-edged way.

Sai Baba, while still in his Shirdi body, stated that he would lead hundreds of thousands of people onto the path and take them to the goal, right up to the very end; right to God. On this work he is still energetically engaged.

Narasimha Swami, and others who have imbibed deeply at the Sai fountain, have stated that the universalist religion of love and brotherhood as taught by Sai Baba is destined to embrace the world. Certainly, it is spreading through the length and breadth of India and beginning to take root in places abroad. Satya Sai Baba made his first trip overseas in July 1968. He went to Uganda in East Africa, where there was already a nucleus of devotees. His visit became a national event. Great crowds swarmed around him, not only the few thousand Indians there but also the many thousands of Africans, not only the masses of the "lowly" but the "high-ups" as well. Government ministers, the Inspector-General of Police, the Army Chief of Staff and other top officials gathered to pay homage to

Baba. Crowds danced with joy at the sight of him, and ranks of police guards went on their knees as he walked between them.

There is little doubt that all continents and all peoples will have the chance to see Sai Baba in the years ahead. So here is something never known before in the world's history. A God-man, a living worker of miracles, will be able through the use of modern global communications to travel the world, and make his message known to all people during his lifetime.

Of old, this could not happen, and tidings of such amazing events reached the mass of mankind either through verbal reports or by accounts written long after the events took place. Now the sceptic, the doubting Thomas, who cannot believe in either the greater or the lesser miracles, can prove their reality for himself. If keen enough, he can visit Prashānti Nílayam to witness them; otherwise he can wait until Sai Baba comes nearer to his part of the globe.

The miracles of Christ and Krishna must be taken on trust or through faith; those of Sai Baba you can see for yourself.

Truth stands on its own evidence, it does not require any other testimony to prove it true, it is self-effulgent.

Swami Vivekananda

19

SOME SAI TEACHINGS

Readers who have not yet had the opportunity of enjoying English translations of Sai Baba's spiritual discourses would no doubt like to have some idea of the verbal teachings of this God-powered man of miracles. It is no easy task to give in a chapter even the gist of these vital, luminous teachings. But I am somewhat helped by the fact that the truism "there is nothing new under the sun" applies also to spiritual instruction and philosophy.

Christ's Sermon on the Mount, for instance, seemed no doubt to be quite revolutionary to its original hearers, and to many people since. In fact all its "new" teachings can be found in the age-old but ageless sacred writings of the East. It seems, indeed, that all the great spiritual truths man is capable of understanding at his present stage of evolution were given out long ago by the ancient masters of India. Since then the basic stock of wisdom has been many times revived, restated, revitalised by the great world teachers who have come. Each presents it with different accent, different emphasis, new interpretations and up-to-date illustrations to suit the age to which he teaches. But a study of the recorded ancient wisdom – in the 'Védas', the 'Upanishads', the 'Pūrānas', the 'Shāstras' (Hindu scriptures) – show that all the fundamental truths that can be stated have been stated already in some form or another.

This does not mean that the recurrence of new teachers is unnecessary or unimportant. In time any temple built to truth becomes its sepulchre. Enlightening words between the covers of ancient manuscripts or books are inevitably forgotten or misunderstood, or twisted by knavish priests to make a trap for the unwary and ignorant. The ancient wisdom has to be brought out and re-dressed, re-energised to give it a new interest and living significance. This can only be done by one who *really* knows; knows not from books but from his own being. His words will not have the speculative note of the philosophers but the confident certainty of true knowledge.

Every great teacher who speaks this self-effulgent truth has his own individual approach and method of presentation. Some have addressed only the few, in their own lifetimes, others the many. Those like Christ who spoke to crowds, have cast the wisdom largely in the form of parables, to be easily understood by untutored minds.

Sai Baba has many similarities to Christ, not only in the miracles but in the style of his presentation. In his discourses he uses an abundance of parables, figures of speech, analogies and homely illustrations. This is no doubt one of the reasons why he draws the great crowds; another reason is the authority that sounds through his words. He speaks as one who *knows*, and he is not afraid to hammer his lessons home, to repeat, to re-emphasise. In this he demonstrates the fact, as all great teachers have done, that it is not enough for men to hear and know about the truths; they must live them. The knowledge and the action must become as one. Now I will try to give some little idea of what he teaches.

Man is essentially the *ātma* (which may be translated as "spirit"). He is not the body and must never identify himself with the body which is merely a temporary vestment. Even those who agree with this truth intellectually act most of the time as if they were no more than the body; so Baba is never tired of hammering in this fundamental truth.

He says, for instance, "You are the invincible *ātma*, unaffected by the ups and downs of life. The shadow you cast while trudging along the road falls on dirt and dust, bush and briar, stone and sand, but you are not worried at all, for you walk unscathed. So too, as the *ātma* substance, you have no reason to be worried over the fate of its shadow, the body."

This true self of man is "something subtler than water or air or ether; for it must go into the eye in order that you may see; into the hand so that you may hold; into the feet to enable you to walk. The senses themselves are inert materials; the self must operate before they can function."

The *ātma* itself is formless, but it creates the forms it requires. It has created the five sheaths of man. The grossest of these is the *annamaya kosha* (food sheath). More subtle is the *prānamaya kosha* (sheath of vital breath). These two are part of the physical body. Two more sheaths make up the subtle or astral body. These are the *manômaya kosha* (mind sheath) and the *vijnānamaya kosha* (sheath of intellect or higher mind). The fifth is the *ānandamaya kosha* (sheath of bliss) which serves the highest body of man, the causal body, known in Sanskrit as the *kārana sharíra*. All these components and compartments serve the lord of the castle, the *jívātma* (individual spirit).

But the lord, fully pre-occupied with these instruments of his own creation and the experiences they bring, has forgotten his true identity. Nevertheless, deep within there is the dim echo of a memory. Sometimes he hears it. So that when a call comes from the immortal regions, he responds. As Baba says: "Man is not a despicable creature, born in slime or sin, to eke out a drab existence for ever. Man is immortal and eternal. So when the call comes from the region of immortality, he responds with his whole heart." He "seeks liberation from his bondage to the trivial and the temporary. Everyone craves for this in his heart of hearts. And it is available in only one shop, that is in the contemplation of the *ātma*, the highest self, which is the basis of all this appearance."

But liberation is a struggle that stretches over a long period of time. It does not come automatically with death as some may think. After shedding the physical body, the *ātma* is still immersed in other vehicles, it still has links with the earth, links of memory and desire, which bring it back into reincarnation again and again.

To reach liberation and eternal bliss, man must get rid of all earthly desires and attachments. In one of Baba's graphic similes he says: "Man is like rice. Provided the husk is removed, it will not grow. Man's husk is his body of desires; if this is liquidated, he will not reincarnate."

Of course, the conquest of earthly desires and attachments is something that calls for long *sādhanā*, or spiritual practices. Most of Baba's teaching is aimed directly towards assisting people in this great struggle, and he uses many homely illustrations to help them grasp and remember the basic principles involved. For instance, he says, "Man's many desires are like the small metal coins he carries about in his pocket. The more he has, the more they weigh him down. But if he can convert them all into one paper note of higher currency, he will not feel any weight. In the same way if he can convert his many desires into one desire, that is, into the aspiration for union with God, then there will be no weight to pull him down to the earth level."

Once man comes through the long school of phenomenal existence - in this world and on other planes as well - he begins to understand that his main aim is to break out of the cocoon that has held him down so long. The cocoon has had its uses, but the time of its usefulness is over. He is ready for his flight into the new life of freedom, the divine life.

The fact is that every man is a spark of divinity; every man is potentially God - not God as we usually think of Him, with form, but the formless God, the divine ocean from which comes all existence. Baba states this plainly: "If you realise the *ātma* principle you become God Himself. . . . Each one of you can become God by merging your separate individual souls in the ocean of the universal *ātma*."

The basis of love and brotherhood between men is the truth that they are all of this one *ātma* principle, no matter what their colour, caste or creed. The analogy that Baba sometimes uses here is that of the electric current lighting globes of many colours, shapes and sizes. The reality behind the globes is the current flowing within them. The same for each. The *ātma* can be likened to the electricity flow. Men are varied expressions of this one current.

God is formless, yet He has form. He is that which lies beyond all forms yet He creates, maintains and destroys everything that exists. God is really in every form, but in man more than in anything else, and in some men more intensely and completely than in others. A few men in the world's history have been one hundred per cent God.

The fact is, though, that God, who expresses some aspect and part of Himself as an essence in every form, can actually manifest Himself as God in any chosen shape, be it human, partly human, or otherwise. Also He can respond to any name. Baba puts it this way: "The Lord can be addressed by any name that tastes sweet to your tongue, or pictured in any form that appeals to your sense of wonder and awe. You can sing of Him as Mūrūga, Ganapati, Shāradā, Jesus, Maitreyí, Shakti, or you can call on Allah or the Formless One, or the Master of all Forms. It makes no difference at all. He is the beginning, the middle and the end; the basis, the substance and the source."

But we must never think that the omnipresent God is completely contained in any particular form of our choosing, or answers exclusively to the one traditional name we have been conditioned to worship. He manifests Himself through such limited finite channels if our worship is sincere, but he is not confined to them. As the Sufi poet writes, "His dust is here, but He is in the Infinite."

In one sense, God is nearer than our hands and feet. We do not have to search for Him out beyond the starry constellations "where the wheeling systems darken, and our benumbed conceiving soars", for the loving merciful God is ever close at hand. He is the very core of our spiritual heart, but particularly, "as the doctor is found where the patients gather, and the surgeon in the operation room," states Sri Sai, "so the Lord is ever with the suffering and the struggling. Wherever people cry out for God, there God will be."

The ultimate object of every man – his true purpose, whether he knows it or not – is to realise the God within himself. How should he live his life, in order to achieve this?

Baba does not teach that the only way to reach this spiritual goal is to go away and live in caves, forest hermitages or walled-in monasteries. It is right for the majority of us to live the ordinary life of the world, but we must not become bond slaves to the world's allurements. A boat, he says, is meant to go into water, but the water must not get into the boat. In the same way we are meant to be in the world, but the world must not get into us. He adds another illustration: "Man must grasp God with the right hand and the world with the left. Gradually, the left will lose its hold. Do not worry about this; it has to be so; that's maybe why the hand is called 'left' – the world will be left behind. But the right hand must not loosen its grip. Being called 'right', it is right for it to grip right and hold on."

How to do this? We must realise that the great drama of this world in which we are now playing a part is no more than a passing show. We must not identify ourselves with the drama, or become attached to its vestures and "properties" which we will soon be leaving behind anyway. In other words we must learn to discriminate between the permanent and the transitory, the substance and the shadow.

The shadow is the great illusion that we are our bodies and that the physical world around us is the ultimate and only reality. The way to correct that error is to keep our thoughts and aspirations towards God, our faces towards the divine light. Baba gives this analogy: "Move forward towards the light and the shadow falls behind, but if you move away from the light, you have to follow your own shadow. Go every moment one step nearer to the Lord and then the great illusion, the shadow, will fall back and will not delude you at all."

Actually, what we all seek is happiness, but through the deluding shadow of our own ignorance, we seek it in the wrong places. "Once you turn towards the path of worldly happiness," says Baba, "you will be led on and on to greater and greater discontent, competition, pride, jealousy. Just stop for a moment and examine your own experience. Are you happier when you grow richer, do you find more peace when your wants are satisfied? You will yourself be witness to the truth that an improved standard of living is no guarantee of happiness."

When we seek happiness through the pleasures of this world, we always find as much pain as pleasure, as much sorrow as joy. The pairs of opposites, the black and white twins, are ever near to each other. But let them come; the pleasures and the pains, the joys and the sorrows, they are part of the divine *leelā*, or play. Beyond them, and inspite of them, we will find a great peace and abiding joy once we turn our faces towards the light and understand that we are a part of the divine substance, the *ātma*, and that our real existence lies beyond this shadow show on the space-time stage.

Is there any special guidance and yogic training that will help men break the grip of the world's allurements; help them make that difficult about-turn from the tinsel glitter to the greater light? Baba often discourses on the three classical yoga pathways to enlightenment. He points out that all of these – *karma* (action), *jnāna* (knowledge) and *bhakti* (devotion) – must be used. They are three lanes on the one great highway to God.

Baba says: "Base your action on knowledge, the knowledge that all is one. Let the action be suffused with *bhakti*; that is to say, humility, love, mercy and non-violence. Let *bhakti* be filled with knowledge, otherwise it will be as light as a balloon which drifts along any current of air, or gust of wind. Mere knowledge will make the heart dry; *bhakti* makes it soft with sympathy, and *karma* gives the hands something to do, something which will sanctify every one of the minutes that have fallen to your lot to live."

I once heard Baba talk in other terms of these three lanes to Self-realisation. He called them "the three Ws": work, worship and wisdom. Work (*karma*) alone is, he said, the slow passenger train, with long stops and some changes at junctions before you reach the end of the journey; but if you add worship (*bhakti*) to the work, you will have an express coach, and get to your destination more quickly and easily. Work and worship together will furthermore develop wisdom, or knowledge of the real (*jnāna*). With this you will then be on a non-stop express train right to your journey's end. So worship while you work, and strive meanwhile for the self-knowledge that will help these two to bring the true wisdom.

Speaking of spiritual books, he says that they are only like maps and guidebooks. "Scanning a map or turning over a guidebook will not give you the thrill of the actual visit, nor will it give you a fraction of the knowledge and joy of a journey through that land."

"In fact," he says in another place, "you need not even read the scriptures, the 'Gítā' or the 'Upanishads'. You will hear a 'Gítā' (divine song) especially designed for you, if only you call upon the Lord in your own heart. He is there, installed as your own charioteer."

So the great scriptures of the world are guidebooks, taking us as far, but only as far, as the written word can. The real knowledge must come from our own inner experience. We must ourselves travel to that land that lies within. But it is very difficult, well nigh impossible, to find one's own way through the forests, though life's dense jungle encircling that divine land. So it is by far the best to have a guide who has been there, who from personal experiences knows the route. In other words, the surest, easiest, swiftest way to Self-realisation is to have a spiritual *gūru* – a *sadgūrū* – who is himself Self-realised. If in ordinary life you have an experienced guide who is taking you through strange forests or deserts or the intricate ways of an unknown city, you do not stop to argue and debate with him about the route. You put your trust in him and submit to his guidance. Likewise with your *sadgūrū*: you must put yourself completely in his hands. Your own foolish ego and pride and self-will will only lead you astray. Your spiritual guide knows how to take you where you want to go, so the first thing you must learn is the difficult science of self-surrender.

Of course, you are greatly helped in this by the love you inevitably feel towards your *sadgūrū*, who has your true welfare at heart, and helps you onwards, with no other motive than that of his selfless love. It is taught in the Hindu spiritual philosophy that there is no difference between the *sadgūrū* and God, and in this *bhakti* love the *sadgūrū* expresses the love of God. "When God loves," wrote Saint Bernard of Clairvaux, "He wants nothing else than to be loved; for He loves for no other purpose than that He may be loved, knowing that those who love Him are blessed by that love."

This selfless love of the *sadgūrū* for the disciple, and the responsive, ever-growing love of the disciple for the *sadgūrū*, is the heart of the *bhakti mārga*, the way of devotion.

So while the other yogic lanes must not be forgotten, and must be utilised as required, *bhakti* is pre-eminently the laneway for the great journey. Or – to change the metaphor – though *bhakti* is not the only ingredient in the alchemical formula for transmuting man's base elements to spiritual gold, it is the most important ingredient. Baba has often said that for this age the *bhakti mārga* is the easiest and surest way to the goal, and many great teachers, from Lord Krishna onwards, have said exactly the same thing.

Baba uses many stories and similes to point the value of the *bhakti mārga*. Here is one:

> A *bhakta* and a *jnāni* (a follower of the *jnāna mārga*) were walking through a forest and became very thirsty. They came to a deep well with water far down and the sides overgrown with bush and briar. There was no way of obtaining water. The *jnāni* overcame the difficulty by expending great psychic force to assume the form of a bird. Then he flew down through the bushes and briars, losing many feathers on the way. On the other hand, the *bhakta* yearned for the Lord's grace and called fervently on His name. The Lord hearing and responding, the waters rose to the level of the *bhakta* who was thus able to slake his thirst completely.

Sometimes Baba likens God to a magnet and says, "Remember that the magnet cannot draw to itself a bit of iron that is rusty and covered with dust. You cannot be drawn by God when your mind is laden with the rust of material desires, and the dust of sensual craving sits heavily upon it."

There is on record a story of how a rich man came to Sai Baba when he was in his Shirdi body and asked to be shown the way to God-realisation. Baba first put the man through several tests, and then gave a dissertation on the qualifications necessary before any person can hope to realise God in his lifetime. A number of Baba's disciples were there, along with the rich man, listening to this dissertation.

I have at various times, and in various places, heard Satya Sai Baba give the same instructions concerning the self-disciplines, training and austerities necessary in order to make progress along the Sai way, which is the *bhakti* way as taught by Sai Baba. So I will give the substance of that memorable Shirdi discourse here. In it Baba elaborated ten points:

> (1) The aspirant must realise the absolute triviality and unimportance of the things of this world and of the next. He must, in fact, feel a disgust for the honours, emoluments and other fruits that his action will bring in both this world and also in the one to follow, for his aim is higher than

that.
(2) He must fully realise that he is in bondage to the lower worlds and have an intense aspiration to get free. He must work earnestly and resolutely to that end, and care for nothing else.
(3) Our senses have been created with a tendency to move outwards and so man always looks outside himself. But he who wants Self-realisation, and the immortal life, must turn his gaze inwards and look to his inner self.
(4) Unless a man has turned away from wrong-doing and composed himself so that his mind is at rest, he cannot gain Self-realisation even though he has great knowledge.
(5) The candidate to the spiritual life must lead a life of truth, penance, insight and right conduct.
(6) Two classes of things constantly present themselves to man for acceptance: the good and the pleasant. A would-be disciple has to think and choose between them. The wise person chooses the good; the unwise, through greed and attachment, chooses the pleasant.
(7) The aspirant must control his mind and senses. If his mind is unrestrained and his senses unmanageable, like wild and vicious horses drawing a chariot, he cannot reach his destination. But when the intellect and enlightened will exercise the control, like the hands of a good driver manipulating the reins (the mind) expertly to guide the horses (the senses) steadily along the right road, then the true self, who is the master of the chariot, reaches his journey's end – the supreme abode of the all-pervading God. Sometimes, using another simile, Baba likens the mind to an electric cable. "Do not establish contact with the mind; that is as bad as contacting the cable! Watch it from a distance; then only can you derive bliss." That is to say, becoming too closely identified and involved with the mind incapacitates one for seeing the reality that lies beyond the mind.
(8) As well as controlling the mind a man must purify it. To do this he must discharge satisfactorily, and at the same time in a non-attached way, the duties of his station in life (his *dharma*). He must get rid of the great delusion: "I am the body", or "I am the mind". This will help him to lose egoism, get rid of avarice and purify the mind of all lower desires.
(9) The aspirant must have a *guru*. The knowledge of the Self is so subtle that no one by his own effort could ever hope to attain it. The help of a great teacher, who has walked the path himself and attained Self-realisation, is absolutely necessary. There is no difficulty about finding a *guru*; when a pupil has done all he can in self-enquiry and self-training the *guru* will come, either in the body or unseen. Baba sometimes says, "If necessary God Himself will come down and be your *guru*."
(10) Last, but not least – in fact, the most important of all – is the Lord's grace. When the pupil goes on trying and failing over and over again, when all seems quite hopeless, and he fully realises his own utter

helplessness, then the divine grace comes, the light shines, the joy flows through him, the miraculous happens. He takes another step forward on the spiritual way.

After the Shirdi dissertation was over, Baba said to the rich man, "Well, sir, in your pocket there is God in the form of two hundred and fifty rupees; please take that out." The man took out his bundle of currency notes and, counting the money, found to his great surprise that there were twenty-five notes of ten rupees each. He had not known previously the exact amount of money in his pocket and so, feeling Baba's omniscience, he fell at the holy feet, and asked for blessings.

Baba said: "Roll up your bundle of God. Unless you completely get rid of greed you will never get the real God. . . . The love of money is a deep whirlpool of pain, full of crocodiles in the form of conceit and jealousy. . . . Greed and God are as poles apart; they are eternally opposed to each other. . . . For a greedy man there is no peace, contentment, nor steadiness. If there is even a little trace of greed in the mind, all the spiritual endeavours are of no avail . . . . The teachings of a *guru* are of no use to a man who is full of egoism, and who always thinks about the sense objects. Purification of the mind is absolutely necessary; without it all spiritual endeavours are nothing but useless show and pomp. It is, therefore, better for one to take only what he can digest and assimilate. My treasury is full and I can give anyone what he wants, but I have first to see whether he is qualified to receive what I give. If you listen to me carefully, you will be certainly benefited . . .".

Baba knew that the rich man to whom he spoke was mean and greedy. His preliminary tests had demonstrated this fact to all present. Having wealth is not in itself a crime. It is our attitude to the wealth that matters. If we are "poor in spirit", that is, unattached to our possessions, understanding that they are held in trust from God and must be used properly, then it does not matter how much or how little we own.

This wealthy man, unlike the rich young man who came to Christ and asked for salvation, apparently did not go sorrowfully away. The chronicler states that, on the contrary, after getting Baba's blessings, he left the place quite happy and contented. He, like the others present, had enjoyed the spiritual feast served by Baba and perhaps he felt some hopes that the insights thus gained would eventually enable him to reduce the size of the camel of his attachments, so that it might pass through the eye of the spiritual needle.

Whether we seek Self-realisation via the *bhakti mārga* or one of the other lanes, it is necessary to purify the heart of greed, desire, hatred, falsehood and the other vices. One of the great purifiers, for those who can practise it, is that inward-looking, self-raising exercise known as *dhyāna* or meditation. As taught by Baba, meditation can be on God with form or the formless God, or on one leading to the other.

Long ago Lord Krishna taught the self-same method (as recorded in the 'Shrimad Bhāgavata'). Speaking, not as the warrior but as the Supreme God, Krishna said: "Having withdrawn his mind from the sense and fixed it on My form, the devotee should now focus it on only one part of it, preferably the smiling face, to the exclusion of all the others. Then, withdrawing it from even there, he should concentrate it on My all-pervading Self which is free like the sky. Leaving that too, and becoming one with Me, he should cease to think of anything. He will see Me, the inner ruler, in himself, and himself in Me, like light that has united with fire. All doubts about matter, knowledge and action will then come to an end."

In his former incarnation Sai Baba struggled valiantly to remove the dangerous misunderstanding and conflict between Hindus and Muslims; in this life he strives constantly to show the basic unity between all religions. Among his devoted disciples are men of all the leading faiths. He shows his approval by materialising appropriate things for each . . . including, for the Christians, Crosses and images of Christ. "This is the greatness of the *Sanātana Dharma*, the eternal spiritual law. . .this insistence on the oneness behind the apparent multiplicity. The *ātma*, which it declares to be the basic truth, does not contradict the doctrines of any faith. God is unlimited by space and time. He is undefinable by names or forms."

Speaking of the evils of our day, Baba says "Nations are arming wildly and breeding hatred. . .. Man has reduced himself to the status of a wild beast . . . . The spark that arises in the individual mind has spread a worldwide conflagration of hate and greed. This has to be scotched in the individual, the family, the village, the city, the nation; in fact, wherever it raises its head. Man is suffering because he is not aware of the treasure he has in himself. Like a beggar ignorant of the millions hidden under the floor of his hovel, he is suffering dire misery." Four firemen are capable of putting out the world conflagration: *satya*, *dharma*, *shānti*, *préma*. Nothing else can do it.

Satya is truth; it is that intellectual clarity which enables us to see beyond all the shams, falsities, illusions, right to the heart of things. Through *satya* we know the truth of our own being, of God, and of the universe.

Dharma is the spiritual law of living. It is the executive power of carrying out *satya*, the basic truth, in the circumstances in which we are placed. Sometimes *dharma* will demand that we act one way, sometimes the opposite way, but in each case it will be in accordance with the unalterable, immortal law of spirit. Through *dharma* we live the truth; *dharma* is *satya* in action.

Shānti is the great peace that comes to men through *satya* and *dharma*, through knowing and living the truth. It is that "peace that passeth understanding, abiding in the hearts of those who live in the eternal".

Préma is the divine love which in all the great religions is named as the highest expression of God on earth. Christ said that God is love and that we must love our neighbours as ourselves. The *Sanātana Dharma* gives the reason for this: that through our real selves, the *ātma*, we are actually one with each other, with all men, and with God.

Defining this *préma*, which flows constantly from God, and which all men are capable of feeling for one another, Sai Baba says: "It is sustained in bad times as well as in good. It is not like the pepper or salt with which you flavour your dishes; it is the very bread and butter, the essential substance itself. It is an unchanging attitude, a desirable bent of the mind, standing steady through joy and grief."

One of the many stories he tells on this theme is about Rādhā's love. One day Yashodā, the foster mother of Krishna, was searching for the child who had strayed away. She sought almost everywhere in vain, and then went to the house of Rādhā, but Krishna was not there either. Then Rādhā closed her eyes and meditated on Krishna for a while, and when she called his name, he appeared. Yashodā shed tears of joy that her beloved was found, but after thinking about the incident, she said to Rādhā, "I love Krishna as a mother, with some egoism and possessiveness in me because he is my son. Your *préma* is pure; it has no egoism prompting it." And so it was more effective.

Pure *préma* has the power to call God into manifestation before our eyes. Sai Baba is himself a personification of pure *préma*, as Christ was. If through his example, influence and power, enough of this love can be sown in the hearts of men, the world will be changed.

Finally, it must be said that Baba's most important teachings and training are given individually through words, hints, directions for action, example and (perhaps most important of all) silent influence. Such spiritual guidance differs for each individual disciple, for it depends on the disciple's temperament, state of progress and needs at the time. As it is personal and secret, it cannot be extracted and expounded by any observer. I can only say that to some he gives *mantras*, to some special guidance in meditation, to some yogic practices and austerities. Others receive none of these, but different types of help. Some followers seem at a certain time to be given much leeway, while others have to keep their sails trimmed close to the wind. The many are taught by simple parables and analogies; the few who can understand are told deeper meanings.

The underlying theme of all his training is that we must seek God through self-surrender and devotion. The soul which has completely surrendered itself, blotting out the lower ego, is able to absorb and gain full benefit from the silent, wordless teaching which the *sadgūrū* radiates.

At the same time, Baba often says, "It is all within you. Try to listen inwardly and follow the directions you get." To show the importance of this inner voice, he tells the story of Lord Krishna and Arjūna taking a walk together.

Seeing a bird in the sky, Krishna said, "There's a dove!"

"Yes, a dove," responded Arjūna.

"No, I think it's a pigeon."

"You're right, it is a pigeon."

"Well, now I can see that it looks more like a crow."

"Beyond doubt it is a crow."

Krishna laughed and chided Arjūna for agreeing to every suggestion, but Arjūna said, "For me your words are more weighty than the evidence of my own eyes. Whatever you say it is, it is."

Here Lord Krishna represents the divine voice within each one of us. Our physical senses may give us a wrong report, but the inner voice will never do so. The purpose of the outer *sadgūrū* is to help us hear the voice of our inner *gūrū* clearly, surely, and at all times, so that it becomes our infallible guide.

Higher and nobler than all ordinary ones are another set of teachers, the Avatārs of Íswara. They are the Teachers of all teachers, the highest manifestations of God through men.

Swami Vivekānanda

20

AVATAR

When I discovered on my first visit to Prashānti Nílayam that most of Sai Baba's devotees spoke of him as an *avatār*, I began to enquire and read all I could find on this Hindu doctrine of divine incarnations. Actually, of course, it is not an exclusively Hindu doctrine. Christianity teaches that Jesus, the carpenter of Nazareth, was an incarnation from the Triune Godhead, but it states that this was the only divine incarnation, a unique event in the long history of man on the earth.

Hinduism, or the *Sanātana Dharma*, and Mahāyana Būddhism on the other hand teach the more reasonable doctrine that there have been many incarnations on earth from the Godhead. In its simplest, most elementary form, this Hindu doctrine means that Vishnu – that member of the Triune Godhead concerned with the maintenance and evolution of the universe – takes human birth. Nārāyana, another name for Vishnu in his all-pervading mode, is considered the origin or seed of *avatārs*.

The 'Shrimad Bhāgavata' states the truth of the *avatār* principle in allegorical language in its first Book. "The *Pūrūsha* (that is, the first person, or God) known by the name of 'Nārāyana' is perceived by the yogis as possessing thousands of heads, of eyes, of arms, of feet, etc., and is the seed of all *avatārs*."

On the same subject it states, "As countless rivers are born from an ocean that never goes dry, so countless are the descents of the Lord; some of these are major, like Rāma, Krishna, etc., but most are minor *amshas* (rays) from His supreme radiance."

So, according to this teaching, there are degrees of "avatārhood" and many of the great spiritual teachers of India are believed to have embodied rays of the divine radiance and to have been partial or minor *avatārs*. The few, the Teachers of teachers, those who have brought about a great forward movement in man's spiritual evolution, are called the major *avatārs*.

But how shall we understand this question in its deeper metaphysical sense? According to the truth-religion, that is, the wisdom at the foundation of all the great religions, *every* human being is a descent of the Divine into matter; but as well as being a descent from God, man also represents an ascent from lower forms of life. Because of the immortal divine spirit that has come into him, man has struggled upward along the path of spiritual evolution, and will continue to ascend until he fully understands and realises himself to be of nature divine; or, to put it another way, until he is merged with God, and *knows* himself to be merged. The end of his long journey of many lifetimes through the phenomenal worlds of matter will be to arrive where he started, as T. S. Eliot says, but to know the place where he is, and who he is, for the first time. Changing the metaphor, the divine seed will have become a fully grown plant.

So man is at present a meeting point of the animal and the Divine. As he climbs upward from the mud and the mire, the higher light descends into him, inspiring and aiding his climb. All men as well as being sons of earth are sons of God, as Christ said. But when an individual has reached the end of the pilgrimage and washed away the dust of earth in the "cool kingdoms of celestial dew", what then? There will be no desires to draw him back to earth, no *karma*, no "unfinished business", to drag him back. If he returns, if he reincarnates, it will be because of his love of mankind, his desire to help his fellow men in their titanic struggle. Great compassion can be the only motive for the descent of one who has reached enlightenment, freedom, divinity.

We must keep in mind that one who has lived as man and finally and fully realised himself as God merges with the divine ground of all being, the Godhead. He becomes, in mythological terms, part of the myriad eyes and hands and feet of Nārāyana. If he incarnates as a human being once more on earth surely this is God incarnating, for the freed soul and God are one.

The metaphysicist may try to draw a distinction between the divine man and the Divine in man, the "descent" and the "ascent". But when a highly intellectual devotee of Baba questioned him on this point, Baba said that there is no real difference, that you can call it "ascent" or "descent" because both are involved and both are true. The fact is that our finite minds cannot really grasp this deep abstruse question. All we can understand is that a major *avatār*, though man in appearance, human in body, is totally God within.

What are the signs and signals by which we may know a major *avatār*? The most obvious are, of course, the *siddhi*, the super-normal powers. Being completely merged with God, he will have command of all of these without the use of *mantra*, *tantra* or *yantra*. He will have, for instance, the power of creating anything on the spot from the *ākāsha*, that is, from apparently nothing and nowhere. The same power enables him to increase or diminish quantities and sizes as required, and to cause objects to vanish or to change their nature.

Important points to note are that, with an *avatār* as distinct from a magician, these *siddhis* do not disappear or decrease no matter how much they are used, and they are never used for personal gain, always to bring blessings and benefits on others, or to glorify God.

Another major *avatāric* sign is the power of bestowing divine grace. Sai Baba says that such grace is really a reward for good things done in the past, perhaps in a past life. It is like personal savings that have been fixed in the *kārmic* bank, and are suddenly released by the power of the *avatār*. We do not remember the good deeds, the causes, and so the windfall is regarded as a gift from heaven.

But, Baba says, there is also special grace. This has nothing to do with past good actions. There are no assets in the *kārmic* bank on which you can draw, but you desperately need some funds. A rich man with understanding and compassion may go guarantor for you, and the bank will advance you the money. Special grace is something like this, and the *avatār* has the power to bestow it. It may come as a result of one's repentance and self-surrender to God, and is thus similar to redemption.

Special grace may change a person's fate, and so also may its opposite, the power of laying dooms. By the laws of *karma*, or moral compensation, all men will suffer sooner or later for their errors and misdeeds. But if the crimes are very great, the *avatār* may hasten and concentrate the *kārmic* effects by laying a doom. Thus Lord Krishna put the doom of prolonged wandering, with physical and spiritual suffering, on Ashvatthama, the killer of infants and sleepers.

If the *avatār* shows anger, it will be righteous anger, to overcome evil and promote human welfare. Behind it will be the sweetening leaven of love. The surface personality may sometimes show human emotions, but behind them is the constant bliss of one who lives in the eternal. From the eternal heights, beyond *māyā* (illusion), where his centre always is in full consciousness, the *avatār* sees the past, present and future. Untrammelled by restrictions of time and space, he perceives causes and effects far beyond our human vision and judges accordingly. Therefore his words and actions are often hard to understand. They may seem puzzling, sometimes even unreasonable, to ordinary humans who see only a small portion of life's great tapestry. So we say that the *avatār* is inscrutable.

These then are some of the outer signs by which men with perception may recognise the God in human form. Minor *avatārs*, possessing perhaps a few of such features, come fairly frequently, particularly in India. Several have lived and taught during the last hundred years, for example. The great *avatārs*, on the contrary, are rare: many centuries elapse between their advents. They come only when conditions on earth have reached a critical stage, when there is grave danger of the evil, demoniac, or backward-pulling forces overpowering the good, *devic*, or forward-pulling forces. They come as a drastic medicine to destroy the evil toxins in humanity, and give a spurt to the evolution of human consciousness. In the oft-quoted verse of the 'Bhagavad-Gítā', Lord Krishna, speaking as God Himself, says, "Whenever virtue subsides and wickedness prevails, I manifest Myself. To establish virtue, to destroy evil, to save the good, I come from age to age."

There is no doubt that we are living today in an age of great crisis. "The world is the body of God," Baba says. "There is a cancer in the body and it must be removed." Can the cancer be treated or must it be removed by drastic surgery? That is the question. In other words, must there be a catastrophic war, an Armageddon, before mankind (what will be left of it) learns to live in brotherhood and peace? Or will a gentler therapy be effective?

Long ago Lord Krishna, both heavenly *avatār* and earthly king, strove first for peace. But he found in the end that the surgery of war was necessary to remove the cancer of that day: a powerful military caste that had grown arrogant and evil and forgotten its *dharma*. Many centuries earlier *Avatār* Rāma was forced to deal with the same problem in the same way. He had to fight to destroy the *rākshasas*, the demons in human form, who were dominating the earth, and obstructing the divine plan of human evolution.

What about today, with the human race riding the precipice of nuclear doom, with ignorance and greed sharing the reins? Can the powers of light take over direction in time? Baba uses a different metaphor: "White ants are in the tree again. In ancient times the tree was cut down. Now we try to save it." So perhaps there is hope.

"But why should an *avatār* be necessary?" the religious-minded man may ask. "If the direct intervention of God is essential, why can't He act from where He is? Why must He incarnate?" Sai Baba once said: "A person wishing to save a man from drowning must jump into the same pool; the Lord must come here in human form to be understood by men."

In taking on human form, we should note, the Divine One takes on certain human features and limitations. He has a physical body to which, as Swami says, he "must pay the taxes". If we study the lives of known *avatārs*, such as Rāma and Christ, we find evidence of some emotional attributes that are more human than divine: sorrow, anxiety, partiality towards certain people, for example.

We may be surprised to find these human touches in the personality of the incarnated God but, actually, they bring him closer to us. Through them we are able to understand him a little, and so come to the divine qualities beyond the human. Hence it is by becoming a human being with some of its imperfections that an *avatār* is able to promote human welfare.

Concerning his mission in the world, Baba has said many things. Here are just two of them: "I have come in order to repair the ancient highway leading man to God. Become sincere, skilful engineers, overseers and workmen, and join me. The 'Védas' the 'Upanishads' and the 'Shāstras' are the road I refer to. I have come to reveal them and revive them." And also: "I came to sow the seeds of faith in religion and God. You might have heard some people say that I became Sai Baba when a scorpion stung me. Well, I challenge any one of you to get stung by a scorpion and transform yourselves into Sai Babas. No, the scorpion had nothing to do with it. In fact, there was no scorpion at all. I came in response to the prayers of sages, saints and seekers for the restoration of *dharma*."

Practically all the close devotees of Baba, especially those who have known him for a number of years, regard him as undoubtedly a major *avatār*. Their personal experiences, their deeper feelings and insights have convinced them of this.

Some people, like Dr. K. M. Munshi, sense the divinity of Baba at the first contact. Writing in his journal soon after his initial interview with Baba, Dr. Munshi said, "The true test of a God-possessed individual is whether he has the capacity to plant the seed of faith in men, a seed which, when it blossoms, will liberate them from greed, hate and fear. This quality Baba has in abundant measure."

People from the West as well as the Indians see Baba as a divine incarnation. After her first visit to Prashanti Nilayam a woman of Germany, a devout and earnest seeker on the path, said, "Baba is the incarnation of purity and love." Later, after spending more time with him, she wrote in a letter: "I get more and more convinced from within that he is Jesus Christ who has come again, in the fullness of Christ, as Satya Sai Baba."

Some people, however, who have visited Baba and seen him as a holy man with supernormal powers, do not regard him as an incarnation of divinity. But this has ever been the way of the world. Most of Krishna's contemporaries saw him only as a man; even some of the great yogis of the time seem to have doubted his "avatarhood"; only a few saw his infinite splendour and knew beyond doubt what he was. The same seems to have been true of Rāma. And how many accepted Christ as of the High Godhead when his sandals trod the dust of Palestine? Even some of his disciples were not convinced.

When one spends days and weeks with Sai Baba, however, be it in the special atmosphere of the *āshram*, or on tour in many places, one soon begins to feel that he is far beyond the measurements of man. Apart from the miracles which show his command of nature, his power to be anywhere and know what his devotees are thinking and doing ("I am a radio and can tune in to your wave," he says), and his ability to bring protection and help; apart from all these superhuman qualities, there is the pure, ego-less love. This above all stands as a sign of a Christ-like divinity. In man sometimes we see flashes of this love shown towards children, the sick, the weak. In Baba it is there all the time, flowing freely from the divine fount of his nature, embracing everybody, collectively and individually.

And this love is backed by a great wisdom, a deep intuitive perception that sees the real beyond the play of shadows. His devotees have countless proofs that Baba sees their past, present and future, that he knows their *karma*, and what suffering they must go through to pay old debts and learn the deeper truths of life, to reach deliverance. And he helps them to bear that suffering when its immediate removal is not expedient. He becomes the kind, gentle, indulgent mother, the courageous, compassionate, merciful father, until his children's hearts and eyes overflow with *bhakti* tears. They wonder: "What have I done to deserve this? Surely I am not worthy."

If we were asked to list the attributes in our concept of God, the spiritual parent, most of us would name these: compassionate concern for our welfare, knowledge of what that welfare truly is, the stern strength to make us take the nasty medicine when necessary, the power to help and guide us along the narrow way to our spiritual home, the forgiveness and mercy of the father who welcomes with joy the returning prodigal, the power to bring essential innovations to the human drama which he has himself created, and a love that is equal towards all his human children. These are surely the salient qualities in man's mental image of God. These qualities, all of them, those who have the eyes to see have seen in Sai Baba.

Furthermore, a tree is judged by its fruit, as the Bible tells us. Baba's fruits are those devotees who have surrendered themselves fully to his influence, and through the years been moulded thereby. After meeting a number of these, several Western visitors have remarked: "Baba's devotees are a wonderful advertisement to him. After being with them, one knows even without meeting him that Baba is something very special." I myself can say that never before, after years of experience in many places among many groups of seekers, have I met a set of people with such fraternity, such generosity, such warm-heartedness and sincerity. It is a joy to be among them, and often I think of the words of Saint John concerning the early followers of Christ: "We love each other because he first loved us."

To a Vedantist devotee of Baba I once said, "Do you think Sai Baba is an *avatār*?" He replied, "That's really a subject well out of my metaphysical depths. But of his God-like love, power, infinitude, inscrutability and final mystery, there is no doubt." I find myself echoing this. Why bother about a metaphysical label over which men will argue anyway? There is certainty concerning the divine attributes, and there is, too, the feeling of unfathomable waters. As I once remarked in an address to one of Baba's mammoth audiences, "Writing a book about him is like trying to enclose the universe in a small room."

The point is put more graphically in a symbolic story. When the child Krishna was running around getting into all sorts of mischief, his foster mother, Yashodā, tried to tie him to a post with a piece of rope. But the rope would not go around his body. She took a longer piece but that also proved a little too short. Whatever length she obtained, it was never quite long enough to encircle the divine child.

So, too, I find that every description of Sai Baba, of his miracles, his personality, his qualities, his teachings, is short of the actuality. There is always something important that eludes and escapes one. On this matter Baba himself says: "No one can understand my mystery. The best thing you can do is to get immersed in it. There is no use arguing about pros and cons; dive and know the depth; eat and know the taste. Then you can discuss me to your heart's content. Develop truth and love and then you need not even pray to be granted this and that. Everything will be added unto you unasked."

At another time he said; "Of course, you must discard all evil in you before you can evaluate the mystery. Do not proclaim before you are convinced; be silent while you are still undecided. When faith dawns, fence it around with discipline and self-control so that the tender shoots are guarded against the goats and cattle, the motley crowd of cynics and unbelievers. When your faith grows into a big tree, those very same goats and cattle can lie down in the shade that it will spread."

GLOSSARY
OF INDIAN WORDS

A

aarati: (see ārati)

abhaya (m): fearlessness; fearless.

abhishéka (m): inauguration or consecration (by sprinkling water or other auspicious substance).

ākāsha: space; sky; emptiness of space.

akshaya: imperishable, undecaying; perennial.

amrita (amruta, amritha): nectar; life-giving celestial liquid; essence of immortality.

amsha (amsa): part, share; fraction.

anāhat: lit. not struck, hence new, unconditioned.

ānanda: joy, bliss; happiness.

ānandamaya kôsha: the fifth or innermost encasement, sheath or body of man, that of bliss, joy.

angávastram: lit. body-clothing, hence an intimate garment.

anna: food, nourishment; cereal.

annamaya kôsha: the first or outermost encasement, sheath or body of man, that of (physical) matter.

anríta: opp. *ríta (q.v.)*., unrighteousness.

ārati (aarati): ritual performed to worship a deity, or venerable person, by circular movements of a lighted lamp, or flame, before his or her image.

āshram (a) (āsram): lit. shelter; hence hermitage, establishment of religious teacher or spiritual master.

ātma: Self. Soul; breath, life; self; essence, nature; universal soul within individual *(Lat. auto)*.

Aum (Om): mystic monosyllable representing the deity, said to be the sound of the universe, cosmos; the sound of creation, of the Divine.

avatār (avatāra, avathār): incarnation; a descent (to earth). [The Author uses it exclusively to denote a divine incarnation.]
avatāric: adjective from *avatār (q.v.)*
ayurvéda: lit. the knowledge of life, of longevity. Name of ancient Indian system of medicine.
ayurvédic: adjective from *ayurvéda (q.v.)*

B

bābā: father (Arabic)
bhajan: n. a devotional song; v. to adore, worship.
bhakta: a worshipper, follower, devotee.
bhakti: worship, adoration, devotion to God.
bhakti mārga: the path of spiritual fulfilment, or self-realisation, through love.
bhakti yôga: in context, used by Author as synonymous with *bhakti mārga (q.v.).*
bilva: wood-apple tree, *aegle marmelos.*
Brahma: one of the three deities of the Hindu trinity, the Creator; God the Creator.
Brahman: the Supreme Impersonal Spirit; the Absolute.
Brahmôpadesham (Brahma + ūpadesham): the imparting of spiritual knowledge; a spiritual teaching and guidance.

C

chakra: a circle, wheel; in the *yôga* system of Patanjali a *chakra* is a centre of energy in the body used to raise the consciousness from matter to spirit in regulated steps of a given discipline.
chélā: pupil, follower; disciple.

D

darshan: view, seeing, looking at, beholding; sight of. Also, doctrine or philosophical system.
déva: heavenly, divine, celestial being; divinity.
dharma: established order; rule; duty; right; justice. In this context, righteousness and the ideal of righteousness.
dhôti: a loose outer garment tied at the waist worn by (Hindu) men.
divya: adj. divine; celestial, heavenly; n. the divine.
diwān (Urdu): minister; chief or prime minister.
divya prema: divine love; universal love; unconditional love.
dhyāna: meditation; religious and/or spiritual contemplation.

F

fakir or *faqir* (Urdu): a wandering (Muslim) holy man; a renunciate, hermit.

G

Ganésha: god of wisdom, remover of obstacles, son of Shiva and Pārvati;

the "elephant-headed" god of auspiciousness.
ghee: clarified butter.
grāma: village; town.
grāma shakti: village goddess; locally worshipped deity.
gūna: fundamental quality *(sattva, rajas* and *tamas);* good quality, virtue, excellence; property or quality of.
gūrū: most frequently used to denote a spiritual initiator or teacher.
gūrūdéva: a term of respect for one's own spiritual initiator; lit. *gūrū* as god.

I

Íshvara; lord, ruler, hence God; name usually referring to Shiva, but not exclusive to him.
Íswara: alternative spelling of *Ishvara.*

J

japa (m): n. muttering or repetition of prayers; v. repeat in an undertone, mutter or murmur (prayers); pray with set words.
japamālā: prayer beads (rosary) consisting of 108 beads.
javār: millet
jíva: individual life, innate (individual) spirit; self, soul.
jívtātma: individual *ātma.*
jnāna: knowledge; true or spiritual knowledge.
jnāna mārga: the path of spiritual fulfilment, or self-realisation, through knowledge.
jnāna yôga: the *yogic* discipline of attaining release *(môksha)* through knowledge.
jnāni: knowing, understanding, wise; a person possessing the higher knowledge.

K

kalpa: wish, wishful imagination. Also, a cosmic period in Hindu understanding.
kalpatāru: wish-fulfilling tree.
kankan: bangle.
kārana: cause; the reason for or of.
kārana sharíra: the causal body, also known as the *ānandamaya kôsha (q.v.).*
karma: action, deed; act; activity, work. Wrongly used in the West to denote only the result of actions past and present.
karma yôga: the yogic discipline of attaining release *(môksha)* through activity.
kārmic: related to activities and/or acts and/or actions past and present; adj. of *karma.*
kôsha: sheath; case; shell; cocoon; hence store-room, abode.
Krishna: eighth incarnation of Vishnū; one of the ten divine *avatārs (q.v.).*

kūmkūm: blood-red powder used in *pūjā (q.v.)* and in ornamentation.

L

leelā: play, diversion; appearance, semblance; charm, grace; by extension, divine play.
lína: absorption; absorbed in (through devotion).
linga(m): emblem, characteristic. The Author uses it exclusively in its *vedantic* sense as the indestructible original of the gross visible body. (N.B. Not phallus or phallic).

M

maddāla: a kind of drum.
mahāsamādhi: final absorption *(nirvāna)* into the Absolute; colloquially used for the death of a religious teacher or spiritual master.
mahātma; lit. great self, being; a courtesy title for some religious or spiritual leaders.
mahimā: glory; majesty. A prayer called *mahimā* is an exaltation, or praise, or singing the glory of a particular deity.
mālā: necklace; also, rosary, prayer beads.
manas: mind (in its widest sense as the seat of intellectual operations and of emotions); hence, understanding; intellect, thought; imagination; inclination, desire; disposition.
mānasa: man; mankind.
mandir: temple.
manômaya kôsha: the third encasement, sheath or body of man, that of the mind.
mantra(m): prayer, hymn; sacred text; mystical verse, incantation; a verbal key to spiritual evolution.
māntric: adj. of *mantra.*
mārga: way, path.
māyā: art, marvellous power; illusory image; illusion. In some philosophic systems, the power that causes the world to appear real.

N

Nārāyana: the personified *Pūrūsha,* identified with Vishnū (therefore Krishna).
neem: a tree with very bitter fruit.
nétra: eye(s).
nétralingam: a *lingam (q.v.)* with an eye mark in or on it.
Nílakanttha: a name of Shiva.
nishkāma: lit. desireless; hence, disinterested or selfless.
nishkāma karma: acts and activity without thought of reward; duty performed selflessly.

O

Ôm: (see *Aum*)

P

paisā: generally, money; specifically, one of 100 units that make up the decimal *rupee.*

paisé: plural of *paisā (q.v.).*

panchalôhā: lit. five metals (said to represent the five elements of earth, water, fire, air and ether); an alloy made either of gold, silver, copper, tin and lead, or of copper, brass, tin, lead and iron.

Paramātma: Supreme or Universal Soul.

prāna: breath; vital spirit; vital air; vigour, energy, power.

prānamaya kôsha: the second encasement, sheath or body of man, that of vitality.

prasād: gracious gift; food offered to an idol or respected person/s and eaten by them; remnants of such food taken as a blessing.

préma: love.

pūjā: ritualistic worship with prayers and chants.

pūjāri: worshipper; the performer of (a) *pūjā.*

pūrūsha: a man, male human.

Pūrūsha: highest universal principle, supreme spirit.

R

ràjas: aspect, quality, characteristeric of passion and energy; forcefulness. One of the three *gūnas.*

rājasic: adj. of *ràjas.*

rākshasa: demoniac being; fiend. Mythological evil-doer.

Rāma: seventh incarnation of Vishnū; one of the ten divine *avatārs (q.v.).*

rangôli: floor and ground decoration made with flowers or coloured powders and dyes as if mosaics.

Rāvana: mythical *rākshasa (q.v.)* king of Lankā slain by *Rāma (q.v.).*

rishi: saint or sage; a special class of revered beings whose number is often limited to seven; one of the great *vedic Illuminati.*

rita: the established way; righteousness, the right way.

rūdrāksha: a tree *(elaeocarpus ganitrus)*, whose berries are used to make prayer beads for the worshippers of Shiva.

S

sadgūrū (sat + gūrū): lit. real or true *gūrū;* supreme *gūrū;* God.

sādhaka: lit. assistant. Worshipper, aspirant (to spiritual knowledge).

sādhanā: (in this context) spiritual endeavour or effort; instrumentality; straightness, directing one's effort.

sādhū: straight, right, unerring; noble, virtuous, good; hence saint, seer. Colloquially, a holy man.

samādhi: deep meditation during which one can achieve union with the Supreme Spirit; also, the physical death of venerated people; also, the memorial structure erected in honour of such a person.

Sanātana: eternal; perennial; from always to always.

Sanātana Dharma: the perennial philosophy; lit. the ever-lasting order.
Sanāthana Dharma: (see *Sanātana Dharma)*
sankalpa: resolve of the mind, will; purpose, definite intention, determination.
sārathi: charioteer.
sāri: six or nine yards of material worn in certain ways by some Indian women.
sathya: (see *satya).*
Sathyanārāyana: (see Satyanārāyana).
sattva: aspect, quality, characteristic of truth, peace, the original state of balance. One of the three *gūnas*.
sātvic: adj. of *sattva*.
satya(m): true (truth); actual, real, genuine; extant.
Satyanārāyana: lit. true Supreme Spirit, true God. Name of Vishnū, sometimes used for Krishna. The given name of Sri Sathya Sai Baba.
shabda: sound; utterance; word.
shabda yóga: the discipline of achieving union (with God) through sound.
Shakti: name of the Goddess, consort of Shiva, from *shakti* = power, strength, capacity; regal power; active power or energy of a deity, especially Shiva.
shankha: shell; conch shell.
shānti: peace.
sharíra: body; human or animal anatomy, body.
shashtipūrti: the completion of sixty (years).
Shiva: one of the three deities of the Hindu trinity, the Destroyer; God the Dissolver.
Shivalingam: mark, sign, emblem of Shiva (see *lingam*); a spheroid dedicated to Shiva worship.
Shivarātri: lit. night of Shiva. A festival dedicated to Shiva (*Mahāshivarātri).*
siddha: lit; accomplished, achieved, fulfilled, realised, successful; perfect, perfected. In this context, spiritually accomplished (person).
siddha pūrūsha: a spiritually fulfilled person.
siddhi: accomplishment; success. In this context, an ability of a supranormal nature achieved through spiritual endeavour.
Siva: (see *Shiva*)
sphatika: crystal.
swāmi (sva = self, *mi* = am): owner, lord, master. A term of respect for holy men; also, a particular order of *sādhūs (q.v.).*

T

tamas: aspect, quality, characteristic of darkness and ignorance; inertia. One of the three *gūnas.*
tāmasic: adj. of *tamas (q.v.).*
tambourā (tambūrā): musical instrument with four strings used as a drone.

tantra: lit. loom, warp. Underlying principle, essence; a class of mystical treatises much maligned as magical, superstitious and orgiastic.
tāntric: adj. of *tantra (q.v.).*
tapas: lit. heat. A spiritual effort or discipline of great physical and mental austerity.
thūmbi: long gourd (*lagenaria vulgaris).*
tongā (Anglo-Ind.): light two-wheeled carriage drawn by a horse.
tūlsi: the holy basil plant (*ocymum sanctum).*

U
ūdhi: ash.
ūpadésha: teaching; an instructional speech; an imparting of spiritual knowledge; a message (of upliftment).
upanayanam: investiture. In this context, an investiture of the sacred thread, a Hindu ritual.

V
vibhūti: mighty, powerful; manifestations of might, power; hence, ash produced by or through spiritual power.
vijnāna: discernment, knowledge; profane knowledge (opp. *jnāna*); science.
vijnānamaya kôsha: the fourth encasement, sheath or body of man, that of discernment.
Vishnū: one of the three deities of the Hindu trinity, the Sustainer; God the Sustainer.

Y
yantra: apparatus, appliance, mechanical contrivance, engine, machine; amulet, mystical diagram.
yôga: lit. union; means expedient; contact with. The yoga system of philosophy; in *Samkhya* philosophy, unity of soul and nature.
yôgi: an adept of *yôga (q.v.).*
yogic: adj. of *yôga (q.v.).*

INDEX